Critical theory and sociological theory

MANCHESTER
1824

Manchester University Press

Critical theory and contemporary society

Series editors:
David M. Berry, Professor of Digital Humanities, University of Sussex

Darrow Schecter, Professor of Critical Theory and Modern European History, University of Sussex

The *Critical Theory and Contemporary Society* series aims to demonstrate the ongoing relevance of multi-disciplinary research in explaining the causes of pressing social problems today and in indicating the possible paths towards a libertarian transformation of twenty-first century society. It builds upon some of the main ideas of first-generation critical theorists, including Horkheimer, Adorno, Benjamin, Marcuse and Fromm, but it does not aim to provide systematic guides to the work of those thinkers. Rather, each volume focuses on ways of thinking about the political dimensions of a particular topic, which include political economy, law, popular culture, globalization, feminism, theology and terrorism. Authors are encouraged to build on the legacy of first generation Frankfurt School theorists and their influences (Kant, Hegel, Kierkegaard, Marx, Nietzsche, Weber and Freud) in a manner that is distinct from, though not necessarily hostile to, the broad lines of second-generation critical theory. The series sets ambitious theoretical standards, aiming to engage and challenge an interdisciplinary readership of students and scholars across political theory, philosophy, sociology, history, media studies and literary studies.

Previously published by Bloomsbury

Critical theory in the twenty-first century Darrow Schecter
Critical theory and the critique of political economy Werner Bonefeld
Critical theory and contemporary Europe William Outhwaite
Critical theory of legal revolutions Hauke Brunkhorst
Critical theory of libertarian socialism Charles Masquelier
Critical theory and film Fabio Vighi
Critical theory and the digital David Berry
Critical theory and disability Teodor Mladenov
Critical theory and the crisis of contemporary capitalism Heiko Feldner and
Fabio Vighi

Previously published by Manchester University Press

Critical theory and epistemology Anastasia Marinopoulou
Critical theory and feeling Simon Mussell
Critical theory and legal autopoiesis Gunther Teubner

Forthcoming from Manchester University Press

Critical theory and contemporary technology Ben Roberts
Critical theory and demagogic populism Paul K. Jones

Critical theory and sociological theory

On late modernity and social statehood

DARROW SCHECTER

Manchester University Press

Published by Manchester University Press
Altrincham Street, Manchester M1 7JA
www.manchesteruniversitypress.co.uk

British Library Cataloguing-in-Publication Data
A catalogue record for this book is available from the British Library

ISBN 978 1 5261 0584 4 hardback
ISBN 978 1 5261 0585 1 paperback

First published 2019

Typeset by Newgen Publishing UK

For Diana, Luca, and our friend, Axel

Contents

Acknowledgements

This book attempts to elaborate some of the ideas initially sketched in *The Critique of Instrumental Reason from Weber to Habermas* and *Critical Theory in the Twenty-First Century*. If it manages to open up some new directions in critical theory, it is undoubtedly due the help provided by students, colleagues, and friends. Many thanks to the students and faculty of the Social & Political Thought (SPT) programme at the University of Sussex, especially Jonathan Bailey, Michael Baines, Nic Baxter, David Berry, Mojo Blyth Piper, Sean Brown, Tim Carter, Denis Chevrier-Bosseau, Andrew Chitty, Martin Davey, Gerard Delanty, Alex Elliott, Beatrice Fazi, Chris Ferguson, Lucy Finchett-Maddock, Gordon Finlayson, David Gonsalves, Alasdair Gray, Nadine Hafez, Neal Harris, James Kelly, Dimitri Kladiskakis, Peter Kolarz, Valentinos Kontoyiannis, Alinafe Luka, Xuran Ma, Iain McDaniel, Karim Mohammadi, Tom Nathan, Jack O'Connor, Max O'Donnell Savage, Faure Perez, Umut Sahverdi, James Stockman, Paul James Williams, and especially to Joseph Backhouse-Barber and Val Whittington.

I have had fantastic support from colleagues in the School of History, Art History, and Philosophy at Sussex, including Liz James, Claire Langhamer, Ambra Moroncini, Vicky Phillips, Paige Thompson, Clive Webb, Gerhard Wolf, and Kim Wünschmann. Very special thanks to Lisa Brown, Jake Norris, and Gerardo Serra.

Exchanges with colleagues at other universities have had a decisive influence on the pages that follow. I've learned a great deal from discussions with Francesco Bilancia, Arianna Bove, Hauke Brunkhorst, Sarah Bufkin, Colin Crouch, Raul Digon Martin, Heiko Feldner, Alessandro Ferrara, Andreas Fischer-Lescano, Kevin Gray, Angelos Koutsourakis, David McGrogan, Lois McNay, Dirk Michel-Schertges, Kolja Möller, Marius Ostrowski, Jaroslav Skupnik, Marcel Stoetzler, Wolfgang Streeck, Fabio Vighi, Jackie Wang, Patrick Wheatley, and Chris Wyatt.

I am particularly indebted to Alberto Febbrajo, Regina Kreide, Ana Marinopoulou, William Outhwaite, Andreas Philippopoulos-Mihalopoulos, Heinz Sünker, Gunther Teubner, and, as ever, to Chris Thornhill.

Friends have challenged lazy thinking on my part and made me re-think crucial issues. I've received particularly valuable insight from Fernand Avila, Ed Cangialosi, Costantino Ciervo, Richard Jemmett, Volker Lorek, Chris Malcolm, Mand Ryaira, Jarret Schecter, Imke Schmincke, and Cristiana Vitali.

Working together with Alun Richards and Caroline Wintersgill on the *Critical Theory and Contemporary Society* series has been easy and enjoyable. They consistently combine the light touch with clear direction in ways that will enable the series to grow in the future.

Although there is probably too much speculation in this book, I can say for a fact that neither this one nor the others would have been possible without Diana Göbel and Luca Lavatori.

Introduction

Which methodological and substantive issues should define the contours of a critical theory of society in the twenty-first century, and why does the relation between critical theory and sociological theory need to be re-articulated today? Some observers may wish to argue that the need for a critical theory of society has in fact gone with the publication of Jürgen Habermas's *Theory of Communicative Action* (1981) and the alleged linguistic turn in social and political thought. Advocates of this assessment maintain that critical theory provided important intellectual resistance to fascism in the 1920s and 1930s, whilst also offering a subsequent warning not to ignore the possible spread of new variants of authoritarian populism after 1945. It is often suggested that the possibility of political implosion became increasingly remote some time ago as a result of the economic boom following World War II.[1] According to this assessment, the dangers facing a post-colonial global world are more likely to be post-modern relativism, 'clash of civilisations' bigotry, ecological disaster or terrorism than authoritarian populism or related threats to democratic legitimacy. It might thus seem to follow that what is really required now is a new kind of post-modern cosmopolitanism rather than the renewal of critical theory as such.[2] Yet the ongoing economic crises that have intensified since 2008 as well as the difficulties encountered by the Syriza government in Greece in 2015 indicate that the problems now facing democracies around the world run deep. It seems difficult to avoid the conclusion that cosmopolitanism may be necessary, but certainly not sufficient to preserve and enrich the democratic model of statehood. In reference to Syriza's victory, Timothy Garton Ash quotes Jyrki Katainen, the Finnish vice president of the European Commission at the time, as saying: 'We don't change our position depending on elections.' This view neatly complements Troika policy that certain banks and other key non-elected institutions are simply 'too big to fail', regardless of what democracy and political equality might happen to stipulate in principle.[3] It is possible, when adding a number of qualifications, to regard the Troika as a kind of combined executive and judiciary with the transnational constitutional design to overrule national-level legislatures and electoral results when deemed necessary. It is therefore equally possible to apply Marx's analysis of Bonapartism in conjunction with Gramsci's concept of the historical bloc to evaluate the dynamics shaping political events in Greece and elsewhere.[4] It will be seen in due course that a number of the socio-economic phenomena first diagnosed by Marx and Gramsci, and subsequently taken up in different guises by the Frankfurt School and bio-political theory, are far from resolved or outdated.

This book examines some of the most important problems besetting democracy today by delving into what can be considered an acute and still very much unresolved issue in democratic theory and practice. On the one hand democracy will appear to be authoritarian and out of step with the complexities of modern society if resolute attempts are undertaken to make it substantive and social rather than formal and political. Twentieth-century history in Eastern Europe and elsewhere indicates that society-wide projects to institute constituent power by expanding democracy usually have to be imposed by a single party with a monopoly on the legal means of justice, information, and repression. On the other hand democracy is susceptible to collapse if its formal and procedural mechanisms are not sufficiently supplemented by educational, cultural, and other institutional resources. These resources require further buttressing through varying degrees of socio-economic planning and related interventions in the workings of the economic system still commonly referred to as capitalism and more recently qualified as neoliberal. It can be plausibly argued that in most known cases, the supplementing in question amounts to different approaches to making democracy substantive and social rather than merely formal and political. It would be very naïve to think that whilst in the first instance the break with formalism is cynical and conducive to totalitarian aberrations, in the second instance it simply implements good common sense and solid pragmatism in line with reliable political tradition. So the question for this introduction and the rest of this book is the following: how does critical theory help illuminate the contemporary dilemmas of democracy and statehood in this regard, and what is meant by a sociological approach to critical theory?

The main question and four central claims

Four central claims are defended in the course of the following chapters. The first claim is that it is imprecise to argue in terms of democratic versus non-democratic if one does so in abstraction from a detailed consideration of specific political constitutions and the plural processes of social constitution in the wider sense implied by the historical bloc and related concepts. When examining political constitutions one is typically looking at how the division of state powers in a specific historical setting has evolved and how the equilibrium of checks and balances is continually renegotiated and restructured. But in terms of wider social processes, one is also investigating power relations as well as the institutionalisation of the various informal compromises that in a more colloquial sense help construct the alliances constituting a given social order.

The second claim addresses what is mentioned above as the need to strengthen democracy beyond the formal mechanism of granting each citizen a vote, without thereby precipitating into some dictatorial version of constituent power. It is relatively uncontroversial to say that democracy is susceptible to collapse if its formal and procedural mechanisms are not sufficiently supplemented. Constitutions in the restricted and wider sense still do this. But in view of some of the phenomena linked with transnational executive-judiciaries and nationalist authoritarian populism just touched upon, one wonders how long the mainstays of the post-1945 order will be able to provide a stable framework. Civil society, a vibrant public sphere, strong trade unions, Keynesianism, social democratic parties with clearly identifiable electoral bases, and what Habermas refers to as the lifeworld all played a crucial role in stabilising democracies in North America, Western Europe, and other parts of the globe during the years 1945–1989. These institutions were constituent dimensions of citizenship and political statehood, mediating between citizens and state authority during a period in which geographical boundaries and national borders were still key points of reference for notions of sovereignty. That epoch is now passing; unions and social democratic parties are now on the defensive. Keynesianism has been largely discredited by the interests and ideologies that have set out to convince financial markets and enough of the public that balanced budgets are somehow more important than investment and employment. Hence the second claim contains a descriptive and a speculative component. In descriptive terms it is explained that the crucial task of dividing and sharing power, which was established at the level of the nation state and fortified by key institutions in various national civil societies in order to supplement formal democracy, is being reconfigured under conditions of global governance. It may be inaccurate or perhaps too early to characterise the situation as post-democratic. But a certain kind of democracy that was known and familiar until the end of the Cold War is slowly becoming more historical than actual. The transformations involved affect the ways in which power is divided and shared. Perhaps most significantly for the argument about the changing composition of statehood developed in subsequent chapters, they affect the mediations between the various economic, educational, juridical, and cultural elements of democracy. In more speculative terms, then, the book explores the possibility that new mediating and representative institutions are emerging, and that these institutions could provide the impetus for a gradual transition from political to social statehood. It is somewhat difficult to assess the chances for this transition just yet. One of the major obstacles to such a prognosis at this stage is that representation in political statehood has normally been rooted in territorially demarcated electoral districts. The spatial dimension of collective decision-making and compromise was usually fairly transparent. Although representation in social statehood will certainly not be able to ignore the specificity of place, it is also likely to be rooted in systemic operations and functions with less straightforward spatial boundaries than electoral districts, local authorities, and nation states (claim three below). The proliferation of digital space and other kinds of extra-territorial spaces under conditions of global governance further complicate any attempt to analyse the quality of statehood in the twenty-first century. One should not overestimate the extent to which the idea of social statehood is a marked departure from the idea of political statehood, however. This becomes clear when trying to determine where, exactly, the state of political statehood is located. In other words, and as Hegel tries to demonstrate, the state and statehood have always been simultaneously concrete and conceptual. Chapter 1 examines his dialectical line of argument.

The third and related claim can be introduced by noting that one of the defining features of modern society is the evolution of social forms into social systems. This development is analysed here in relation to the functional differentiation (henceforth FD) of economic, political, legal, educational, and other systems. For the purposes of this book, then, sociological theory is really concerned with the sociology of FD.[5] It is important to clarify this at the outset given the vast array of sociologies one might consider, such as those of youth, race, gender, class, religion, and many others, including an intersectional approach combining different aspects of each. It is shown that the FD of social systems is not tantamount to their isolation from one another. On the contrary: systems become more dependent on each other as a result of their differentiation. In order to persist and, where possible, expand, individual social systems are obliged to develop the capacity to read and assimilate the communication they receive from neighbouring systems. That communication is coded according to the distinct operations of the system in question. This is evidently a matter of great theoretical complexity; it is treated with care in subsequent chapters. For now it will suffice to observe that there is much disagreement within the relevant literature about how inter-systemic communication actually happens. The disagreement in question is potentially very fertile since, in accordance with the caveat not to exaggerate the differences between political and social statehood, democracy has always been about inter-systemic communication and a matter of co-ordination between economic, political, scientific, legal, educational, and even aesthetic operations. To repeat, however, the modalities of mediation and co-ordination are currently in a process of rapid transformation. Terms such as neoliberalism, globalisation, financialisation, and digitalisation only partially explain the nature of these changes. For a fuller understanding one must also examine social systems, systemic coding, and inter-systemic communication, as well as historically discernible patterns of state formation and FD. The stress on mediation foreshadows the fourth claim and highlights the relation between critical theory and sociological theory informing this study.

The fourth claim is that differentiation does not unfold haphazardly and that social systems do not bounce off each other in purely contingent ways. This means that the economic system is not simply one of many that coexist as equal partners in the reproduction of society. It is of more than passing significance that whilst Keynesianism is deemed to be unwieldy and outdated, bank bailouts are actively employed to steer the strategic de-differentiation of social systems. In other words, diverse models of steering and planning are possible. It is certainly not a question of applauding Syriza or chastising the Troika. Syriza stands out because of the dramatic situation in Greece. This deflects attention away from the incongruities between the political and social models of statehood that uneasily coexist at the national level all around the world. In the longer term, however, these incongruities are likely to affect most political parties and key mediating institutions particular to political statehood and national sovereignty. The discrepancies have to do with the unofficial role played by social systems in the constitution of communication and power relations on a global scale, on the one hand, and the established authority of parties and governments, on the other. One has to look in more detail at the processes through which the alternative models of steering are presented by different parties and governments rooted in territorial realties and national traditions, and how these proposals are then dealt with by the organs of transnational governance. The communication between them is distorted in ways that are not fully explicated by theories of inter-subjective recognition and other varieties of communicative action theory. For the sake of simplicity one can summarise for the moment by remarking that the parties and governments rooted in territorial realities and national traditions seem to enjoy figurative proximity with the citizens of those countries. They may well articulate political demands that seem to be populist to varying extents. It is nonetheless often a kind of populism that may strike many as real and urgent. By contrast, the organs of transnational governance seem to enjoy greater figurative proximity with the operations of global social systems. Judging by the example of the Troika, however, transnational governance is confronted with dynamic processes of differentiation and de-differentiation that it cannot effectively manage. As a result, global policy pronouncements almost invariably seem arrogant and remote from popular concerns.

Just as orthodox Marxism does little to effectively explain these processes, most articulations of academic systems theory are also of questionable value in this endeavour. This book retains determinate aspects of the dialectical approach to mediation found in some first-generation critical theory, but gives dialectics a sociological inflection by applying it to the functioning of social systems in contemporary world society. This approach enables researchers to inquire into the reasons why de-differentiation does not unfold any more haphazardly than differentiation. The aim is to come up with explanations of populism, democratic deficits, dysfunctional differentiation, and other qualitative changes in the conditions of statehood without resorting to conspiracy theories or dubious narratives of inexorable decline. One needs a methodology capable of illuminating the reasons why the state and statehood have always been simultaneously concrete and conceptual, why democracy has always been about inter-systemic communication, and why, finally, statehood, inter-systemic communication, and democracy are currently changing. Critical theory remains one of the best methods for understanding historical evolution, complex power relations, and dynamic social processes. It is nonetheless incomplete without certain elements of Gramscian political sociology. More surprisingly, perhaps, is that critical theory today also needs certain elements of systems theory in order to make sense of FD. The following chapters provide sustained arguments in support of the four claims sketched above.

An incisive historical-analytical explanation of the causes and likely consequences of distinct variants of populism is surely not outdated. In fact, the spectre of 'democratic' populism looks more menacing in the second decade of the twenty-first century than it did in the years immediately following the widespread collapse of parliamentary government in the interwar period of the twentieth century. Important questions are thereby raised about long-term causes, effects, symptoms, and discernible patterns involved in crises of democratic statehood.[6] The supposedly peaceful 1950s and 1960s are closer, in strict chronological terms, to the period of fascist rule in Italy and Germany than they are to the present period, in which parties such as the Front National in France have at times enjoyed considerable electoral success and extra-parliamentary support. The implications go beyond the relatively obvious point that one should be wary of assuming that political pathologies become increasingly harmless the more remote they become from the date of their ostensibly original manifestation. Scholarly research shows that capitalism is prone to cyclical overproduction crises that inexorably drive that economic system to stake out new markets across national boundaries. It is a mode of production that demonstrably extends the domain of contractual and quantifiable capital/wage labour relations to areas of social life that had previously been informally regulated by feudal status, different kinds of community, clan loyalty, and personalised lifeworld bonds. It is not easy to assess the extent to which positive law, human rights, and social rights have been able to provide the institutional frameworks needed for the establishment of rational instances of modern solidarity that replace communal traditions with effectively binding civic ties and what Habermas refers to as constitutional patriotism. The project to supplement the procedural mechanisms of democracy cannot really succeed unless these ties are actively nurtured. In anticipation of some of the main lines of argument developed in this book it is necessary to bear two points in mind in this regard.[7]

First, positive law and rights are not simply used to impose capitalist economic relations to the detriment of community and solidarity. In theory, modern law adheres to universally generalisable principles and facts. Severing legal decisions from religious loyalty, ethnic status, and moral Puritanism should in principle help make the rule of law incompatible with religious bigotry, sexism, racism, xenophobia, and homophobia. Historical experience from a variety of contexts indicates that the very possibility of legal process and a judicial trial – as opposed to a legally stamped executive political judgement – depends on the formal separation of law and politics. Few would dispute that there must also be provisions to ensure the greatest possible independence of the courts and the media. The impersonal character of law and rights may seem to undermine the less codified registers of solidarity and community that are needed to sustain a democratic culture. Depending on the specific ways in which rights are institutionalised, however, consistent formalism can also help undermine different instances of naturally conferred status, politically exploited kinship ties, and semi-legal power networks. There is in short nothing inherently exclusionary or capitalist about rights. Rights require a certain level of abstraction in order to be inclusive and effective in terms of normative integration, lest they depend on privately negotiated deals and favours for their implementation. In this case abstraction is by no means synonymous with a priori disembodiment, and indeed, rights provide a tangible example of what is both concrete and conceptual about distinct forms of statehood. This becomes evident when social and economic rights are curtailed, as in times of austerity. Social and economic welfare rights in matters of childcare, housing, education, pensions, health, and transport palliate the contradictions between formal political equality and the manifest inequality generated by de-regulated market economies. To this extent it can be maintained that these rights preserve the differentiation between the legal, economic, and political systems of modern society; to varying extents they ensure that one social system does not dominate the others. They therefore help maintain a precarious balance of power and institute a set of unofficial compromises capable of complementing the official separation of state powers. De-regulation and outsourcing are typically defended as ways of alleviating cumbersome bureaucratic interference in what many elites may like to characterise as free market situations. It is frequently alleged that in order to achieve maximum efficiency, competition and officially recognised expertise, often in the guise of high-level academic and administrative qualifications, should be allowed to rule. As just remarked, however, rescinding rights can be analysed instead as an example of selective de-differentiation and part of a war of position designed to alter the existing balance of power in society. In such cases the substance of the compromises that have sustained that balance can be either ignored or quietly reframed without the consent of the citizens involved.[8]

Second, the war of position first theorised by Gramsci has to be reconceptualised in the light of some of the manifest implications of FD. It is improbable that the post-traditional tendency towards perpetual systemic expansion is an exclusively economic phenomenon. It is far more likely that political, legal, aesthetic, religious, epistemological, medical, media, educational, and other crises recur according to cyclical patterns. At present, these configurations seem to be characterised by the horizontal, de-centred dialectics of systemic expansion, on the one hand, and legal-normative checks on the expansionist tendencies of social systems, on the other. Yet legal-normative checks and balances do more than simply moderate systemic expansion and counter de-differentiation by instituting social rights. One cannot fully understand the dynamics of differentiation and de-differentiation without also examining the ways that social systems are coupled, de-coupled, and re-coupled. Systemic re-coupling can, in some instances, be analysed in terms of inter-systemic communication and mediation. One is not thereby observing the attempted construction of mini states within a given nation state, as was sometimes alleged with regard to some trade union movements under post-1945 corporatism in Western Europe. At the current historical juncture one is more likely to be observing attempts by social systems to enhance their capacity for self-steering. There is fairly widespread agreement in the academic literature on systems theory that individual systems cannot significantly enhance their capacity for self-steering without knowledge about the functioning of neighbouring systems, and that this knowledge is limited to the communication provided by binary codes such as legal/illegal. This book investigates the extent to which this particular knowledge process is changing, and if systems increasingly require the input of citizens capable of thinking and acting more flexibly than most binary codes permit. If this can be shown to be true, as the present study attempts to do, it will mark an important theoretical advance over the hierarchical paradigms of power and legitimacy implied by the centre/periphery, public/private, government/citizens, and state/society dichotomies that continue to structure a great deal of official political discourse in the press and official government documents. Political parties generally accept and have to work within the premises stipulated by these paradigms. This is especially noteworthy in instances such as the case of Katainen speaking on behalf of the European Commission, where the authority of political parties acting within national frameworks is blatantly contested by the International Monetary Fund (IMF), Commission, and other bodies acting transnationally. The point made previously about Syriza and the Commission holds: it is not primarily an issue about who is right or who has been mistreated. It is more centrally about managing the flows of social communication under conditions of FD, systemic re-coupling, and inter-systemic mediation.

The chapters to come raise questions about the extent to which the territorially demarcated nation state is still empowered to steer and regulate specific systems in ways that were possible in the years roughly spanning the end of World War II and the end of the Cold War. The arguments address political and epistemological questions about the extra-juridical components of law in complex societies, and the juridical components of the economic and other social systems as well. As legal and political systems tend to become differentiated in late modern societies, law simultaneously exhibits the capacity to assimilate into its statutes the findings and experiences of non-governmental organisations, New Social Movements, trade unions, research bodies, as well as the experiences of occupations and other protests. Law thus becomes differentiated from politics whilst also becoming increasingly coupled to it. A similar set of mediating dynamics can be seen at work between the law and other social systems. Major doubts can thus be cast on the idea that legality supplies rational political form to the legitimate democratic essence of 'the people'. These issues are introduced in chapter 1 in the discussion linking the concept of mediated unity with the consolidation of the modern nation state, and are then explored in more detail throughout the rest of this book. Chapters 1 and 2 draw out a number of the consequences for our understanding of democracy.[9]

In consequence it would be mistaken to suppose that modern societies are the passive victims of systemic expansion and periodic dysfunction. The example of Keynesian economic management and the establishment of the welfare state and post-war consensus in Britain, for example, show that post-traditional societies can adapt to complexity, learn from crises, and introduce new normative orders in reflexive response to historically evolving needs, values, and possibilities. Without relying on an uncritical notion of historical progress, it can be shown that they are in fact better adapted to do so than hierarchical social orders dependent on the rule of the elders, organic unity, and monolithic belief systems. To the extent that they generate collective resources and flexible steering capacities (until relatively recently associated with states and strictly national constitutions), the more complex societies are not subject to direct, immediate de-stabilisation when one or more systems encounter self-steering problems. Later chapters show how and why there exists a spatial and temporal distance between events in one system and the stability or volatility of a functionally differentiated society as a whole. The distinction between immediately stable/unstable societies relying on organic ethnic-religious unity and complex societies characterised by overlapping and intersecting processes of mediation is not trivial. Adorno might be doubtful about the claim that post-traditional societies can draw on accumulated knowledge to learn from the past, and thereby cope with the challenges that face them. One of his central insights is nonetheless borne in mind here. This is that the humanity–nature relationship, institutionalised in the course of history as society, is mediated and dialectical rather than direct and static. He convincingly shows that humanity is neither fused with nature nor separated from it. Following Hegel on the modalities of objective spirit to a certain qualified extent, Adorno suggests that the antagonistic structure of internally divided industrial societies opens up a critical distance between individuals and institutions that potentially enables each citizen to subject the socio-historical mediations between humanity and nature to an immanent critique. Internal social division, and, by extension, FD, are primarily related to the reality of mediation and are therefore not synonymous with alienation.[10] The enduring power of immanent critique resides in the fact that it brings an explicit methodological 'is' to normative issues in socio-historical analysis. It thereby eschews some of the problems inherent in positivist attempts to remain 'objectively distant' from social reality (which generally end up justifying existing power relations and thereby showing that distance to be speciously objective), whilst also avoiding the pathos of passionate appeals for immediate change (which may be moving rather than incisive).

Part of the problem involved in assessing Adorno's contemporary relevance is illustrated by the difficulty that whilst he correctly evokes a critical space anchored in the dialectical structure of modern society, he then sometimes incorrectly dismisses it with his musings about total administration and universal *Verblendung* (delusion).[11] In clear anticipation of a recurrent theme in the work of several prominent post-structuralist thinkers, Adorno asserts that modern society is never unified enough to be completely manipulated or comprehensively represented religiously, politically, economically, or in any other homologous fashion mapping a one-to-one correspondence between society and any one particular social system. This approach is clearly at odds with the notion that the economic system holds the theoretical as well as the practical key of interpretation, thus foreshadowing Habermas's distinction between lifeworld and system. Two significant conclusions can be drawn. First, it is plausible to argue that fascist and state socialist political systems tried in vain to rely on relatively traditional societal organisation in order to realise their respective visions of a society managed from an imaginary central axis capable of imposing one-to-one correspondence. Neither was revolutionary despite whatever other claims each of them may have put forward in terms of self-definition. It can be shown that neither managed to institute modern instances of political statehood. Second, in the absence of such a central axis, the total mobilisation of society in the service of any vaguely articulated collective project, including democracy, is likely to fail. This highlights the point that the formal dimensions of political democracy have to be supplemented in different ways at different times; what worked during 1945–1989 will not work forever. Adorno shows that the conflicts proper to internally divided societies are dialectical rather than simply random or mechanically determined. In accordance with his reading, the concepts 'internally divided' and 'dialectical' presuppose each other. Simultaneous polarisation (class, exploitation, marginalisation) and homogenisation (coerced integration, reconciliation under duress) is therefore a paradoxical reality, not an incoherent or illogical contradiction.[12]

But this epistemological insight does not sufficiently inform Adorno's analysis of social evolution, thus casting some measure of doubt upon his sociological relevance and the sociological import of first-generation critical theory more generally. This issue is touched upon below by very briefly returning to the example of the post-war consensus and welfare state, and asking how best to explain these and similar instances of institutionalised compromise in which polarisation and homogenisation coexist across the public/private divide. Although there may be doubts about the sociological relevance of the first generation, one also finds a great deal of fruitful epistemological thinking about identity, difference, and mediation in their writings, much of which is in fact relevant to questions of social complexity and internal division today. At their hermeneutical best these works disclose the possibility that normative integration might cease to be a process of coerced integration. Much depends on translating critical distance into new practices of representation. That possibility, in turn, requires us to dispense with the idea that unity is the foundational basis of acceptable difference. It is possible, in other words, to imagine that a plurality of internal divisions could be mediated according to a plurality of incommensurable codes and logics. More fundamentally it demands the articulation of a critical theory capable of re-imagining the links between differentiation processes, inter-systemic mediations, and representation linked to extra-territorial spaces. There is no way to do this by relying on static unities like 'the nation' or 'the people', or by hankering after a-historical essences relying on various notions of the most popular class or ethnicity of the people. The tasks go beyond cosmopolitanism and will not be properly addressed by nostalgia or by attempts to revive the actors and compromises that constituted the post-war consensus.

The post-war consensus can be understood in a number of ways. It can be analysed as an instance of evolving collective learning and flexible adaptation to democratic demands. One might ask if it is more properly characterised as an instrumental compromise between distinct strategic actors, or if it presents a case of benign populism. Perhaps it is best explained in terms of a very intricate combination of expedient political compromise and effective application of accrued and qualitatively enhanced institutional resources. Leaving aside the provisional answers one might come up with for the moment, ascertaining how these resources can be fortified is now a matter of urgency and one of the primary tasks of immanent critique. Citizens need to know if the capacity for flexible planning can be renewed in ways that have worked well in the past. To what extent can we still learn from the historical lessons of active participation in key moments of transition and resistance, such as in Germany in 1918 and Spain in 1975? Citizens also need to know how new methods of generating societal resources can be developed in order to meet the challenges of global society and climate change. Orthodox Marxism, poststructuralism, bio-political theory, and many other methodologies do not pay sufficient regard to the crucial roles played by FD and social systems in modern society. Mainstream systems theory is often a-historical and in any case too dogmatic in its understanding of the relation between social systems and their respective environments; its most powerful insights are almost exclusively descriptive in many instances. Much of the literature on the changing conditions of statehood and democracy is too narrowly framed as a question for political science or constitutional law. A look at the trajectory from traditional to critical theory will set the stage for an introductory statement of the challenges facing the re-articulation of critical theory today.

From traditional to critical theory

It may be true to some extent that critical theory was initially conceived in terms of a staunch intellectual resistance to fascism and as a warning against historically new forms of authoritarian populism. But it also developed as a response to some of the methodological inadequacies of neo-Kantianism, positivism, Marxism-Leninism, phenomenology, psychoanalysis, and other epistemological currents that emerged in the wake of the crises of idealism and Marxism. This book attempts to retain and update the founders' belief that epistemological questions are framed by sociological and historical processes, and that, as Adorno says, 'the critique of knowledge is social critique, and vice versa'.[13] The implication is that epistemological issues have political ramifications and can therefore never be purely logical or neatly analytical, and, by extension, that an interdisciplinary approach is needed to examine the relations between knowledge, social communication, and the exercise of power. What the founding theorists did not take into full account, and what lends their approach to interdisciplinary research a somewhat eclectic feel, is the point touched upon above, namely, that modern societies tend to differentiate their respective legal, political, economic, media, religious, aesthetic, scientific, and other systems. Consequently, the relation between knowledge and social communication is de-centred in the sense that it does not ultimately rely on what are still very often treated as unified foundations, such as consciousness, capitalism, or the state. The relation between social systems and the state is key for this study and merits an additional explanatory word before proceeding.

Social systems develop codes to help them maintain their boundaries with other systems. Each system does this in order to process information coming from the others, and to reproduce the unique conditions needed to guarantee the continued functioning of that system.[14] Although the relations between the various systems are mediated, there is no central mediator capable of co-ordinating all of the major systems without coercing some of them into what are often artificially constructed combinations. In accordance with the fourth claim introduced above, strategies of governance are used to manage selective de-differentiation. Systems clearly need steering of some kind as well as a rigorous constitutional framework promoting steady inter-systemic communication. From the time of the early modern revolutions (in Britain, the United States, and France) until the present day, the state has been entrusted with this task. Without wishing to indulge in excessive speculation, it is possible that *centralised mediation* was the dystopian unconscious dream of fascist and state socialist political systems. Be that as it may, states that are generally considered to be stable and democratic have always depended on government cabinets and state ministries to preside over and guide specific social systems. In practice it has usually been possible, until relatively recently, for purportedly stable democratic states to ignore or seemingly diminish the glaring implausibility of centralised mediation. This is typically accomplished by relying on steady economic growth of the kind available in Western Europe between 1945 and 1973. It can also be accomplished by enlisting a variety of other techniques to maintain a given hegemony or prop it up in times of inter-systemic crisis. In theory these techniques are undergirded by various conceptions of mediated unity between citizens and the state that are implicitly called into question by Simmel and explicitly called into question by Gramsci and systems theorists like Niklas Luhmann. Some of the most important theories of mediated unity are examined in chapter 1 with a particular focus on Hegel.

It may seem curious to draw attention to the methodological compatibilities linking Adorno's negative dialectics with the systems-theoretical approach to de-centred mediation. Adorno is after all remembered as a critical theorist; systems theory seems to be defined by an inherently conservative bias towards reproducing already existing social relations. The point is certainly not that democracies are in fact dictatorships in disguise. It is nonetheless advisable to carefully investigate the theoretical and historical affinities between openly authoritarian centralised mediation and ostensibly democratic mediated unity. Critical theorists like Adorno and systems theorists such as Luhmann deploy theories of de-centred mediation to very different ends. It will be seen that the critical-theoretical and systems-theoretical approaches to de-centred mediation can nonetheless be very fruitfully combined in the endeavour to better understand the points of continuity between centralised mediation and mediated unity. It is moreover urgent to re-think the possibilities of de-centred mediation at a time when government cabinets and state ministries are very obviously overburdened and incapable of co-ordinating the operations of the relevant social systems in the ways that they once could. If it is obvious that statehood cannot function on the basis of centralised mediation, it is becoming increasingly clear that it cannot function on the basis of mediated unity, either.

Subsequent chapters return to this point in detail in an attempt to develop a critical theory of society with contemporary sociological relevance. For the purposes of this introduction the point is that the emphasis on interdisciplinary investigation in the work of Horkheimer, Adorno and the other members and associates of the Institute for Social Research is limited to a philosophical and aesthetic appreciation of the fact that the relation between humanity and nature is de-centred and mediated. First-generation thinkers stress that mediations, in turn, materialise as partial, protean syntheses that join disparate phenomena by way of conceptual form. To phrase the matter in a manner that makes the link between epistemology and sociology a bit more explicit, mediations materialise in conceptual and institutional form. They thereby unify distinct phenomena that are not really united. The point is that un-mediated, essential knowledge and un-mediated social unity are likely to yield metaphysical epistemology and authoritarian social steering.[15] The task of finding the right mediations in both endeavours is therefore absolutely crucial for the possibility of redeeming the promise of non-instrumental reason and non-coercive integration. Adorno, Benjamin, Horkheimer, and Sohn-Rethel broadly follow a number of the methodological principles set out in the sociology of Georg Simmel. Simmel helps them elaborate the implications of the thesis that the critique of knowledge is social critique. He does so by pointing out how the critique of knowledge helps ascertain the complex interaction between conceptual form and institutional form. Simmel thus provides the bridge between Hegel's understanding of concept and institution and a decidedly less foundational account of that relation. This becomes evident if one bears in mind that whilst Hegel provides a dialectical analysis of the state, Simmel provides a dialectical relation of something much more amorphous and fluid, i.e. society. Yet his retention of a dialectical method indicates that society moves in ways that are not random, and that a plurality of mediations can be discerned. To this extent the author of the *Philosophy of Money* foreshadows the work of Adorno and early critical theory.[16]

Adorno writes about the *mediated* non-identity of concept and institution to distinguish his position from an outright Hegelian one stressing the mediated unity of concept and institution. It will be seen in chapter 1 that the notion of mediated unity is of fundamental importance in terms of deconstructing the presuppositions of modern political theory and for grasping the reliance of traditional dialectical theory on the concept of totality. Adorno retains Hegel's stress on mediation and dialectics to show that attempts to divest thinking completely of its conceptual moment are likely to result in obfuscation that forfeits the potentially critical capacity of conceptual thinking to challenge authoritarian syntheses in the day-to-day life of social institutions. In response to Hegel he shows that the project to capture all of reality in thought amounts to an attempt to conceptualise non-conceptual reality along with conceptual reality. The synthesis that thereby emerges integrates into thought what is non-identical to it. For Adorno integration of this kind has to be coercive in real historical practice. Adorno is an acute reader of the *Phenomenology* who spots the parallels between the mediated unity of A and non-A in that work, and the supposedly harmonious unity of the individual and state in the *Philosophy of Right*. One of his guiding insights is that there is more than a casual connection between attempts at seamless representation in epistemology and coercive normative integration relying on flawed political representation. To reiterate, this word of caution on Adorno's part is emphatically not tantamount to a call to abandon conceptual thought. If it is the case that concepts threaten particularity, they nonetheless remain the most effective weapons against authoritarian syntheses and repressive institutional form. They are, in other words, both a tremendous problem as well as a crucial resource for explaining how social divisions illuminate the dynamics of antagonistic institutional mediation processes. More specifically, they help show how those divisions point to problems in inter-systemic mediation that might be substantially rectified with inter-systemic reform. In this respect concepts can be compared to rights. Concepts, like rights, threaten particularity and non-identity. To repeat, however, depending on how they are institutionalised, rights can also help stabilise a certain kind of imperfect individual autonomy that might be drastically improved in qualitative terms – though probably not perfected. Just as inter-systemic communication is always likely to be characterised by a certain degree of contingency, rights establishing perfect individual autonomy would no longer really be rights. Hence in response to Heidegger and others Adorno demonstrates that the flight from conceptual work glorifies very arbitrary accounts of non-identity, such as the supposed non-identity of thinking and being. In his view being remains a concept whether one reverts to its traditional spelling or draws a line through it. In this instance it is an obscure concept celebrating an illusory reconciliation between humanity and communitarian destiny.[17]

Rather than consistently pursuing a programme of interdisciplinary research, the first Frankfurt School thinkers spot elective affinities between subjectively manipulated mediations between humanity and nature, instrumental reason, oppressive institutional syntheses of humanity and nature, and coerced integration. Complex issues related to the synthesising function of form and mediation, the manifold distortions of instrumental reason, and the cognitive dialectics of intellectual stringency and sensual creativity are often handled with striking originality. Adorno, in particular, ably speculates about the absent conditions of truthful reconciliation between humanity and nature, and the absent conditions for a just reconciliation between the different groups and classes of a humanity estranged from itself. He resists the temptation to harmonise humanity and nature in conceptual union. Similarly, he refuses to flee the problems of conceptual syntheses and dialectics with recourse to abstractions such as being as the ontological *unmediated* (absolute, metaphysical) non-identity of thought and its intangible other. But he and other Institute colleagues develop an approach that commits them, to varying degrees depending on the thinker in question, to placing the central epistemological and political questions of their work on the humanity–nature axis. Instrumental reason and the division of labour are consistently regarded as paradigm instances of flawed mediation and failed reconciliation, with the result that the possibilities for non-instrumental reason and un-coerced reconciliation can only be glimpsed in terms of their manifest absence, or, very fleetingly and occasionally, in aesthetic originality and brilliance.[18]

For the purposes of the present study it is not really important whether or not one chooses to call this framework the philosophy of consciousness, negative idealism, or something else. Given the inadequacy of the public/private, citizens/government, and state/society dichotomies, it is far more pressing to re-articulate the relation between epistemological critique and social critique. More specifically, it is important to re-articulate it with a view to understanding how inter-systemic, horizontally structured mediations work today. Early critical theory offers an appropriate but somewhat limited point of departure. This question is closely related to the issues connected with replenishing political resources and discovering new ones.[19] Horkheimer, Adorno, Benjamin,

Marcuse, and Fromm imagine that at some unspecified historical juncture, the hegemonic elites of most post-feudal societies become obsessed with the idea that industrial progress and technological innovation endow Western humanity with the capacity to subjugate external nature for the purpose of conquering natural scarcity. In their official capacity as political leaders, these elites tirelessly repeat that markets can spontaneously co-ordinate supply and demand, that tolerance should hold sway over dogmatism as a result of the rule of law, and that the state must remain neutral with regard to competing conceptions of what it means to lead a good life. Neutrality is thus widely held to be especially important in complex societies in which there are many contrasting views concerning how best to pursue individual and group projects. In view of this uncertainty, complexity, and diversity, official sources maintain that it is impossible and undesirable to plan economies or propose positive, prescriptive visions of political liberty. A number of early critical theorists are mainly correct to reply that despite official proclamations to the contrary there is a definite plan, just as, for Marx, the modern state is an impersonal but decidedly non-neutral arbitrator. The plan is to usher in a socio-political order based on efficiency and productive rationality, and to do so with dogmatic determination, or, as one might say today, in accordance with the dictate that 'there is no alternative'. According to the interpretation offered in the *Dialectic of Enlightenment*, humanity's earliest known trauma is not so much the individual's deprivation of the love of the mother as much as it is the species' fear of the otherness of nature, and human helplessness before nature's whimsical unpredictability.[20] Each in their own way, then, first-generation critical theorists maintain that the conquest of external nature through scientific rationality and industrial organisation may indeed elevate collective humanity above scarcity and subsistence economies at some point in the future. But these organisational and administrative techniques can only do so at the great price of enmeshing individual internal human nature in the increasingly mechanised and comprehensive project to master external nature. This dynamic leads to a threefold problem that cannot be properly analysed and understood without a methodological shift from traditional to critical theory.[21]

First, the subordination of external nature creates the potential for post-scarcity and freedom from want. Yet it does so at the very high price of acute class antagonism and related conflicts about ownership of the means of production and distribution of the fruits of the labour process. Stated slightly differently, the attempt to subjugate external nature indirectly subjugates humanity by pitting humans against one another in a struggle marked by recurrent economic crisis, interpersonal antagonism, and an overwhelmingly technical approach to epistemology that distorts the sensual and non-conceptual dimensions of the knowledge process. As Marx observes, humans are alienated from nature, from the products of their labour, and from each other, thus making the state necessary. Indeed, the more acute alienation and social division become, the more the state seeks to present itself as the state of all citizens on an equal basis.[22] Second, as Nietzsche and Weber observe, the discipline and renunciation required to impose industrial efficiency on external nature leads to the gradual elaboration of ascetic norms and punitive values. The subsequent internalisation of repressive norms domesticates individual internal human nature, thus creating longer-living, though ultimately very unhappy and neurotic, people who tend to be mentally passive whilst also being emotionally susceptible to authoritarian populist mobilisation. However, the founding members of the Institute for Social Research are all doubtful about the prospects for re-appropriating alienated essences linked to the capitalist labour process or any other specifically human activity. Since the collective struggle against external nature triggers a kind of boomerang effect that isolates individuals and places them in conflict with their own most basic desires and sensual impulses, Freud must inform the transition from traditional to critical theory as much as Marx, Nietzsche, and Weber. Third, and in some ways anticipating more contemporary discussions about algorithmic learning and artificial intelligence, there is a marked tendency for notions of science, progress, and technological innovation to become synonymous with reality itself.[23]

In technological civilisation, then, science and progress function much in the way that myth, magic, and religion had done so in traditional pre-modern societies. The important difference is that scientific findings become axioms of objective truth and supposedly impartial reason. In this way instances of industrial rationality prevailing in the economy are able to marginalise the capacity for aesthetic observation and mimetic reflection. To the extent that these processes become automatic and are widely described as having the capacity for self-steering, reason becomes irrational, and progress acquires a number of the regressive characteristics formerly attributed to myth. What is more troubling to Horkheimer and Adorno, however, is not merely the fact that scientific rationality becomes a pervasive reality principle that excludes and marginalises philosophical, poetic, aesthetic, and other reality principles. In traditional societies governed by myth, magic, religion, and naturalised rank, hierarchies are usually relatively transparent and openly authoritarian. Under the sway of instrumental reason, a specifically capitalist version of modernity declares its right to offer the only feasible version of post-traditional society. Diverse hierarchies are legitimated through performance ideologies and accepted as meritocratic, democratic, impartial, and enlightened.[24] For critical theorists the implication is that hierarchy and power have not been dismantled. Power is transformed into institutions that are far less transparent and openly brutal than traditional ones, thus opening up the concrete possibility for the potentially complete conquest of inner human nature and the eradication of meaningful difference between individuals.

Hence first-generation Frankfurt School thinkers generally seek a synthesis of Marx on the dynamic between humanity and external nature as this relates to the economy, on the one hand, with Nietzsche, Freud, and Weber on the dynamics of normalisation and the relentless disciplining of internal, human nature, on the other. The synthesis is deployed in various articulations to explain how reason, which had been subversive of ecclesiastical and feudal hierarchies during the historical period culminating in the Enlightenment, is gradually transformed into a legal-rational domination at the institutional level and compulsive self-preservation at the individual level. Instead of contrasting the fascist parenthesis with post-war democracy, Horkheimer and Adorno are convinced that there is a fundamental continuity from the two World Wars, fascism, and genocide, to the post-1945 era of regulated capitalism, consumerism, and mass culture. Therein lies critical theory's polemical charge and deep pessimism in the years spanning the publication of *Traditional and Critical Theory* (Max Horkheimer, 1937), *The Change in the Function of Law in Modern Society* (Franz Neumann, 1937), *Theses on the Philosophy of History* (Walter Benjamin, 1940), *Changes in the Structure of Political Compromise* (Otto Kirchheimer, 1941), the *Dialectic of Enlightenment* (Max Horkheimer and Theodor Adorno, 1944), *One-Dimensional Man* (Herbert Marcuse, 1964), *Negative Dialectics* (Theodor Adorno, 1966), and the publication of *Structural Transformation of the Public Sphere* (Jürgen Habermas, 1962) and *Legitimation Crisis* (Jürgen Habermas, 1973). In different guises it is affirmed that European and North American society after 1945 may seem to be democratic, governed by the principle of equality before the law, and economically productive. But the pathologically instrumental dialectics of internal nature and external nature that seemed to have come to the fore with fascism and atomic warfare were never really addressed after 1945, with the result that new and even more catastrophic results had to be expected despite the euphoria of the post-war economic consumer boom.[25]

On this reading one can see why, from the perspective of someone like Habermas, the first generation offers highly original, important, but ultimately inadequate responses to the challenges of modernisation and, more recently and perhaps more acutely, of globalisation. Although incisive as readers of Kant, Hegel, Marx, and Heidegger, several prominent Institute members seem to want to argue that in the course of what Weber analyses in terms of rationalisation and disenchantment, law becomes codified violence, Enlightenment becomes myth, reason becomes irrational, society becomes total administration or repressively tolerant, and culture expands to the point that it is reduced to mass culture. As a result, the subtlety of Adorno's dialectics often cedes place to a far less dialectical, less immanently critical perspective on law, reason, and the tasks of critical theory. In his writings following *Legitimation Crisis*, Habermas warns that Horkheimer and Adorno conjure up an eschatological historical perspective on the dialectics of external and internal nature that fails to consider how humanity learns from history, accumulates knowledge through pragmatic trial and error, and develops collective resources such as modern law, the legal state with its independent judiciary, and constitutions. In his view, these palpable gains constitute genuine knowledge and confute the trans-historical pessimism of the *Dialectic of Enlightenment* and other writings. In his writings following *Legitimation Crisis* Habermas makes clear that reason is not permanently eclipsed by impersonal command and other modalities of illegitimate power in the modern world.[26]

Instead, he thinks that the rationalisation of diverse lifeworlds in the spheres of work, independent scientific research, the formation of public political opinion, religious belief and a variety of others leads to a plurality of stable interactive contexts. Each context is marked by the fruitful collaboration of technically trained experts and ordinary educated citizens in what can be broadly characterised as a democratic civic culture. When these collaborative discussions are channelled upward into the system of official political authority, the findings are capable of generating legal norms based on legitimate consensus. The great gain of rationalised lifeworlds with respect to the pre-modern organic communities preceding them is that modern integration is achieved on the basis of discursively achieved agreement rather than coerced integration dictated by fixed roles, assigned status, or traditional hierarchies. So instead of juxtaposing a nearly ubiquitous rationalised system with occasional instances of exceptional art, as Adorno and other Institute members do at times, Habermas distinguishes systemic imperatives steered by money, power, and instrumental reason from lifeworld interaction guided by communicative action. He is alive to the possibility that the binary dimension of systemic logic can at times colonise the spontaneity of lifeworld interaction. In *Between Facts and Norms* (1992) he provides a detailed explanation outlining how lifeworld communication can resist this tendency and retain its extra-systemic interactive quality. In this work he defends the thesis that the lifeworld does not have to resist colonisation through splendid isolation. On the contrary, and in ways reminiscent of Hegel's reflections on the divisive conflicts of civil society in relation to the harmonising function of the state outlined in the *Philosophy of Right*, the non-identity of lifeworld and system provides a supple elasticity to post-traditional societies. Lifeworld communication therefore exerts influence on administrative and economic systems through the media of law, associations in civil society and the public sphere, and democratic politics more generally. To this extent Habermas believes that intermittent crises provide guidance for necessary adjustments, so that a stable equilibrium can be consistently reached between lifeworld communication and systemic imperatives. It is therefore possible to regard his position as a further development of Adorno's belief that modern society is never unified enough to be completely subordinated to any single vision of technocratic programming and control. Retrospectively, these must have seemed like very persuasive conclusions in the light of German reunification and the promise of European co-operation signalled by the Maastricht Treaty.[27]

The challenges facing a critical theory with contemporary sociological relevance

The present book makes little further mention of figures like Horkheimer, Benjamin, and Marcuse. It does not argue in favour of an unqualified return to Adorno. Nor does it offer a modified version of the distinctions between lifeworld and system informing Habermas's theory of communicative action. Instead, it seeks to contribute to a critical theory of complex societies capable of mapping out the main tensions between centralised territorial authority and the FD of social systems. Territorial authority and social systems have developed broadly speaking constitutional resources for making collectively binding decisions and for sharing and dividing power. Both have developed varying capacities for planning and steering. Fundamental differences become apparent when considering how systems are coded – they definitely do not consistently adopt the political principle of one equal vote for each equal citizen, nor do they respect national or geographical boundaries. The tensions in question thus have major implications for the ways we think about democracy and legitimacy. In marked departure from mainstream systems theory, however, this book argues that systems are not coded in natural, neutral, or a-historical ways. On the contrary, it is explained how and why efforts to re-code them are part of a war of position in the battle for hegemony. The book thus builds on the work of a number of contemporary thinkers who have observed discernible continuities as well as notable ruptures in the evolving relations between solidarity, social conflict, legal positivisation, the gradual emergence of post-traditional authority, and globalisation.[28] It broadly accepts the historical accounts of Simmel, Weber, the early Habermas, and others, according to which informal, communal solidarity goes hand in hand with instances of oppression sustained by traditional roles in the family, workplace, and public office. It also accepts the main lines of the thesis that the transition from informal solidarity and traditional oppression to individual rights and rationalised forms of political integration is marked by the emergence of political parties and the separation of powers animating the constitutional frameworks of most stable modern states. But it rejects the notion implicit in the *Dialectic of Enlightenment* that there is no significant difference between traditional, personalised oppression and modern, juridical integration, apart from the fact that the latter is ostensibly concealed by legal-rational domination. It therefore also rejects the corollary thesis that this supposed continuity neutralises or offsets the palpable conceptual and normative gains accompanying abstractly formulated rights vis-à-vis the conventional obligations demanded by traditional notions of inclusion and exclusion. In the feudal period the latter were commonly defended with naturalist fallacies and implemented according to inherently hierarchical privileges. More recent instances of integration can and sometimes do rely on various inequalities and hierarchies to achieve governable order. There is in fact a notable tendency for this to happen as a result of the politics of austerity currently dominant in the eurozone and beyond. But there is no inherent, necessary reason why this has to be the case, and there would be no need or role for critical theory if it were somehow inevitable. Post-traditional integration is examined here as part of the still incomplete transition from naturalised stratification to complex stratification and beyond to FD. As the title of the conclusion suggests, however, FD can be and often is dysfunctional. The evolution of norms defining the legitimacy of states is investigated as part of a series of ongoing processes that can be broadly characterised as sociological rather than natural, organic, or even humanist in any unqualified sense. The first-generation emphasis on mediation, dialectics, and immanent critique is retained. It is updated and revised in an attempt to illuminate the relations between contemporary socio-economic, political, and cultural phenomena that may at times appear to be unconnected, without, however, relying on some notion of totality to do so. Instead of adopting Habermas's distinction between system and lifeworld to explain the mutual dependence of facts and norms, the approach here explores the implications of the point made at the outset of this introduction about the volatile dynamics structuring systemic expansion and legal-normative checks to control it. In chapters 4–5 questions about the possibilities for inter-systemic mediations and developing new sources of political integration are posed in relation to the declining fortunes of unions, parties, and other institutions that acted as primary mediators within European and North American nation states in the period prior to full-blown globalisation.[29]

It is in the light of this well-documented crisis of primary mediation and political representation that one might ask a number of preliminary questions about the continued pertinence of the distinction between lifeworld and system. The discussion to follow in chapter 1 demonstrates that this distinction can be interpreted as an inconclusive break with Hegel and other thinkers who posit a mediated unity of integration, representation, and legitimacy in the institutions of the modern state.[30] It is questionable if such a unity ever really obtained for any significant historical period. In any case, it is not yet entirely clear what kind of dialectic is at work in terms of delineating the links between integration, representation, and legitimacy in the current period. It now seems implausible that the links can best be thought of as a pragmatic combination of clearly defined, vertically structured representational authority, supported and upheld by the horizontally structured inter-subjective dynamics of recognition, communicative action, and diverse instances of *phronēsis*.[31] As Simmel suggested more than a hundred years ago, it is more likely to be a set of de-centred dialectics that does not culminate in a political apex or condense in an authoritative centre or any similarly conceived political foundation. As such it is important to pose a series of further queries about the capacity often attributed to the public sphere and civil society to continue to mediate between rights-bearing individuals and the legal state.

Reference to the public sphere and civil society as intermediary instances of communication and information invoked by Kant, Hegel, and other early modern thinkers can be seen as a way of grappling with the reality that individual citizens are rarely permitted to experience the state directly in complex societies. It is clear to these thinkers that it is mistaken to draw direct parallels between citizenship in the Greek polis, citizenship in the Renaissance city-state, and citizenship in the modern state. In their writings the public sphere and civil society can therefore be said to engage and integrate the modern citizen, without, save perhaps fleetingly, allowing politics to become the key to *eudemonia* or *virtù*. Hence they correctly intuit that the politics of the modern public sphere and civil society is not really comparable with the politics of the *General Will*. On this account the break between Hegel and Rousseau is in some ways more decisive than that between Hegel and Marx.[32] But Habermas's distinction between lifeworld and system can also be read as a modified restatement of the dichotomy between internally conscious, human nature (private, ethical, rational), and institutionally objectified, external nature (public, administrative, political). The key mediating role played by the public sphere in Habermas's early writings is taken over by law and civil society in *Between Facts and Norms* and subsequent works. In *Between Facts and Norms* he maintains that it is unlikely that the rule of law can function without the supporting political culture provided by radical democracy. In short, although there are important differences demarcating Habermas from idealism and first-generation critical theory, he can nonetheless be regarded as a theorist of mediated unity in matters of legitimacy, reason, and representation.[33] His research on these issues is astonishingly rich in nuance and rigorously substantiated with coherent theoretical argument and historical evidence, which is why it is so important to raise questions about some of the problems with his position. Thus to conclude this introduction it is worth explaining how the approach to rights and systems adopted here differs from Habermas's in 1992.[34]

From the *Structural Transformation of the Public Sphere* to *Between Facts and Norms* and beyond to his more recent reflections on globalisation and post-national politics, Habermas's work has consistently been informed by Kant's thesis that rational duty rather than inclination or material interest supplies cognitive content to democratic law.[35] It is this epistemological aspect of post-traditional law, which is discursively redeemed by the admittedly bourgeois protagonists of the early modern public sphere, that in principle makes eighteenth- and nineteenth-century law in Western and Central Europe legal in format as well as legitimate in terms of content. The basic tenet is that if compelled, through necessity or any other motives, to let their political stances be determined by economic interests, citizens are no longer required to reason and think about their actions, duties, and ends. Their interests can be aggregated through administrative expertise or a variety of other organisational means which in effect render public reasoning superfluous. If this happens, Hobbes's dictum about authority making the law triumphs over Kant's demonstration that legitimate law is informed by public reason.[36]

From the *Theory of Communicative Action* onwards, Habermas changes his emphasis from the ideal of legitimate law grounded in the individually shared maxims of private bourgeois individuals assembled in public sphere institutions. That function is transferred to interpersonally generated instances of extra-systemic, non-strategic communicative action in the rationalised lifeworlds of industrial societies. It is at this juncture that Habermas shifts from earlier positions on the public sphere influenced by his reading of Kant to a more democratic notion of socially shared and collectively communicated norms exerting an analogous ethical-political pressure on state-level legislative processes. At the historical level, this shift reflects the further consolidation and development of the legal state in Europe and North America from the nineteenth century until the end of the Cold War. At the personal level, it reflects his own move away from first-generation critical theory and what he calls the philosophy of consciousness to legal theory and political sociology. These two periods of his work remain linked, however, just as, in a related vein, he sees an intimate connection between extra-systemic communicative action and the possibility of specifically political democratic legitimacy. For him it is the extra-systemic substrate of communication that provides the

quintessentially human dimension to politics that can stem systemic colonisation of the lifeworld. In his early writings he submits that duty rather than
interest provides democratic law with a non-instrumentally rational dimension that it must not forfeit, lest democracy become plebiscitary and populist.
Democracy may be destabilised if rational obligation is institutionally conflated
with the strategic interest that in his view should really belong to the domain
of systemic rationality. From the 1980s onwards, he thinks that communicative action is likely to degenerate into repressive steering if lifeworlds are
entrusted with the task of guiding systemic operations. He thus implies that
communication can possibly divert, inflect, and re-channel power. But it cannot assume the functions of systemic power without jeopardising the juridical integrity of the autonomous individual emerging from the differentiation
of law, politics, science, art, and ethics. Such a re-suturing would in effect
reverse the very learning processes that make radical democracy a real possibility in post-traditional societies.[37] Habermas believes that the distinction
between system and lifeworld is not necessarily de-stabilising or inherently
populist as long as the boundaries between them are maintained and systemic colonisation of lifeworld rationality is held in check by a steady flow of
extra-systemic communication. His acceptance of sociological theories linking modernity, complexity, and FD is substantially qualified by the following
caveat. Crises of legitimacy will result if social systems detach the private
actor from the public citizen and the public citizen from the state. He suggests
that this is likely to happen if the civic channels linking up the lifeworld and
state are broken, interrupted, or diverted.

This is the crux and the point of departure for the chapters to come. He
and many others continue to suggest that what separates democratic and
non-democratic cultures is the privileged access individual citizens in democracies have to the state via law, the public sphere, and civil society. It is time
to ask if the emphasis on extra-systemic communication must cede place to
an enquiry into the possibilities of inter-systemic communication and a new
model of statehood stemming from it. This is because it is quite evidently
the case that social systems have indeed detached the private actor from the
public citizen, and that, as a consequence, they have fundamentally changed
the relation between the citizen and the institutions of statehood from one
of mediated unity (however fleetingly) to one of mediated non-identity. Any
critical theory with contemporary sociological relevance is obliged to address
this point. In *Between Facts and Norms* Habermas states that democracy
and the rule of law depend on citizen confidence in the belief that they are
the authors of the laws that govern them.[38] He therefore insists on the co-
instantiation of the system and the lifeworld as well as the normative and
political priority of the latter over the former. Consequently, it can be said

that he anticipates some of the potential normative deficits of the systems-theoretical version of sociological theory. Further, it can be seen that he attempts to meet these looming deficits with the defence of anthropological postulates about the human faculty for mutual recognition, discursive inter-action, and juridical subjectivity, which he buttresses with arguments drawn from various linguistic, psychological, republican, and hermeneutic sources. From a current standpoint this is not an entirely convincing solution to the problems of globalisation and the eroded sovereignty of the nation state. The ongoing crisis of unions, parties, universities, welfare states, and a variety of other institutions suggests that the boundaries between system and lifeworld have become blurred and that the channels between citizens and centralised political authority have been comprehensively overhauled since 1945. It is moreover doubtful if questions concerning vital, strategic interest and expert knowledge can be separated from questions about the ways social systems function in modern societies. *Critical Theory and Sociological Theory* therefore borrows from the work of Adorno, Habermas, and Luhmann, but it does so without relying on distinctions they variously deploy to distinguish between system and aesthetic reason, system and communicative reason, or system and systemic environment.

The first stage in the de-traditionalisation and de-personalisation of power is clearly marked by the consolidation of the modern state and the constitu-tional division of powers, the positivisation of law, the formation of political parties, the evolution of guilds into trade unions, and the emergence of a public sphere. De-personalisation in this sense constitutes a marked gain in several senses even if, as Marx, Weber, and Foucault caution, impersonal and impartial are far from being synonymous. This book thus begins by noting that we are now entering or at least approaching a second stage in the dialectics of the de-personalisation of political power and the personal accountability of elected political figures. Trump's incessant tweets and the debacles concern-ing national debt and the Troika illustrate that the dangers of re-personalisation of power and highly selective de-differentiation have not yet been met with sufficient theoretical clarity or practical imagination. The first stage of de-personalisation has often been analysed with the use of vertical paradigms such as those denoted by the centre/periphery, citizens/government, and state/society dichotomies. The discussion in preceding pages raise a num-ber of questions about the continuing validity of those dichotomies, and also asks if we are now in a transition to a second stage marked by a new set of inter-systemic mediations, requiring decisively more horizontal paradigms to explain how social communication now works and how social statehood might eventually be able to work.

Notes

1 This period is often described with the French notion of the thirty glorious years ('les trente glorieuses'), denoting the persistence of steady growth and nearly full employment which came to an end with the oil crises of the 1970s and the subsequent election of Thatcher, Reagan, and Kohl. The austerity imposed by the governments of those political leaders found its counterpart in the frustrations of the first Mitterrand government, which was forced to retreat on virtually all of its major socio-economic reforms because of the threat of capital flight and the pressure on the franc imposed by international financial markets. The implications of these events have not yet been fully explored. Although few people used the terms neoliberalism, austerity, or globalisation to describe those phenomena at the time, it now seems highly probable that almost every state seeking to pursue a national road to social democracy (let alone socialism) would encounter problems similar to those experienced by the French Socialist Party in the early 1980s. See Robert Boyer and Jean-Pierre Durand, *L'Après-fordisme* (Paris: Syros, 1993). The very difficult post-election victory negotiations between Syriza and the Troika in February and March of 2015 offer a reminder of the enormous problems faced by any democratically elected government with a political mandate to challenge the politics of austerity. For an analysis of some of the key factors in play, see Yanis Varoufakis, 'How I became an erratic Marxist', *Guardian* (18 February 2015), pp. 29–32, and *The Global Minotaur: America, the True Origins of the Financial Crisis and the Future of the World Economy* (London: Zed, 2011).

2 There are also those who argue that with the possible exception of Franz Neumann's *Behemoth* (1942/1944), first-generation critical theory was not even very adept at theorising fascism, to say nothing of post-World War II social and political phenomena. For a representative of this line of interpretation, see Michael Schäfer, *Die 'Rationalität' des Nationalsozialismus: Zur Kritik philosophischer Faschismustheorien am Beispiel der Kritischen Theorie* (Weinheim: Beltz Athenäum, 1994). For a more positive assessment of the different interpretations of fascism offered by the main theorists of the Frankfurt School, see William E. Scheuerman, *Between the Norm and the Exception: The Frankfurt School and the Rule of Law* (Cambridge, MA: MIT Press, 1994). The most influential statement advocating a shift from critical theory to a theory of communicative action is articulated by Jürgen Habermas, *Theorie des kommunikativen Handelns*, 2 vols (Frankfurt: Suhrkamp, 1981), available in English as *The Theory of Communicative Action*, 2 vols (Cambridge: Polity, 1984). See in particular Part VIII, chapter 3, on the 'Tasks of a Critical Theory of Society'.

3 Timothy Garton Ash, 'Europe is being torn apart – but the torture will be slow', *Guardian* (9 March 2015), p. 29. The palpable reality that transnationally organised institutions and forces will prop up select national governments and try to undermine others has prompted an at times analytical and at times polemical debate about what neoliberalism is, and the extent to which it contributes to political polarisation. See David Harvey, *A Brief History of Neoliberalism* (Oxford: Oxford University Press, 2005). For an assessment that skilfully combines analytical research and polemical flair, see Jodi Dean, *Democracy and Other Neoliberal Fantasies: Communicative Capitalism and Left Politics* (Durham, NC: Duke University Press, 2009). It should not be assumed, however, that national states enjoyed sovereign autonomy in the period from the end of feudalism until 1945, after which they progressively ceded more and more of their sovereignty, until it was more or less absorbed by neoliberal, global forces after 1989. Some scholars believe that it is more accurate to

say that since the time of the earliest experiments in constitutionalism in medieval Europe, the preconditions of *political* sovereignty have been transnational and social rather than national and *political* (a tautology). See Chris Thornhill, *A Sociology of Constitutions: Constitutions and State Legitimacy in Historical-Sociological Perspective* (Cambridge: Cambridge University Press, 2011), and 'The Future of the State', in Poul F. Kjaer, Gunther Teubner, and Alberto Febbrajo (eds), *The Financial Crisis in Constitutional Perspective: The Dark Side of Functional Differentiation* (Oxford: Hart, 2011), pp. 357–93.

4 Gramsci indicates that it is not always precise enough to speak in generic terms about the Italian state or the French state when analysing power relations in the domestic and international arena. This methodology tends to portray complex sets of relations as monolithic and juxtaposed entities, as when, for example, one reads about the confrontation between the German and the Greek state in the conflict over debt repayment. For Gramsci it is more accurate to investigate how inter-ministerial and extra-parliamentary alliances in political society, civil society, and the economy are formed and constantly re-shuffled in order to bypass or neutralise institutions of democratic control. In an attempt to explain how power is exercised in ways that significantly differ from orthodox Marxist and liberal democratic accounts, he refers to these informal alliances as historical blocs. In short, Gramsci deconstructs the modern state and anticipates a number of contemporary democratic deficits. He shows that the political unity between citizens and the state premised in much normative thinking about legitimacy is in fact a very fragile disunity in most contexts. To borrow from his terminology, lack of attention to these details can distract attention from passive revolutions, wars of position, and other strategic realignments of the forces in play. See Antonio Gramsci, *Quaderni del carcere*, ed. Valentino Gerratana, 4 vols, Vol. II, Edizione critica dell'Istituto Gramsci (Torino: G. Einaudi, 1975), pp. 457–8. Originally written between 1928 and 1935, Gramsci's *Prison Notebooks* are available in English in a number of reliable translations, e.g. *Prison Notebooks*, trans. and ed. Joseph A. Buttigieg (New York: Columbia University Press, 1991). For a detailed analysis of Gramsci's historical bloc as an alternative to the base-superstructure model of political causality and action, see Darrow Schecter, 'The Historical Bloc: Toward a Typology of Weak States and Contemporary Legitimation Crises', in Mark McNally (ed.), *Antonio Gramsci* (Basingstoke: Palgrave Macmillan, 2015), pp. 179–94.

5 This book develops further ideas on social form and functional differentiation introduced in *The Critique of Instrumental Reason from Weber to Habermas* (2010) and *Critical Theory in the Twenty-First Century* (2013). In comparison with those studies, this one contains relatively little explicit treatment of Simmel's theory of social form. For a more recent analysis of Simmel's writings on social form that explicitly links him with critical theory, see Elizabeth S. Goodstein, *Georg Simmel and the Disciplinary Imaginary* (Stanford: Stanford University Press, 2017).

6 Although the Front National in France attracts a great deal of media attention, the phenomenon of right populism has become a pressing issue in Scandinavia and other places which until recently were considered social democratic bastions of welfare solidarity and multi-cultural pluralism. For the Scandinavian political scene, see Susi Meret and Birte Siim, 'Multiculturalism, Right-Wing Populism and the Crisis of Social Democracy', in Michael Keating and David McCrone (eds), *The Crisis of Social Democracy in Europe* (Edinburgh: Edinburgh University Press, 2013), pp. 125–39. For a more theoretical analysis engaging with Lacan, Žižek, and Rancière, see Ernesto Laclau, *On Populist Reason* (London: Verso, 2005) and Tariq Ali, *The Extreme Centre: A Warning* (London: Verso, 2015).

7 Jürgen Habermas, *Die postnationale Konstellation: Politische Essays* (Frankfurt: Suhrkamp, 1998), chapter 4, available in English as *The Postnational Constellation: Political Essays*, trans. and ed. Max Pensky (Cambridge, MA: MIT Press, 2001), and *Zur Verfassung Europas: Ein Essay*, Edition Suhrkamp: Sonderdruck (Berlin: Suhrkamp, 5th edn, 2014), pp. 48–55, available in English as *The Crisis of the European Union: A Response*, trans. Ciaran Cronin (Cambridge: Polity, 2012), pp. 12–20. For a very good exposition of Habermas's ideas on constitutional patriotism, see Jan-Werner Müller, *Constitutional Patriotism* (Princeton: Princeton University Press, 2007).

8 Kolja Möller, 'Struggles for Law: Global Social Rights as an Alternative to Financial Market Capitalism', in Poul F. Kjaer, Gunther Teubner, and Alberto Febbrajo (eds), *The Financial Crisis in Constitutional Perspective: The Dark Side of Functional Differentiation* (Oxford: Hart, 2011), pp. 326–32.

9 Gunther Teubner, 'A Constitutional Moment? The Logics of Hitting Rock Bottom', in Poul F. Kjaer, Gunther Teubner, and Alberto Febbrajo (eds), *The Financial Crisis in Constitutional Perspective: The Dark Side of Functional Differentiation* (Oxford: Hart, 2011), pp. 13–15, also available in Gunther Teubner, *Critical Theory and Legal Autopoiesis: The Case for Societal Constitutionalism*, Critical Theory and Contemporary Society (Manchester: Manchester University Press, 2019); Poul F. Kjaer, *Constitutionalism in the Global Realm: A Sociological Approach* (London: Routledge, 2014), Part III, and Colin Crouch, *Post-Democracy* (Cambridge: Polity, 2004), chapter 1.

10 Theodor W. Adorno, 'Gesellschaft', in *Soziologische Schriften I* (Frankfurt: Suhrkamp, 1979 [1965]), pp. 9–19. Like Adorno and other members of the Frankfurt School, Brecht is very adept at explaining why existing social relations are not the only ones possible because the possibility of qualitatively different social relations is implied by existing ones. Broadly following the Hegelian concept of determinate negation, Adorno and Brecht indicate that it is methodologically suspect and politically ineffective to reject existing relations outright as simply wrong or pervasively unjust in some kind of overarching, ontological sense. For a cinematographic analysis along these lines with contemporary sociological relevance, see Angelos Koutsourakis, *Politics as Form in Lars von Trier: A Post-Brechtian Reading* (New York: Bloomsbury, 2013), chapters 1–2.

11 Theodor W. Adorno, *Negative Dialektik* (Frankfurt am Main: Suhrkamp, 1975 [1966]), available in English as *Negative Dialectics*, trans. E. B. Ashton (London: Routledge, 1973), Part III, chapter 1.

12 Theodor W. Adorno, *Nachgelassene Schriften: Vorlesung über Negative Dialektik – Fragmente zur Vorlesung 1965/66*, ed. Rolf Tiedemann (Frankfurt: Suhrkamp, 2003), pp. 129–43 (ninth lecture), available in English as *Lectures on Negative Dialectics: Fragments of a Lecture Course 1965/1966* (Cambridge: Polity, 2008), pp. 87–97.

13 Theodor W. Adorno 'Zu Subjekt und Objekt', in *Stichworte: Kritische Modelle 2* (Frankfurt: Suhrkamp, 1969), pp. 151–68. This essay provides a very succinct account of some of the ideas developed in much greater length in *Negative Dialectics*. It is available in English as 'On Subject and Object', trans. Henry W. Pickford, in *Critical Models: Interventions and Catchwords* (New York: Columbia University Press, 1998), pp. 245–58, and as 'Subject and Object', trans. E. B. Ashton, in Andrew Arato and Eike Gebhardt (eds), *The Essential Frankfurt School Reader* (New York: Continuum, new edn, 1982), pp. 497–511.

14 The most comprehensive articulation of this perspective on sociological theory can be found in the writings of Niklas Luhmann (1927–1998). See in particular Niklas

Luhmann, *Soziale Systeme* (Frankfurt: Suhrkamp, 1987 [1984]), available in English as *Social Systems* (Stanford: Stanford University Press, 1995), chapters 11–12, and *Die Gesellschaft der Gesellschaft*, 2 vols (Frankfurt: Suhrkamp, 1997), available in English as *Theory of Society*, 2 vols (Stanford: Stanford University Press, 2012–2013), Vol. II, chapter 4. For a very good introduction to Luhmann and systems theory, see Scott Veitch, Emilios A. Christodoulidis, and Lindsay Farmer, *Jurisprudence: Themes and Concepts* (London: Routledge, 2nd edn, 2012), pp. 278–89. Luhmann's ideas have been developed in very fruitful ways by sociologists, legal theorists, critical theorists, and sociologists of law and constitutions. For approaches with much relevance to the arguments developed in this book, see Gunther Teubner, *Verfassungsfragmente: Gesellschaftlicher Konstitutionalismus in der Globalisierung* (Berlin: Suhrkamp, 2012), available in English as *Constitutional Fragments: Societal Constitutionalism and Globalization* (Oxford: Oxford University Press, 2012), and Andreas Philippopoulos-Mihalopoulos, *Niklas Luhmann: Law, Justice, Society* (London: Routledge, 2010).

15 This is the point of ostensible agreement between Heidegger and Derrida, encapsulated in Jacques Derrida, 'Violence et métaphysique', in *L'Ecriture et la différence* (Paris: Seuil, 1967), pp. 117–228, available in English as *Writing and Difference*, trans. Alan Bass (London: Routledge, 1997). An anthropologist might counter that it is perfectly conceivable, depending on the society in question, to have both metaphysical knowledge and harmonious patterns of social integration. Adorno and Luhmann would in all likelihood disagree for reasons that differ from those of Heidegger and Derrida. It will become clear why the line of inquiry pursued here is informed by the theories of negative dialectics and social systems rather than the theories of fundamental ontology and deconstruction.

16 Simmel's influence on the development of early critical theory is brilliantly portrayed in two excellent exegetical works. See Goodstein, *Georg Simmel and the Disciplinary Imaginary*, and Klaus Christian Köhnke, *Der junge Simmel in Theoriebeziehungen und sozialen Bewegungen* (Frankfurt: Suhrkamp, revised edn, 1996), Part III. By contrast, see Herbert Marcuse, 'Philosophy and Critical Theory', trans. Jeremy J. Shapiro, in *Negations: Essays in Critical Theory* (London: Allen Lane The Penguin Press, 1968), pp. 134–41. In this essay Marcuse equates sociology with the sociology of knowledge in ways that commit him to a modified version of the base/superstructure model.

17 Adorno, *Negativo Dialektik*, in English available as *Negative Dialectics*, Part I, chapters 1–2, and Part III, chapter 2. The point about communitarian destiny is a reference to Heidegger's notion of an expressly national community of fate conjured up in paragraph 74 of *Being and Time* (1927). See Martin Heidegger, *Sein und Zeit* (Tübingen: Niemeyer, 17th edn, 1993 [1927]), paragraph 74, pp. 382–7, available in English as *Being and Time*, trans. Joan Stambaugh, revised and with an introduction by Dennis J. Schmidt (Albany: State University of New York Press, 2010), pp. 364–8.

18 Theodor W. Adorno, *Ästhetische Theorie*, ed. Gretel Adorno and Rolf Tiedemann, Gesammelte Schriften, 7 (Frankfurt: Suhrkamp, 1970), pp. 76–84, available in English as *Aesthetic Theory*, ed. Gretel Adorno and Rolf Tiedemann (London: Athlone, 1997), pp. 46–53. Marcuse was admittedly far more optimistic than Adorno about the possibilities for radically reforming organised capitalism. For a very good analysis of their respective assessments, see Douglas Kellner, *Critical Theory, Marxism, and Modernity* (Baltimore: Johns Hopkins University Press, 1989).

19 Oskar Negt and Alexander Kluge offer an original approach in their *Public Sphere and Experience: Toward an Analysis of the Bourgeois and Proletarian Public Sphere*, trans. Peter Labanyi, Jamie Owen Daniel, and Assenka Oksiloff (London: Verso,

2016). This reprinted English translation of a text dedicated to Adorno and first published in German in 1972, one year before Habermas's *Legitimation Crisis*, contains a very useful foreword by Miriam Hansen, written in 1991.

20 Max Horkheimer and Theodor W. Adorno, *Dialektik der Aufklärung: Philosophische Fragmente* (Frankfurt: Fischer Taschenbuch Verlag, 1995 [1944]), pp. 38–9, available in English as *Dialectic of Enlightenment*, trans. John Cumming (New York: Herder and Herder, 1972), pp. 31–3.

21 Max Horkheimer, 'Traditionelle und kritische Theorie', in *Traditionelle und kritische Theorie: vier Aufsätze* (Frankfurt: Fischer Taschenbuch Verlag, 1968), pp. 12–64, available in English as 'Traditional and Critical Theory', in *Critical Theory: Selected Essays* (New York: Continuum, 1982), pp. 188–252; Herbert Marcuse, *One-Dimensional Man: Studies in the Ideology of Advanced Industrial Society* (London: Routledge, 2nd edn, 2002 [1964]), Part I; and Erich Fromm, *Beyond the Chains of Illusion: My Encounter with Marx and Freud* (New York: Simon & Schuster, 1962), chapters 4, 5, and 8. These issues are ably covered by John Abromeit, *Max Horkheimer and the Foundations of the Frankfurt School* (Cambridge: Cambridge University Press, 2011).

22 Marx fluctuates somewhat between the highly polemical account of state power in the *Communist Manifesto* (written with Friedrich Engels) to the much more nuanced tones of the *Eighteenth Brumaire of Louis Bonaparte* and other writings. Despite these differences in tone, the explanation of interpersonal and class conflict is consistently situated within the overall struggle between the buyers and sellers of labour power. Within a certain strand of second-generation critical theory, a normative evolutionary capacity to generate mutual understanding and reciprocal respect is ascribed to such conflicts. See Axel Honneth, *Kampf um Anerkennung: Zur moralischen Grammatik sozialer Konflikte* (Frankfurt: Suhrkamp, 1994), available in English as *The Struggle for Recognition: The Moral Grammar of Social Conflicts* (Oxford: Polity, 2005); and Nancy Fraser and Rachel Jaeggi, *Capitalism: A Conversation in Critical Theory* (Cambridge: Polity, 2018).

23 For a similar perspective that builds on the legacy of the first generation whilst also departing from some of its dialectical and Hegelian motifs, see Bernard Stiegler, *La Télécratie contre la démocratie: Lettre ouverte aux représentants politiques* (Paris: Flammarion, 2006).

24 Horkheimer and Adorno, *Dialektik der Aufklärung*, available in English as *Dialectic of Enlightenment*, chapter 1. Stated in these terms, one can detect similarities between critical theory and certain themes recurring in post-structuralism. On the specific phenomenon of discourses enlisted in the legitimation of power relations, there are clear parallels between the main theses developed in the *Dialectic of Enlightenment*, and those defended by Jean-François Lyotard, *La Condition postmoderne: Rapport sur le savoir* (Paris: Minuit, 1979), available in English as *The Postmodern Condition: A Report on Knowledge*, trans. Geoff Bennington and Brian Massumi (Manchester: Manchester University Press, 1984).

25 Hence 'damaged life', as Adorno calls it, does not cease to be damaged in postfascist peacetime, since, he thinks, progress and barbarism are inextricably interwoven in mass culture. See Theodor W. Adorno, *Minima moralia: Reflexionen aus dem beschädigten Leben* (Berlin and Frankfurt: Suhrkamp, 1951), pp. 57–8, available in English as *Minima Moralia: Reflections from Damaged Life* (London: Verso, 1978), pp. 50–1.

26 He does this very effectively, if somewhat hastily at times given the large number of thinkers he passes under review, in Jürgen Habermas, *Der philosophische Diskurs der Moderne: Zwölf Vorlesungen* (Frankfurt: Suhrkamp, 3rd edn, 1985), available

in English as *The Philosophical Discourse of Modernity*, trans. Frederik Lawrence (Cambridge: Polity, 1987).

27 Jürgen Habermas, *Faktizität und Geltung* (Frankfurt: Suhrkamp, 1992), available in English as *Between Facts and Norms: Contributions to a Discourse Theory of Law and Democracy*, trans. William Rehg (Oxford: Polity, 1997), chapters 7–8. For a decidedly more pessimistic assessment of the possibilities for equilibrium between the capitalist economy and other social systems, written in light of recent controversies in the eurozone, see Heiko Feldner and Fabio Vighi, *Critical Theory and the Crisis of Contemporary Capitalism*, Critical Theory and Contemporary Society (New York: Bloomsbury, 2015), especially chapter 4 and the epilogue.

28 Highly original and influential research on this topic has been done by Harold Berman and David Sciulli, and more recently by Chris Thornhill, Hauke Brunkhorst, Gunther Teubner, Andreas Fischer-Lescano, and Kolja Möller. See the introduction to Harold J. Berman, *Law and Revolution: The Formation of the Western Legal Tradition* (Cambridge, MA: Harvard University Press, 1983); David Sciulli, *Theory of Societal Constitutionalism: Foundations of a Non-Marxist Critical Theory* (Cambridge: Cambridge University Press, 1992), chapters 4–5; Thornhill, *Sociology of Constitutions*, chapters 3 and 5; Hauke Brunkhorst, *Critical Theory of Legal Revolutions: Evolutionary Perspectives*, Critical Theory and Contemporary Society (New York: Bloomsbury, 2014), Part III; Teubner, *Constitutional Fragments*, chapters 4–5; Andreas Fischer-Lescano and Gunther Teubner, *Regime-Kollisionen: Zur Fragmentierung des globalen Rechts* (Frankfurt: Suhrkamp, 2006); and Kolja Möller, *Formwandel der Verfassung: Die postdemokratische Verfasstheit des Transnationalen* (Bielefeld: Transcript, 2015). The ideas and intellectual generosity of Thornhill, Brunkhorst, Teubner, Fischer-Lescano, and Möller exercise a considerable influence on the arguments developed in the present book.

29 For a brilliant analysis explaining how the declining fortunes of social democratic parties are part of a larger mediation crisis likely to grip the entire spectrum of political parties, see Franz Walter, *Vom Milieu zum Parteienstaat: Lebenswelten, Leitfiguren und Politik im historischen Wandel* (Wiesbaden: VS Verlag für Sozialwissenschaften, 2010). Walter analyses declining social democratic vote totals and party membership figures in Germany, but his study raises wider issues taken up by Crouch in *Post-Democracy*. For a far more optimistic assessment of the prospects for social democracy see David Held, *Global Covenant: The Social Democratic Alternative to the Washington Consensus* (Oxford: Polity, 2004). Further scholarship on this topic is provided by Herbert Kitschelt, *The Transformation of European Social Democracy* (Cambridge: Cambridge University Press, 1994); Christopher Pierson, *Hard Choices: Social Democracy in the Twenty-First Century* (Cambridge: Polity Press, 2001); and by Michael Keating and David McCrone (eds), *The Crisis of Social Democracy in Europe* (Edinburgh: Edinburgh University Press, 2013).

30 This point is made in complementary ways in the chapters included in Markus Linden and Winfried Thaa (eds), *Krise und Reform politischer Repräsentation* (Baden-Baden: Nomos, 2011), and articulated as well in the chapters included in Danny Michelsen and Franz Walter (eds), *Unpolitische Demokratie: Zur Krise der Repräsentation* (Berlin: Suhrkamp, 2013).

31 For a far more appreciative assessment of the continued political significance of the inter-subjective dynamics of recognition, communicative action, and *phronēsis*, see Richard J. Bernstein, *Beyond Objectivism and Relativism: Science, Hermeneutics, and Praxis* (Philadelphia: University of Pennsylvania Press, 1983).

32 Isaac Nakhimovsky, *The Closed Commercial State: Perpetual Peace and Commercial Society from Rousseau to Fichte* (Princeton: Princeton University Press, 2011), chapter 4 and conclusion.

33 Habermas, *Faktizität und Geltung*, p. 13, available in English as *Between Facts and Norms*, pp. xlii–xliii. It is true that whereas Hegel attributes mediating primacy to the state, Habermas attributes mediating primacy first to the public sphere and the lifeworld, and thereafter to communicative action and civil society. Both thinkers, however, share the belief that the nation state provides the legal and rational framework within which all citizens are united with political authority. Habermas's writings on the post-national constellation and the EU certainly do provide evidence of a more transnational approach to democracy than those articulated up until *Between Facts and Norms*. Some of his concerns about the risks involved in fully embracing what one might call constitutional patriotic cosmopolitanism are expressed in *Zur Verfassung Europas*, pp. 69–85, available in English as *Crisis of the European Union*, pp. 37–57.

34 A collection of essays resulting from a recent conference in Wuppertal indicates the immense range and depth of Habermas's work. See Smail Rapic (ed.), *Habermas und der historische Materialismus* (Munich: Karl Alber, 2014), especially the chapters by Kreide, Outhwaite, and Brunkhorst.

35 For a statement illustrating the continuity of his views, see Jürgen Habermas, 'Hat die Demokratie noch eine epistemische Dimension? Empirische Forschung und normative Theorie', in *Philosophische Texte*, Vol. IV (Frankfurt: Suhrkamp, 2009), pp. 87–149.

36 Jürgen Habermas, *Strukturwandel der Öffentlichkeit: Untersuchungen zu einer Kategorie der bürgerlichen Gesellschaft* (Frankfurt: Suhrkamp, 2nd edn, 1991 [1962]), available in English as *The Structural Transformation of the Public Sphere: An Inquiry into a Category of Bourgeois Society*, trans. Thomas Burger with the assistance of Frederick Lawrence (Cambridge: Polity, 1992), chapters 4–6.

37 Habermas, *Faktizität und Geltung*, available in English as *Between Facts and Norms*, chapter 9.

38 Habermas, *Faktizität und Geltung*, p. 13, available in English as *Between Facts and Norms*, pp. xlii–xliii.

1

Reconsidering the theoretical preconditions of modern democratic statehood: on mediated unity and overarching legal-political form

This chapter examines two of the central premises underlying most standard explanations of the construction of modern democratic statehood and its preconditions and raises fundamental questions about their continuing relevance. The presuppositions in question must be deconstructed because they offer an inaccurate account of the rights of citizens and the resources of states in the twenty-first century. This preliminary work is necessary in order fully to understand what resources states might realistically rely on today to deal with the internal pressures of conflict and social fragmentation, on the one hand, and the external pressures stemming from globalisation and transnational governance, on the other. The complex relation between internal divisions, external strategic constraints, and collective political resources for coping with tensions is complicated further by the fact that the national and international dimensions of state authority have not been neatly separable for some time now, and certainly not since 1945.[1]

The first premise of post-feudal statehood is that there exists a mediated unity binding individual citizens, law, government, and the nation state. This idea is often implicitly or explicitly invoked in tandem with the second, closely related premise according to which democracy functions as an all-inclusive political form capable of reconciling the unified foundation of popular sovereign power with the normative ideal of extensive citizen participation on an equal basis. Some scholars argue that although conceptual constructions of mediated unity, constituent citizen power, popular sovereignty, democratic inclusivity, and the like can be interpreted as celebrating the agency of the people in theory, one should be wary, for functional and political reasons, of literal readings of these ideas when attempting to explain how nominally democratic states really operate in historical practice.[2] The approach adopted here shares this point of methodological caution. But instead of contrasting theories of the constituent power of the demos with a demonstration of the limitations on the actual exercise of popular power, this book begins by examining how affirmations of mediated unity by some highly influential political philosophers (chapter 1) uneasily coexist with insistence on the functional separation of law, politics, and justice found in the writings of historians of the modern state, constitutional theorists, and sociological theorists (chapter 2). The political and sociological significance of this contradiction will attain greater clarity in chapters 3–5, where the real capacity of political parties substantially to reform functionally differentiated societies is called into question. The investigation in those chapters thus raises a number of fundamental questions about democracy in general and about the future of social democracy in particular.

There is clearly much at stake when defining terms such as 'mediated', 'unity', 'binding', and 'reconciling'. There is also much at stake when framing arguments about the quality and composition of the synthesis between the individual and authority implied by institutions that unite, bind, and reconcile. These issues, in turn, prompt a further set of questions about the extent to which the institutions in question manage to produce political unity without resorting to force, ideological accounts of national origins, and dubious narratives about the sources of cultural identity. Some of the arguments involved in these debates need to be introduced before taking up the central theme of this chapter. The discussion of mediated unity and overarching political form is therefore preceded by a series of preliminary remarks. Whilst the first of these take up questions about the legal and political dynamics of institutional syntheses and mediation processes, the second examine the defining characteristics of the modern state, in contrast with its feudal predecessor in early modern Europe. Although these observations may seem like digressions, they illustrate the extent to which a great variety of arguments about political legitimacy stem from suppositions about the mediated unity of humanity and nature. These premises are frequently translated into assertions about the political unity of the governors and the governed achieved through parliamentary representation. From the sociological standpoint developed in this book, the suppositions in question are shown to be conjectural and speculative in crucial ways.

A number of openly authoritarian thinkers are happy to endorse the idea that the concrete unity of the people and state in a truly democratic community can be effectuated as a synthesis in which preoccupations with the proper relation between theory and practice, as well as careful thinking about constitutional mechanisms capable of limiting the exercise of political power, can be considered superfluous because of spontaneous solidarity and communal bonds. In the *Genesis and Structure of Society* (1943), Giovanni Gentile argues that just as one cannot really separate theory and practice, one cannot distinguish between citizens and the state because society exists inside the individual as language, law, politics, and history.[3] Carl Schmitt recognises the functional separation of law and politics as a distinctive constitutional feature of modern democracies.[4] He nonetheless insists that the irreconcilable antagonisms proper to politics do not disappear with the consolidation of the state of law (*Rechtsstaat*), even if, in times of domestic peace, law seems to limit the exercise of power and neutralise political enmity through juridical formalism. He suggests that what enables the law to function in times of relative stability is the political foundation to which the law is irrevocably tied. According to Schmitt, the unification of the people and political authority is achieved when a state of exception makes the suspension of the law a requirement, thus enabling politics to re-assert its primacy over legal reasoning and strategic corporatist compromise. In this moment of clarity and transparence, sovereign unity is manifested in the rightful authority of the state to resolve a friend–enemy conflict with extra-legal means when the law cannot perform its usual adjudicating functions. This idea runs throughout Schmitt's writings prior to 1945, and is especially prominent in *Political Theology* (1922) and *The Concept of the Political* (1932).[5]

The idea that the relation between citizens and states can be thought of as a synthesis at all may seem inherently authoritarian and abhorrent to many. Yet Hegel enlists powerful arguments to show that unless one thinks of the relation as a synthesis capable of stipulating reciprocally binding and mutual long-term obligations between citizens and nation states, one is likely to have to accept that it is a private and contractual relation that citizens can ignore or cancel at any time, if they so choose. In Hegel's estimation this would set up a permanent war between private, particular interests and collective, public interests. Such conflict might yield illusory unity and dubious legitimacy at times. But it is a war that he presciently thinks will eventually result in either the reversion of law to neo-feudal status and privilege or in the reversion of state unity into loose aggregates of private power, that is, the end of the state. Moreover, as the first thinker to distinguish systematically between civil society and the state, he points out that the kind of unity and agreement required to generate a valid contract presupposes a valid state of some kind. Stated simply, contractual agreement needs and presupposes an extra-contractual agreement that is more elastic and genuinely consensual than the contractual mode of bargained compromise.[6] It can therefore be argued, he intimates, that when analysing the interaction between citizens and states, the question is not whether or not the relation can or cannot be understood as a synthesis. The question is really concerned with the composition and quality of the synthesis, and the mediations that produce synthetic unity. With specific reference to the central thesis developed in the *Philosophy of Right*, the composition and quality of the synthetic mediations performed by the family, civil society, and the state indicate if one is observing harmoniously mediated unity between citizens and authority, as the mature Hegel seems to think, or if one is really observing a series of relations that can be more accurately described as antagonistically mediated disunity, as the young Marx will subsequently say. Despite their manifest differences, these two thinkers are agreed on the methodological and political importance of ascertaining the modalities of mediation at work in *any* political community.[7] But can society in the second decade of the twenty-first century be meaningfully conceived as a political community in which there are institutional forces capable of binding and reconciling the individual citizen and political authority? This strand of the overall argument will be taken up in chapters 4–5.

In anticipation of that debate, the discussion to follow in this chapter will comment on the similarities and differences between Hegel and Marx in relation to the two central premises of modern statehood mentioned at the outset. Hegel is of central importance in this context for several reasons. His thinking has a profound impact on Marx and first-generation critical theory and he initiates a dialectical method of socio-historical investigation discernible in the work of contemporary theorists such as Žižek and many others.[8] Most important, however, is that one can clearly discern Hegelian motifs related to mediated unity in the political theory of what are usually considered liberal, democratic, Marxist, and generally non-Hegelian approaches to the central questions of law and the state. These affinities will become evident in the second section below on weak dialectical and strong dialectical models of political cohesion and agreement. In that discussion it will be shown that whether implicitly or explicitly, theories of dialectics and mediation underpin virtually all explanations of the modalities of modern political representation that underscore the close links between legitimacy and the workings of reason in modern institutions. This is particularly striking in arguments for secular political obligation that regard reason as the only consistently viable alternative to religion, tradition, or command.[9] Hence a key question taken up at a later stage concerns the possibility of developing methodologies of critical theory that manage to retain a modified version of dialectics without relying on the foundational dialectics of mediated unity that underpin virtually all theories of the modern state, and which are so clearly at work in the *Philosophy of Right*. It has already been seen that for Hegel one is grappling with a *synthesis*. This means that one is also struggling to define the precise nature of the *mediations* structuring the dialectic at work in the construction of the specific synthesis under consideration. A very brief preliminary word on the function of synthesis in his philosophy in broader terms is therefore useful.

Hegel intimates that knowledge is achieved through the construction of concepts that give form and unity to contradictory impulses and ideas such as intuitions, thoughts, sentiments, and experience more generally. Concepts aim at syntheses capable of reconciling duty and inclination, thought and emotion, power and authority, sense of reality and imaginative vision, and so on. It is the task of conceptual philosophy to break down the barriers separating the speculative and concrete/immediate aspects of reality and experience, though without fusing them in some kind of implausible union. He thinks that one can attempt to bypass the task of creating conceptual syntheses by asserting the priority of already unified essences, noting that the latter often pose as concrete, immediate, and therefore irrefutable truths about humanity and nature. Hegel points out that the resulting affirmation will usually have to appeal to a philosophically suspect notion of an unconditioned, self-sufficient being or an originary, self-moving mover. By contrast, good philosophy effectively shows that if one attempts to deduce something about nature by resorting to hunches about the nature of nature, or if one tries to identify a fundamental property of humanity by invoking one anecdotal version of human nature whilst dismissing countless others that are equally plausible, one has probably come up with a tautology or mere opinion rather than a convincing account of the phenomenology of worldly forms structuring human life in society. If it is true that nature cannot know nature, that is, if a fully natural entity has no other perspective apart from a natural one that is unreliable because it is dependent on its own, necessarily biased account of itself, the question arises as to how humanity can be known, if human self-knowledge does not suffice to comply with the epistemological demands of objectivity. In this case, the analogy with nature holds: a fully natural account of nature is as unsatisfactory as a fully human account of humanity. In other words, every *unmediated* account of reality is unconvincing, since it can offer no other perspective than the necessarily biased account of itself that it can produce (leaving aside the question, in this specific case, whether nature is even capable of interrogating the premises of its own existence). Hegel therefore suggests that in order to have politically relevant knowledge, one must transform the question about the essence of humanity into a question about the forms and functioning of human institutions as they evolve over the course of history. The way one frames and answers this question about the possibility of knowledge of society has quite obvious implications for the way one understands reason, law, and the attempt by the modern state to use power to limit the use of power.[10]

It is not speculative to think that humanity can know nature because although it is part of nature, humanity is not identical or reducible to it. One might say that humanity is neither separated from nor unified with nature. There is enough proximity in the relation for knowledge to be possible, and also enough metaphorical distance so that knowledge is not superfluous. More will be said in what follows in order to explain why this point about the dynamics between identity-separation and proximity-distance is very relevant to understanding what are still prevalent approaches to the relation between reason, representation, foundational dialectics, and notions of political community. Kant and others adduce good arguments in support of the claim that the question as to whether knowledge is to be sought in the human mind (internal) or in nature (external) is falsely posed, and that the far more pertinent question is the following: under what conditions is knowledge possible, given that humanity is neither fused with nature nor separate from it? As is well known, Kant concludes that the fundamental condition of knowledge is a human subject that experiences the phenomena of the world and events in time and space, with the help of the twelve categories of the understanding. Explanatory problems multiply when one extrapolates from what humanity might know about nature, presupposing the foundation of an individual epistemological subject, to the possible knowledge of the forms and functioning of institutions, presupposing the foundation of a collective epistemological subject such as the people or the proletariat. The question about the phenomena experienced by a natural, a-historically conceived individual cannot simply be re-phrased as a sociological question about institutions and social forms experienced by a collective in a specific historical context. The only way to do so is by positing an overarching political form capable of harmonising the discrepant realities constantly negotiated by overlapping and conflicting partial social forms and systems. If such harmony actually existed, legitimate representation would be a straightforward matter of channelling horizontal patterns of interpersonal interaction into vertical structures of collective authority. This dilemma illustrates the connections between epistemological and sociological matters. Simmel comments on the problems involved in transferring the Kantian approach to human knowledge of nature to the study of human interaction in society. The problem is compounded, Simmel notes, by the fact that although no direct transfer is possible, in one important respect there is a qualified symmetry in approach between Kantian and sociological methodologies. Kant shows that our knowledge of nature is mediated by the anthropological forms (time and space together with the twelve categories of the understanding) that our knowledge takes; Simmel observes that our knowledge of society is mediated by the interactive forms through which our knowledge of society becomes possible. In both cases knowledge is formal rather than metaphysical or essential. The problem is that society is plural and de-centred, and offers no stable epistemological foundation analogous to the individual knower of nature, or, stated differently, there is no direct correspondence between anthropological and social forms. Hence there are qualitatively different kinds of sociological knowledge that pertain to discrete social forms and systems. The implication is that one cannot generate a model of political representation or a theory of political obligation on the assumption that the state can play the role of an overarching mediator capable of synthesising those forms. Nor can one assume that the category of 'the political' somehow distils the plurality of social forms and systems into a clearly demarcated path joining the people and the state by way of a charismatic leader, in the openly authoritarian account of this process, or via political parties and the lifeworld, according to seemingly more acceptable, mainstream versions. Nationalism, populism, and similar movements can be analysed as attempts to distort a complex set of social mediations into an 'imagined community' of political immediacy and collective agency. It can be argued that they usually do this by trading on unwarranted essentialist assumptions. Nationalism and populism may at times stand out as virulent and pathological attempts to bypass accepted channels of representation and thereby to expose those channels as out of touch with popular experience, needs, and capacities for self-government. Depending on the specific socio-historical context, such protest may actually reveal real weaknesses in existing patterns of interest aggregation and the structure of political compromise. The more centrally relevant point for this study is that the critique of essentialist populism raises acute questions about the validity of popular sovereignty, constituent power, and vertical models of political representation that presuppose a mediated unity between citizens and the state. This presupposition typically conflates anthropological and social forms in syntheses that do not synthesise so much as they force together.[11]

For millennia it seemed apparent to many that science, philosophy, and aesthetics offer the most systematic approaches to the human endeavour to know nature. Discoveries in these fields of inquiry eventually contributed to the construction of paradigms with implications for other fields. The work of Galileo and others indicated that religion and tradition could no longer provide plausible explanations of political power and normative order. The Renaissance famously makes humanity the measure of reality in human affairs. But as increasingly complex patterns of stratification became observable, questions arose about the internal divisions and political inequalities shaping the proximity and distance between unique human beings and distinct groups of individuals. How would these divisions affect knowledge of society and the construction of normative orders? This became an urgent matter, as developments in science, trade, and industry seemed to indicate that patterns of social structure play a far larger part than supposed 'natural' talent in explaining divisions and inequalities. With the passing of feudalism, the normative expectations of relatively large segments of European society underwent a profound transformation. In this novel situation, it no longer seemed fanciful to insist that norms backed by the force of knowledge are more legitimate than appeals to natural difference, seigniorial whim, or the weight of tradition. The question of rational norms turned into an urgent problem with the gradual demise of antiquated structures of representative authority. If the divisions in question would no longer be accepted as natural or ordained by God, could they be stabilised by new conceptual syntheses and institutional forms?

Hegel believes that the development of the modern state provides rational grounds for affirmative responses. He addresses questions of difference, division, and conflict through an analysis of the historical processes linking the methodology of conceptual synthesis with the empirical specificities observable in institutional form. That link is crucial for his attempt to show why reliable epistemology depends on establishing a close symmetry between method of inquiry and object of inquiry. He thereby opens up a line of inquiry prefiguring sociological and aesthetic innovations that successfully detach the reality of form from epistemological criteria demanding the imitation of nature. The implications of this move towards de-naturalisation point beyond Hegel's theory of state to a series of wider developments in sociological and aesthetic theory. By separating the reality of form from the imitation of nature, Hegel paves the way for an understanding of a post-foundational theory of legitimacy, without ever articulating such a theory himself. His political writings foreshadow conceptions of inclusion that cease to rely on notions of ethnic homogeneity or unreflective national allegiance even if, on the basis of a literal reading of texts such as the *Philosophy of Right*, he sometimes seems to justify colonialism, Eurocentrism, and excesses of executive power.[12] Although his theory of state has been consistently translated as a 'philosophy of right', the theory is more centrally concerned with the mediating functions performed by *Sittlichkeit* (usually translated as ethical life) in general, and by law in particular. As the second premise of post-feudal statehood suggests, it would be difficult to argue that force is the predominant factor in the synthesis if it can be shown that citizens and government are mediated through laws that are ultimately made by the citizens, such that the citizens are represented by their own laws.[13] This idea is neatly expressed considerably later, well after Hegel's day, in the idiomatic claim that 'we live in a democratic society' that is capable of integrating people through a combination of social solidarity and formal political rights, without relying on ideological deception or unlawful coercion. As signalled in the introduction, it will be seen that this claim fails to distinguish between legal, political, economic, scientific, and other systemic dynamics that tend, in complex societies, to develop semi-autonomous codes and operations. It may well be that the political system of any given state demonstrates features that can be accurately described as democratic. Chapters 4–5 demonstrate why this does not mean that the same can be said in any unqualified way about the economic, educational, legal, and other systems.

The citizen–state synthesis implied by the second premise of post-feudal statehood proposes that citizens play an active role in making the laws that govern them, via representative institutions, and that citizens are simultane-ously subject to the legal authority they have indirectly endorsed, within the borders of their territorially delimited nation state.[14] The recurrent postulate is that the harmonious condition of being empowered to make the laws to which one owes allegiance establishes a symmetry or continuum between individual autonomy and collective autonomy. Whilst Hegel is the key theorist of medi-ated unity, Rousseau as well as more recent republican thinkers and theorists of positive liberty tend to regard juridical-political primacy as the precondition of political democracy.[15] Despite attributing a preeminent legislative role to the civil service in his theory of state, Hegel's thinking exhibits elements of both approaches, and in his thoughts on contract, abstract right, and moral-ity, he acknowledges the validity and importance of arguments for negative liberty, private law, and what is discussed in the second section of this chap-ter as a weak dialectical position.[16] He also demonstrates that the dialectical method captures something palpably real about the dynamic and conflictual character of complex conceptual thought and the structure of modern society, whilst also showing that the parallel between conceptual and social complex-ity is more than casual. This is why Hegel is confident that attempts to ground authority in non-dialectical terms are very likely to be predicated on 'necessary fictions', such as the idea of the social contract or the state of nature. In his eyes necessary fictions tend to assume the validity of unified essences bereft of any discernible patterns of historical development or internal tensions, such as those predicated on the postulate of 'man in the state of nature'. These kinds of a-historical abstractions do not offer adequate responses to the chal-lenges of re-thinking inclusion and integration along post-feudal, secular lines. They may beguile through coherence and simplicity, but they cannot account for conflict, agreement, and the causes of historical change.

Although he does not resort to a-historical abstractions, he evidently does rely on what he takes to be a symmetry between method of inquiry and object of inquiry and this, in turn, relies on the idealist belief in a conceptual reality that adequately synthesises subject and object. Just as idealist syntheses do not so much synthesise as they force together, the symmetry between method and object is achieved to the detriment of the non-conceptual, which ends up being dismissed as neither real nor rational. The transitions Hegel sees at work in the mediations of ethical life supposedly reconcile individuals and institutions. But they do so in ways that effectively have been called into question by Marx, Simmel, and Adorno. As a consequence, even the most convincing case in support of mediated unity, as it was developed in 1821, does not fully convince today.[17] The rest of this chapter shows why postulated mediated unity and overarching legal-political form can no longer be invoked to provide stringent sociological or normative accounts of the ways in which law and other instances of social communication are produced and function in complex, functionally differentiated societies. The arguments developed will also show how this explanatory deficit impedes an accurate understanding of the conditions under which contemporary states work. Hence the analysis proceeds by reconstructing the preconditions of modern democratic statehood as an historically distinct form of political authority.

Democratic statehood as the mediated unity of law and politics

Ideas of sovereign democratic statehood were developed by a variety of thinkers and social actors as part of a sustained attempt to build a stable polity with sufficient control over key areas of jurisdiction which, under feudal institutional arrangements in most European regions, were markedly undemocratic and normally governed by confessional dogmas, rank, tradition, privilege, and other naturalised hierarchies, rather than by uniformly applied positive law.[18] How much centralisation and what kind of unity would be needed to secure sufficient steering capacities, without subjugating individual citizens and groups? One can begin to approach the matter with the help of ideal types. In ideal-typical terms, a key precondition of post-feudal political authority capable of exercising control over crucial areas of policy is non-interference from ecclesiastical authority.[19] Another is the elimination (or at least greatest possible marginalisation) of rival military factions, and the subordination of the official police and armed forces at sea and on land (and eventually in the air) to centralised political power. Professionalisation of public office across the board – especially in the civil service – tends to accompany the centralisation of military and security authorities and their subordination to the state, so that

the allocation of posts and organisation of responsibility is guided by meritocratic criteria and standard qualifications, rather than by personal connections
or private debts and obligations. In principle, there should also be a unified legal
system that is valid for all citizens regardless of status, social class, religion,
race, gender, and so on, which is empowered to raise revenues through taxation on a similarly uniform, universally applicable basis. This of course meant
the end of taxation by the church and other corporate bodies; the latter could
henceforth ask for contributions, dues, membership fees, and the like, but
were no longer empowered to tax as such. Moreover, there should be a unified system of public courts rather than an arbitrary amalgam of public courts
and private tribunals.[20] Then there is the difficult question of education for all
citizens on an equal basis. The ambiguities attached to the domain of national
education raise a series of difficult debates that are of great contemporary
significance. Many people around the world continue to regard the nation as
a naturally and essentially unified organic body. If one accepts this premise,
it is not difficult to conclude that educational practices should be committed
to the preservation and perpetuation of specific belief systems and cultural
traditions. Nor is it difficult to see that conservatism of this kind can impede
the diversification of social learning processes and hinder the consolidation of
collective political resources. Does this mean that states should refrain from
obliging schools to teach patriotic accounts of national history, or should they,
on the contrary, encourage schools to help create a sense of identity and
belonging conducive to mediated unity and order? Conflicts related to secular
education versus religious education and the questions raised thereby for various possible models of political integration continue to confront multicultural
and post-colonial societies with difficult choices.

In any case, historical and empirical facts contradict theoretical self-
definition and ideal types in fairly dramatic fashion: remnants of hereditary
rank, recurrent class conflict, unequal access to secondary and tertiary education, persistent racial discrimination, gender inequality, and religious sectar-
ianism have consistently posed immense questions to the self-understanding
of democratic states as regards the accountability of the police and army, the
fairness of the tax and educational systems, and the universality and impartiality of the law. One can leave aside the fact that consistently enforced universal suffrage did not arrive in a number of European states until after 1945, and
that it really did not arrive in the United States until 1965. Many people still
regard the tax system as unjust, the court system as unpredictable, and the
law, in more general terms, as erratic.[21] In many countries a sense of fatalism
persists about class, gender, race, and other manifest inequalities.[22] These
problems continue to sow doubts about the institutional reliability of reason,
thus highlighting the difficulties involved in measuring progress and assessing

what one might think of as qualitative change, as opposed to dubiously quantified notions of performance and efficiency. One might also ask why it is that within this framework of putative fairness, universality, and impartiality, the one central division allowed to persist in many influential accounts of statehood and nationhood is that between the public and private spheres. This would seem to be an especially urgent matter, given that it affects the ways in which access to housing, education, health care, and the job market is structured.[23] Hegel and many other influential thinkers respond by intimating that the very distinction between public and private presupposes their mediation and ultimate unity in the state. The premises underlying this view are analysed below as part of the re-articulation of the relation between epistemological critique and social critique attempted in this book.

However flawed in conception, norms of accountability, fairness, and impartiality help shape the evolution of real practices that can be debated and reformed – once they have been comprehensively critiqued and de-naturalised.[24] At first glance it would seem that the dialectical impulse to replace fixed essences with an emphasis on synthesis and mediation accomplishes this task. But as the previous discussion of Hegel indicates, and as will be shown in more detail going forward, the normative power of critique depends very much on what specific kind of dialectics is invoked in order to de-naturalise. Questions concerning normative and institutional reform will be taken up in some detail in the last two chapters of this book, but it is worth making two relevant points at this juncture, before turning to the central theme of this chapter. First, comprehensive critique refers to an endeavour carefully to evaluate the relations between social process and normativity: this means avoiding both the uncritical approval of existing norms and dismissing them outright as ideology. Second, whether one is talking in theory about the exercise of military, fiscal, or legal power, the terms 'sufficient control' and 'centralised' in practice designate the authority to dispense power and enforce collectively binding decisions in an unrivalled, rather than in an all-encompassing way. The distinction between unrivalled and all-encompassing refers to the need to restrict the simultaneous existence of rival powers *within* military authorities, taxation systems, the courts, and so on to a bare minimum, lest one be faced with 'a state within the state'. At the same time, the distinction alludes to a complementary need to refrain from applying military, religious, educational, and other principles *across* spheres and into areas external to military, educational, and other functions in some kind of overarching way, lest one have to manage a militarised judiciary, a religiously motivated economy, a politicised scientific community, and so on. In order for the modern state to be the state of all citizens rather than the protective shield and guarantor of privileged access of any caste, class, race, gender, ethnicity, or religion, this particular state form has to refrain from personal identification with any and every specific social actor, and should in principle respect – but not absolutise – the boundaries between distinct spheres of social communication guided by different codes and logics. This means that discrete spheres of social communication should not be colonised by others, and yet, communication within one sphere cannot function well if it proceeds in ignorance of what goes on in other spheres. Here one is confronted with the question of the most appropriate methodology needed to analyse the state and its constitution in both restricted and extended senses. Although the overall argument has been scarcely developed at this early stage, it is nonetheless worth reiterating the two points just raised concerning the distinction between unrivalled versus all-encompassing inclusion *within* systems, and the need to respect but not absolutise the difference *between* individual social systems guided by distinct codes. Whilst the first point underscores the ways in which modern democratic statehood is functionally compatible with social-systemic differentiation, the second offers a reminder of the mediated and therefore dialectical dynamic characterising the regulation of relations between systems. Taken together, these two points foreshadow the theme of inter-systemic communication that will receive far more explicit attention in the discussion of societal constitutionalism in chapter 5.

It may be fairly clear why a militarised judiciary and politicised scientific community are likely to produce poor judicial decisions and unreliable scientific arguments. But matters become much more complicated when evaluating arguments for the legality of religious (private) education or, crucially, when considering the steering advantages gained when legislating various degrees of political management of the economy or outlawing strikes deemed to be political. Most modern states tolerate a combination of private and public education and therewith a plurality of religious approaches to pedagogy and faith. At the very least since Keynes, states have relied on various degrees of political planning and stimulation of consumer demand in the face of manifest market failure and the inability of economic systems to develop self-steering capacities. Why, exactly, should inter-systemic hybrids be allowed to exist with regard to religion and education and not be so readily accepted, say, with regard to the integration of socio-economic interests into the institutions of political representation and decision-making? One may ask if such representation was economically viable and politically scientific when the conditions for social democratic corporatist compromise were available, but ceased to be viable and scientific when these conditions were altered by the collapse of the former USSR, decline in the power of trade unions, and the wave of privatisation and de-regulation accompanying globalisation in many states since the end of the Cold War. If political management of the economy intrudes upon individual choice and freedom of initiative, governments should really refrain from bailing out banks in the name of those values.[25]

Stating the matter in these terms raises a series of further preliminary questions. What is the best way of understanding the relationship between the epistemological dimensions of dialectics and mediation, on the one hand, and the political practices of representation and democracy, on the other? Why should questions of knowledge and method of this kind even be considered when examining questions of power and authority? One can sketch a series of provisional answers with reference to the preceding remarks about fairness, universality, and impartiality, and the demarcation between public and private. Modern societies are confronted with the challenge of coming up with rational, post-traditional norms of political integration, bearing in mind that reason can mean different things in different contexts. The relations between reason, post-traditional law, knowledge, and norms are complex; it is unlikely that whilst knowledge is scientific, norms are quite simply humanist.[26] It is perhaps somewhat simplified but by no means inaccurate to suggest that some of the hopes attached to the project of an enlightened alternative to feudal obscurantism focus on the possibility of producing post-traditional norms that are egalitarian, anti-hierarchical, and based, to paraphrase one of the ideals of the French Revolution, on the principles and practice of solidarity. It is also perhaps a little simplistic but by no means false to think that if one abandons egalitarianism and solidarity, one will in effect embrace new forms of obscurantism and hierarchy by wasting individual potential and collective resources, and by protecting irresponsible leadership cliques from scrutiny and accountability.[27] First-generation critical theorists make this argument in diverse ways by showing that overcoming different kinds of ignorance is a theoretical project bound up with the practical political project of overcoming individual and collective dependence on powerful elites.[28]

Re-articulating critical theory means challenging lazy justifications of entrenched hierarchy that accept hierarchies as natural, inevitable, the reasonable price of meritocracy, or the just trade-off for political freedom. Part of what this entails is an historical examination of the reasons why certain kinds of hierarchy, which at one stage of social evolution may have been needed for steering purposes and in order to make binding decisions in parlous times, have become obstacles to efficient planning and collective decision-making. Re-articulation also entails challenging the assumption that meritocracy and solidarity are intrinsically at odds with one another. As in the case of differentiation discussed in the introduction and to be taken up in some detail later in chapter 5, the question is *how* meritocracy and solidarity are understood and instituted. It might be possible to endow social systems with partial constitutions enabling them better to co-ordinate their respective operations.[29]

This kind of de-centralised planning would surely yield a model of differentiation that is qualitatively distinct from the current ones promulgated through austerity, imposed as privatisation, and defended on the grounds that 'there is no alternative'. These policies are patently not conducive to investment, growth, political stability, or efficient use of human and natural resources. They tend, on the contrary, to produce damaging swings from de-regulation to erratic re-regulation, and the rather haphazard introduction of government regulators. Today one is frequently confronted with the evident reality that states around the globe are not successfully coping with these problems, and that the imperative to plan flexibly and steer in a de-centralised fashion has to be re-thought outside of the established national frameworks if there are going to be solutions to state failure, climate change, economic instability, and the movement of refugees across the world. That means breaking with the conservatism inherent in plan-versus-market and nationalisation-versus-privatisation approaches to the economy. But it also means re-examining, in more general terms, the premises that continue to inform prevailing notions of democratic statehood and citizenship, starting with the central theme of this chapter.

The term mediated unity expresses the idea that, if there was no way to bridge the political distance between citizens and the state through intermediary instances of public and private communication, the representation of interests as well as the enforcement of obligations would be *impossible*. Following this logic, therefore, the practice of mediation and the possibility of representation are intrinsically linked with the assumption of an underlying unity, which, in this particular model, is mediated rather than organic or seamless. The corollary is that if there was immediacy in the sense of identity or fusion between citizens and the state, the distinction between formal reason and substantive reason would disappear, mediation would be unnecessary, and representation would be *superfluous*. Hence the poles of impossibility and superfluity point to an unreal, dystopian world somewhere beyond knowledge, communication, and mediation. In such a world knowledge and politics are either chimerical and unattainable, or mythically re-embedded into monolithic metaphysical structures of hierarchical authority. It would in any case be a pre-modern world where tradition and command stand in for reason and accountability. Ascertaining the quality of the mediations in play in any given context is therefore important. That quality is indicative of the extent to which the distance just alluded to can be bridged without being distorted and misconceived. To return very briefly to Hegel and Marx, this means that one needs to enlist the methodology of philosophy, political theory, and sociology in order to determine the extent to which that quality can be characterised as harmoniously mediated unity or antagonistically mediated disunity.

For Hegel, the truth content of absolute spirit (philosophy, religion, art) finds its counterpart in the truth content of objective spirit (abstract right, morality, and ethical life, i.e. institutions); objective spirit ensures that political representation in the modern state is juridical and rational rather than arbitrary and authoritarian. According to the dynamic of ethical life depicted in the *Philosophy of Right*, the unmediated unity of the family is re-articulated at a higher, richer level in the state, where mediated unity is strengthened by virtue of containing civil society. Civil society embodies the moment of contractual rationality, mediated disunity, conflict, and strategic compromise within ethical life. It is central to Hegel's argument that diverse instances of conflict strengthen the fabric of the state because they help foster a complex type of unity that can bear the strains of individualism, difference, and exploitation, without, however, unravelling as a result of antagonistic pluralism.[30] It is this kind of *unity* that in principle could build a stable polity with sufficient *control* over key areas of jurisdiction, thus providing a framework for reaching binding collective decisions capable of dealing with the internal divisions and external constraints mentioned at the outset of this chapter. There is fairly wide agreement that during feudalism these areas of jurisdiction were somewhat chaotically bundled together according to a pre-modern model of legitimacy that the young Marx designates as 'the politics of un-freedom'.[31] In Hegel's account of civil society, negotiations and disagreements between two contracting parties can only be adjudicated if there is fundamental agreement on the principle and the institutional reality that the power to enforce contract is vested in a third instance which is non-negotiable.[32]

Although there is a qualitative difference between the kinds of rationality and the kinds of unity operative in the family, civil society, and the state, reason pervades all areas of ethical life. The state is definitely not simply a big family, any more than a city is simply a big town. Hegel's point is that if familial relations will often work as the basis of tribes, kingdoms, clans, and other instances of pre-modern political authority, familial relations cannot function as the foundation of a state in the modern sense, where the mediated unity of the state is fortified by the unmediated unity of the family and the mediated disunity of civil society. The spontaneity of the family and natural ties do not provide a permanent foundation for the long-term development of the family, which, like every institution, will eventually have to evolve in response to changing socio-historical conditions. By extension, the structure of private relations and calculations characteristic of the civil sphere will implode without a public regulatory framework that is also capable of reforming the operations proper to the civil sphere – Hegel rejects the idea that the actions stemming from private incentives will serve the public good. He is adamant that without that public political framework, these relations are likely to break down into the irresolvable conflicts that Marx anticipates in his critique of Hegel. Although Marx acknowledges the existence of a variety of problems in industrial societies, he comes to see private property, the division of labour, and private control over the organisation of labour power as the key to explaining why the reality of supposed mediated unity is antagonistically mediated disunity.

However, if mediated unity is not synonymous with fusion, identity, or spontaneous co-ordination for Hegel, badly mediated disunity does not mean random violence, casual exploitation, or unsystematic stratification for Marx. Marx thinks that labour power is the decisive factor in the historically evolving mediation between humanity and nature, and that each mode of production yields a determinate set of economic outputs and socio-political conflicts. He reckons further that whilst it is important to understand changing state forms, the modern state will never be able to play the fundamental role in organising humanity's productive capacities because of its lack of institutional proximity to the labour process and social production – including communication – in more general terms. It may someday attain this organisational planning power once the antagonism between the buyers and sellers of labour power has been eliminated and superseded in a new political form for collective decisions and conflict resolution. If and when this happens, however, one will no longer be speaking about the modern state, since the irrationality inherent in the condition of mediated disunity will have been overcome. Hence Marx sees a close connection between the kinds of rationality citizens can rely on to plan, steer, and organise their common affairs, and the kinds of integration that are likely to obtain in any particular historical period. In his view modern states are always susceptible to acute crisis because their politics are constitutionally designed to lack proximity to the fundamental mediating process uniting and separating humanity and nature. Conflict can be postponed but never really resolved, since there is a structural tension between the dynamism of the labour process and the constitutional imperative to preserve a specific configuration of relations between the buyers and sellers of labour power. He believes that the institutional contours of the political form of the future can be fleetingly glimpsed in the Paris Commune and other instances of radical democracy capable of co-ordinating productive and political functions. It is in this precise sense that Marx regards the Commune as 'the political form at last discovered to work out the economic emancipation of labour', and adds that '[o]ne thing especially was proved by the Paris Commune, and that is, that the working class cannot lay hold of the ready-made state and wield it for its own purposes'.[33] He reckons that once the antagonism between the buyers and sellers of labour power has been replaced by a co-operative and participatory mode of production, joint ownership of the means of production and social control of collectively produced wealth in goods, services, and organised solidarity can become the basis of political authority. At this point political authority will cease to be state authority as such. It will be the authority of all the citizens, as the institutional expression of the power vested in all of them. Marx suggests that genuine mediated unity will thus be attained in the place of its pale imitation which Hegel sees at work in the civil service, police, crown, and representative estates.[34]

By contrast, in the modern state Hegel believes to observe the workings of a highly elastic form of union capable of providing the institutions of unmediated unity and mediated disunity with a significant capacity for self-steering. Self-steering stops well short of fully developed autonomy, however; it is conditioned by the state, as the mediating third instance. One might say that for Hegel mediated unity is the contradictory culmination of a movement in which being and consciousness are reconciled – neither fused nor separated – and indeed, the idea of a relationship between elements that are neither fused nor separated illustrates how a system of rational political representation is a concept that becomes real in the modern state. This is not just true for Hegel, as will be seen in the next section. Virtually every theorist of the modern state accepts the state as an institutional necessity and an instance of normative rationality.[35] In his writings on world history and objective spirit, Hegel argues that mere being and conscious being are intertwined in a continual process of conflict and conflict resolution that is eventually moving towards a non-coercive synthesis in fully rational institutions capable of harmonising the spontaneity of nature with the rational capacities of mind through the medium of historical evolution. His emphasis on the dynamism of mediation can be contrasted with the more static notion of a natural bond just as, in a parallel vein, his understanding of modern rights can be contrasted with decidedly more personal modes of dependence such as those embodied in the hierarchical command structures of the old regime. Contractual ties are qualitatively more supple and elastic than natural bonds. But they are underpinned by a weak dialectical rationality proper to civil society that is limited by the privatised logic of non-infringement and mutual gain through exchange. Hegel successfully shows that the weak dialectical rationality of civil society cannot match the strong dialectical rationality of the state in terms of adaptive responsiveness to historical change. This becomes evident when one examines the constant flow of different kinds of social communication between the family, civil society, and state in the Hegelian model, and compares it with the abstract calculation of individual interest motivating the atomised individuals of the state of nature in the social contract model. It remains to be seen below how both dialectics are underpinned by foundational premises. It will then be possible in later chapters to examine why these foundations misconstrue the de-centred plurality of communication in functionally differentiated societies.[36]

Strong dialectical and weak dialectical models of foundational representation

The immediate question is not so much whether Hegel is correct or incorrect in this remarkably affirmative assessment of the integrative capacities of public political authority in post-feudal times. In insisting that one cannot come up with convincing grounds of political obligation in contractual terms because a valid contract presupposes a valid state, Hegel's thinking about the foundations of the state is symptomatic of a widespread tendency in modern Western theorising about political authority and normative order.[37] He makes original unity the basis of subsequent unity and re-presented unity (representation) and, in addition, he uses original unity to define the tolerable limits of dissent and alienation. To say that law and government are capable of integrating private individuals into a public normative order that respects individual rights, whilst also making rights dependent on publicly administered power, is to incorporate a dialectical dimension into one's defence of the authority of authority. Returning to the points made earlier in relation to the poles of impossible representation and superfluous representation, on the one hand, and figurative proximity and distance between citizens and states, on the other, the most important question for Hegel and those to follow him is not whether integration can be approached dialectically. It consists instead in defining the precise modalities of dialectical mediation shaping the institutions of ethical life, and evaluating the extent to which distance in this specifically juridical-political sense is mediated. Will these modalities rely mainly on individual interest, contract, property, and exchange to mediate, or will contract, property, and exchange be subsumed within a more overarching and substantial conception of political community? For Hegel, it is not a matter of choosing between the state of nature and a contractual model of civil society – the question he asks is which kind of state will guarantee the most rational mediations and which mediations will safeguard the most rational state.[38]

   In Hegel's highly influential usage, ethical life is a movement and a process whose internal tensions are resolved in positive terms such as mutual recognition between individual citizens, integration of citizens within the community of the nation state, and historical progress. He does not deny the existence of neglect in the family, exploitation in civil society, colonialism in international affairs, and alienation between humanity and nature in the realms of epistemology and politics. In his view these instances of deficient knowledge and political conflict function as preconditions for the establishment of a qualitatively richer, more complex instantiation of harmony between humanity and nature than the type of very strained, tenuously mediated unity that prevailed during European feudalism and early modern absolutism. The implication is that mediated unity precedes conflict and difference, and that a more perfected mediated unity results from these antagonisms, too. Difficulties of interpretation arise because the stages of these overlapping moments do not adhere to a straightforwardly linear, quantitative logic. A wide variety of institutional forms arrive on the historical stage and leave it eventually, but the processes of mediation and the generation of new social forms continue to evolve and unfold.[39]

Is the modern nation state one of those transient political forms, now preparing to exit the historical stage, or are the functions of what was formerly recognisable as the state now devolving upon international bodies in the first stages towards the establishment of an international state? Will populist forces reclaim the state as the property and prerogative of the nation? What other scenarios are plausible? Debates on the Transatlantic Trade and Investment Partnership (TTIP) confirm some of Hegel's misgivings that the state may shrink to a series of private agreements between international military, socio-economic, technocratic, bureaucratic, and political elites. This is probably more likely than an outright authoritarian reversion of law to command of the kind witnessed in the interwar period of the twentieth century. It is not inconceivable, however, that a combination of private deals between international elites and authoritarian steering at the national level could define the exercise of political power. Parts of Central and Eastern Europe have already experienced this particular version of neoliberalism since 1989.[40] The answers to these questions cannot be sketched at this juncture. Before they can be approached later on in this book, it must first be seen why the dialectical approach to mediated unity is not a Hegelian idiosyncrasy, but is instead a feature common to virtually all of modern thinking about the state in both spatial terms of distance/boundaries, and in temporal terms of putative origins. One can construct the main lines of argument starting with a few broad observations about how suppositions about the relation between humanity and nature typically figure in some guise in most theories of individual and collective autonomy. These suppositions will take the discussion beyond Hegel to issues of wider contemporary relevance.

It is often assumed or casually asserted that humanity is part of nature and subject to natural facts such as mortality and a variety of other factors that for the most part have to do with necessity and mechanical/biological causality beyond human control. Gravity, environmental realities, and sheer contingency thus place limits on autonomy. Given that humanity is neither identical with

nature nor completely detached from it, humanity can be said to enjoy a relation of mediated non-identity with nature.[41] According to this approach, the
extent to which humanity can overcome its dependence on nature without
detaching itself from the reality of natural processes and the life cycle therefore
crucially depends on the structure of the mediations that simultaneously unite
and separate humanity and nature. Distinct forms of property and the division
of labour do so in qualitatively different ways. Agriculture and other processes
unite humanity with the life cycle, making human life beyond mere subsistence and survival possible. They also distance humanity from direct subordination to natural scarcity and unpredictability in the guises of illness, drought,
earthquakes, flooding, etc.[42] It is sometimes argued further that practical reason in combination with various socio-economic and technological innovations
can in theory enable citizens to transcend need in two specific senses. Whilst
economies can guide humanity beyond poverty and scarcity, law and government can control and perhaps even reduce instances of un-accountable power
to a bare minimum. The examples of poverty/economy and un-accountable
power/government indicate that fundamental democratic issues are at stake in
deciding (1) how citizens plan to transcend the necessities inherent in the life
cycle, and in deciding (2) how they plan to limit the arbitrariness characteristic of political tyranny. Questions of democratic planning and decision-making
cannot be considered in abstraction from the specific modalities of knowledge
relevant to the workings of the economy, government, education, etc. Citizens
around the globe today need to devise democratic processes capable of clar-
ifying difficult choices about priorities in the struggle to transcend material
necessity and contain arbitrary exercises of power. There will certainly be disagreement about how best to organise shared productive resources in these
matters. In an attempt to anticipate and deal with some of the conflicts likely
to arise when these questions are answered in practice, standard narratives
propose that one ideally needs *to know* how to combine *knowledge* (tautology deliberately underscored) about the essence of liberty with the authoritative means required spatially to demarcate where liberty stops, and where,
logically, liberty-curtailing interventions begin. Knowledge of this kind should
by definition be formal and neutral and not, in the first instance, an explicitly
revealed matter of socio-economic interest, political loyalty, or other factors
where neutral means are distorted and undermined by power struggles and
unequal access to vital information.[43] It is in this context that one can begin to
see how notions of negative liberty/positive liberty, and weak dialectics/strong
dialectics are related to questions about legality, democracy, and legitimacy.
In what follows it will become clear how weak dialectics can be used to try to
demarcate where negative liberty stops according to the dictates of what is
meant to be formal and neutral knowledge.[44]

According to a negative theory of liberty informed by a weak dialectical epistemology, one cannot achieve essential knowledge of liberty, or for that matter, essential knowledge of any kind. The price to pay for objective knowledge is relinquishing absolute knowledge. This means that knowledge has to be concerned with the formal, negative knowledge of the limits and the means of knowledge. The supposition informing this stance is that one cannot take up issues related to the substantive, positive affirmation of the ends of knowledge without lapsing into metaphysics and dogma. What little remains of such positive affirmation after the end of metaphysics and the separation of church and state must be considered a private, ethical, or aesthetic matter, lest the temptation arise to legislate a politics of ends that could only be achieved by way of brutal imposition or manipulation.[45] In light of this epistemological and political uncertainty, one must settle for a politics of legal means that is open to all conceptions of the good life, and which is vehemently opposed to each and every politics of legitimate ends, since every one of these, in its own way, privileges one possible good life at the expense of all the others.[46] It is often claimed by theorists of negative liberty that the authority to decide where freedom is violated by unwarranted interventions should be vested in the people – not forced upon them. It is argued further that the best means of respecting this difference is through protection of a free press, unimpeded communication, and similarly free exchanges of goods, services, and information, so that the citizens can decide for themselves how they prefer to be free – unless they happen to be refugees, since these freedoms seem somehow not to include free circulation of people beyond the natural borders of nation states.[47]

In any case, one might regard the demarcation of these lines as the enforcement of the non-enforcement needed to complement the politics of legal means. Neutral and objective law founds legitimacy – not extra-legal conceptions of the legitimate good. It is therefore the case that for champions of positive and negative liberty alike, there is no directly legitimate means to legitimate ends – the relation is considered to be mediated and dialectical rather than direct and immediate. Extra-legal conceptions are moreover irrational or in any case purely subjective. It follows for the exponents of negative liberty that reason should indicate the boundaries of legitimate state intervention, but, more importantly, that freedom requires that the claims of reason and legitimacy stop with the delineation of those boundaries: these are epistemological and political boundaries beyond which reason becomes irrational and states become illegitimate. Political *legitimacy* that limits itself to *legitimate* (tautology again deliberately underscored) intervention and enforcement of law that is itself neutral with regard to competing conceptions of the best way to live is therefore the indispensable precondition of liberty.[48]

This argument proceeds from a temporal starting point that is simultaneously taken to be an achieved outcome: proponents of negative liberty know what the preconditions of liberty are. This means that they must have tangible experience of ways of living that are already emancipated from illegitimate political intrusion into a naturally legitimate private sphere of private interaction, communication, and exchange. It is presumably from this already emancipated and naturally legitimate position that the difference between the practice of legitimate law enforcement and the illegitimate abuse of law is ascertainable and susceptible to correction. Once the necessary corrections have been made, self-setting private/public boundary adjustment should be reliable once again, just as, by analogy, naturally optimal functioning markets should be relied on to function properly as a consequence of the periodic corrections to market dysfunction taken by governments whose interventions are held in check by constitutional strictures of imposed self-limitation. The enforcement of non-enforcement and the periodic restoration of self-setting boundary setting thus complement each other in the imposition of a very particular kind of 'neutrality' on all citizens sometimes referred to as governance. But who, exactly, is doing the enforcing and restoring, and how neutral or impartial could they/it possibly be? Boundaries would not have to be enforced if they were truly self-setting – this presents considerable problems for liberal democratic and orthodox systems-theoretical accounts of tacit consent and harmonious FD. The boundaries between public and private spheres or those between diverse social systems could only be neutral if there was a somehow demonstrably natural basis to all of humanity that could be re-set, re-stored, and re-presented as eternally (metaphysically) natural. But that thesis fails to convince unless one accepts that humanity can be said to enjoy a relation of mediated unity with nature, where the mediation is performed by democratic law made by and for the majority of the (naturally democratic) people. This argument does not depart decisively from the main lines of Hegelian thought; it is the weak dialectical version of Hegel's notion that mediated unity precedes and simultaneously results from conflict and difference. Hegel does not rely on an uneasy mixture of a-historical dialectics and human essences; he consistently comes up with the better arguments even if, from a contemporary standpoint, they are inadequate. Those inadequacies foreshadow a number of the arguments to be developed in subsequent chapters about the history of states and the sociology of FD. There are many epistemological and normative challenges bound up with questions as to who is doing the enforcing and restoring, how neutral or impartial these processes could possibly be (especially if a 'who' is involved), and how self-setting boundaries operate in practice. If the steering in question is not performed by Hegelian *Geist*, at present it is demonstrably not performed by automatically self-adjusting markets, impromptu planning, or spontaneous individual and collective decision-making, either.

The invocation of a naturally legitimate position creates a series of unresolved tensions in the negative liberty/weak dialectical model. The main tension is that between the legality/legitimacy distinction needed to demarcate boundaries and the legality/legitimacy fusion needed to solve the problem of demarcating boundaries without identifying the boundary-maker, lest that crucial function be revealed as the prerogative of a particular set of interests. The boundary-maker must remain unknown and impersonal if he/she/it is to have any chance of being widely regarded as rational, neutral, above all suspicion of bribery, and impervious to populist incursions from the political right and left. That raises the question as to what, specifically, is objectionably populist about using the law as a means to express the democratic will of the people. It would be more coherent to conclude that democracy is fundamentally and intrinsically populist, and that democratic law re-presents the legislative capacity of the demos (*pouvoir constituant* or constituting power) to reform the (its) state (*pouvoir constitué* or constituted power) in accordance with its collective will. This approach to these matters obscures the fact that the most pertinent question is not so much whether negative liberty or positive liberty is most conducive to democracy. That issue is better approached by investigating the relations obtaining between the political system and neighbouring social systems as they currently function and then examining how those relations might evolve in different directions under conditions of qualitatively enhanced inter-systemic communication. The response to the question about the composition of constituent power can only be answered in terms of the unqualified political agency of the people if it is accepted that there is an overarching legal-political form capable of uniting the citizens and the state in a relation that is neither fused nor separated. That answer amounts to a plea for strong dialectical legitimacy and positive liberty. It is usually met with the reply that negative liberty and formal legitimacy are the only possible and therefore necessary safeguards against the authoritarian paternalism that would result from strong dialectical legitimacy and positive liberty in practice. This kind of legitimacy can be thought of as the identifiable essence of a collective subject empowered to make law and justice work as a means in the service of substantive rather than merely formal political ends. On this reading of democracy it is difficult to avoid the conclusion that real democracy is intrinsically populist and that, as a corollary, there is nothing particularly democratic about negative liberty and formal legitimacy. In retrospect it is not difficult to see that after 1945, state socialist regimes set themselves the task of settling the key substantive question concerning the struggle to transcend material necessity; assessments differ as to the extent to which and why they did do this in ways which largely forfeited control over the arbitrary exercise of power. It would in any case be difficult to argue that the people (or parliament) is really sovereign if it is not authorised to shape such fundamental dimensions of the constitution of the state and society. On the one hand, major questions are raised about what is left of democracy once the possibilities for substantive reform and the scope for difficult choices and active participation have been scaled down to reading about the personalities and gaffes of professional politicians. On the other hand, the perceived (and actual) neutrality of mediation is largely forfeited if it becomes apparent that a decidedly non-neutral political subject is required to preside over the institutional mediations suturing the demos to the democratic state. It may seem constitutionally worrying if a party or loosely organised group of private interests is in a position to control decisions and agendas in this way; but it would be naïve to think that these ordering functions happen according to the free play of spontaneously consensual interactions or spontaneously self-setting boundaries.

There is an obvious dilemma here. If one insists on the neutrality of mediation, one loses the legislative agency of the citizenry. If one abandons the neutrality of mediation, the independence of the judiciary seems to be forfeited to the desideratum of securing the political integrity of the will of the demos to make fundamental changes. One might insist on the separation of powers to resolve these issues. But the enforcement of non-enforcement and the occasional restoration of self-setting boundaries finds its complement in a separation of powers which is simultaneously a complex ensemble of powers once, that is, it is accepted that (a) legal form enjoys (implicitly political, explicitly constitutional) priority over legitimate essence, and (b) that there is a private or civil sphere of naturally legitimate exchange that is not susceptible to meaningful legal reform. Research shows that various combinations of (a) and (b) can be invoked to handle conflicts arising in that sphere as if the law has already decided how the conflicts have to be managed before any serious alternatives can even be considered. Returning to the point in the introduction that the European Commission does not feel compelled to change policies in the light of election results, it is *as if* compelling objections to whatever happens to be legal at a given historical juncture are not, and cannot be, admitted as valid. At that point, citizens have to accept commands *as if* they were laws – especially in what are deemed to be emergency situations. The enforcement of non-enforcement thus becomes extremely problematic if it tends to efface the difference between law and force, whilst also blurring the criteria that might make that distinction intelligible and politically relevant. Many observers are likely to associate these phenomena with the crisis of the Weimar Republic and the collapse of democracy in several states in twentieth-century Europe. Yet it is clear that the contemporary crisis of Greek democracy is inextricably bound up with the legal enforcement of austerity and decisions that have already been made in notable instances of transnational intervention in national political processes. It seems highly unlikely that the Greek example will remain an isolated case.[49]

One can attempt to approach these issues by guessing about what people might agree to in a hypothetical state of nature, or, as has been attempted more recently, one can speculate about the kinds of risk they might accept behind a veil of ignorance. The theoretical constructs suggested by the state of nature and veil of ignorance cannot really address the problem that, from the moment exchange is not susceptible to meaningful legal reform, *exchange processes* in both the economic and wider senses analysed by Simmel and others tend to develop extra-legal means of auto-enforcement based on systemic codes that elude the weak and strong foundational dialectics of mediated unity and the respective models of normative integration that they each imply. The anthropological assumptions underpinning both negative conceptions of liberty (the human as an acquirer and exchanger of property) and positive ones (the human as a political animal and civic guardian of the public good) are thereby called into question. If legality was ever a means to legitimate ends, it ceases to be so when complexity and differentiation accelerate and deepen these sociologically verified tendencies towards *autopoiesis* on the part of discrete social forms and processes. Once the reality of these processes has been verified by critical research, the privileged relations between law, politics, and the people is similarly susceptible to contestation. The lines between legislation and illegitimate command become blurred to the point where there is acute analytical and normative confusion about what is law, what is command, and what is enforcement of democratically agreed norms.[50]

One can try to circumvent some of the problems posed by this confusion by arguing that law is not legitimate unless it conforms to the maxims furnished by the practical reason of a morally autonomous subject with a rational will. In some versions, this is a subject who transcends economic necessity through private means, i.e. through property ownership and/or the lucrative exercise of a profession. In *An Answer to the Question: What is Enlightenment?*, Kant maintains that it is really only a reasoning public, individually endowed with economic self-sufficiency and rational self-control, that can exert the requisite political pressure for positively enacted law to integrate ethical and epistemological principles into its statutes. The subversive dimension of Kantian epistemology can be found in his insistence that the conditions of possible experience are the same for all human beings. He argues further that this universality is politically relevant when codified in juridical form. Legality in Kant can be interpreted as both the condition of the possibility of objects of experience, whose existence is governed by laws, and the condition of the possibility of humanity (as opposed to other organic life and mechanical causality), whose freedom is enacted in rational self-legislation. He therefore offers a very good example of a theorist of negative liberty who relies on a weak dialectical epistemology. Whereas the concept of essence would normally be contrasted with form, as the content contained or framed by the latter, his version of idealism achieves what might seem like a paradoxical result – a formal theory of human essence. In refraining from a positive definition of freedom, and insisting on the primacy of legality over legitimacy, Kant defends a formal conception of human essence that never discloses what that essence is. It is difficult to overestimate the political significance of this position for the question of neutral mediation and impartial boundaries. It signals the articulation of an inchoately liberal worldview which makes a substantial claim about reason at the same time that it imagines to know what constitutes the essence of humanity. That essence is juridical and rational for Kant and for most post-Kantian liberals who regard their work as a further contribution to continuing the project of Enlightenment. Kant's theory of overarching legal-political form, which is re-worked by Rawls, Habermas, and many others, accepts the thesis that a reasoning public can exert the requisite political pressure for positively enacted law to integrate ethical and epistemological principles into its statutes.[51]

Habermas correctly sees this as a far more promising approach to legitimacy than updating the state of nature argument or joining the analytical political theorists in the debates on the veil of ignorance and ideas of justice. He democratises Kant's version of the public sphere thesis by eliminating the Kantian restriction on participation to economically self-sufficient professional men and 'softens' criteria of inclusion by rescinding the stipulation that this already restricted number should be restricted further to those that can control their emotions and aesthetic impulses, so that rationality and reasonable boundaries can be made to prevail over whim, caprice, intuition, and impulse. Habermas does not completely reject Kant's warning that any attempt to make legitimacy the form as well as the essence of legality will be tantamount to the abolition or at least dilution of legality in the name of some group or leader's arbitrary definition of the substantive bases of legitimate order. Such attempts amount to the desire to bend juridical formalism to meet the infinitely varied, extra-legal demands of happiness and human emancipation. The likely result is a lurch from objective rationality governing the objects of experience (Kant) or a deviation from communicative rationality and the post-traditional dialectics of facts and norms (Habermas). What Habermas retains, elaborates, and updates is the belief that juridical norms are not simply derivative of material interests. In his view they conform to a rational format that is universally human, and are shared on an equal foundation that is constitutive of citizenship, as opposed to inclusion in a clan, social class, or ethnic group.[52] It is not so important where one might want to position Habermas in relation to liberal democratic thinking past and future; perhaps it is now more accurate to view him as a constitutional and cosmopolitan thinker. It is important to evaluate the explicit claim that (1) the public sphere, embedded within the various lifeworlds of civil society, mediates between individual citizens and constitutional arrangements for impeding the private usurpation of political power, and the implicitly Hegelian presupposition that (2) rational mediation of this kind reproduces the mediated unity of citizens and the state without sacrificing *the primacy of legal form* in modern democratic societies. Habermas updates Hegel's defence of the state by reinstating and democratising the Kantian category of publicity that Hegel largely dismisses in the *Philosophy of Right*. Habermas is confident that legal form does not degenerate into legal formalism or positivism because of the ethical and cognitive inputs to the political process supplied by the combined forces of the lifeworlds of civil society and widespread communicative rationality.[53]

This chapter shows that the primacy of legal form cannot be relied on to enforce democratically agreed norms. There is no leading political or juridical form capable of mediating between the plurality of social forms and systems operative in society, on the one hand, and a supposedly democratic political centre that is still referred to as the modern state, on the other. A final point can be made to conclude this chapter. For the social contract theorists Hobbes, Locke, Rousseau, and Kant, the legitimacy of the early modern state is not directly founded upon a calculation of interest. It is founded instead on the supposedly unanimous agreement that prompts people with powers in the state of nature to renounce these powers in order to become citizens with rights in civil society, bearing in mind that the state and civil society are synonymous until Hegel's theory of ethical life dispenses with the idea of the state of nature. In contrast to this abstract, contractually mediated theory of individualistic agreement, non-infringement, and optional participation in civic affairs (negative liberty, weak dialectics), a number of Hegel's interpreters envisage a much more organic kind of collective and communally mediated agreement secured through the constant participation that Marx applauds in the Paris Commune, and which Lenin in 1917 sees at work in the radical democracy of the soviets (positive liberty, strong dialectics). Marx initiates a line of thinking and political action that abandons the a-historical state of nature in favour of what he takes to be the ground of history. For Marx, this means that class struggle provides the framework defining the terms of possible agreement, and not, emphatically, a fictitious assembly of property holders striving to make stable property out of their precarious possessions. Marx and his followers broadly adhere to this line of enquiry by assuming that the task of the working class consists in abolishing private property by collectivising it, or, in the social democratic variant, by nationalising it. This is the crux in this discussion of weak versus strong dialectics: private property is regarded to be the ideological mediating institution maintaining formal democracy and enforcing negative liberty, thus precluding the institutionalisation of substantive democracy and positive liberty. The tautological implication is that the working class is the most popular class of the people. It is the democratic essence of the people that is revealed when formal citizenship is exposed as ideological. This is a labouring essence fully capable of instituting democratic processes to make fundamental choices about priorities in the struggle to transcend material necessity and contain arbitrary exercises of power. It is oppressed and concealed by what are mistakenly taken to be the free exchanges of goods and services. The mistake consists in confusing free and transparent with privately owned and hierarchically organised. Once property is collectively owned and the allocation of labour power is carefully planned rather than haphazardly sold in search of profit, a transition can be made to the more consistently democratic modalities of action and agreement that would liberate genuine legitimacy from its parliamentary instantiation. As Marx suggests in relation to the Commune, the emancipation of labour power from private appropriation and wage slavery requires expansive political form rather than parliamentary democracy. Although this statement of the matter races through some complex issues and simplifies some of the theories involved, it helps illustrate the point that the foundational dialectics of people–government–state yields a model of representation that can be conceived of in liberal (ostensibly more liberal, less democratic) or social democratic and eventually socialist (ostensibly more democratic, less liberal) terms, as if there was a graduated scale linking liberal, social democratic, and socialist positions on the basis of fundamental, underlying unity that is mediated by juridical-political form. The crucial question of facts and norms has to be posed anew without relying on the existence of that continuum.

Notes

1 On this point see Kjaer, *Constitutionalism in the Global Realm*, chapters 2–3, and the essays included in Mikael Rask Madsen and Chris Thornhill (eds), *Law and the Formation of Modern Europe: Perspectives from the Historical Sociology of Law* (Cambridge: Cambridge University Press, 2014), Part III.
2 Chris Thornhill makes a very good case for caution in this regard. See Chris Thornhill, 'Contemporary constitutionalism and the dialectic of constituent power', *Global Constitutionalism*, 1:3 (2012), 369–404. The term 'mediated unity' captures some of the ambiguity involved. Depending on the structure of the institutional

mediations and historical context, the term mediated can denote a relation ranging in qualitative composition from highly attenuated to closely sutured. It is therefore important to be clear about context when discussing the constitutional character-istics of specific states. It is arguable that this issue can be traced back to the ambiguities inherent in the distinction between *le pouvoir constituant* (the people taken as the constituting political power of the state) and *le pouvoir constitué* (state institutions proper) exemplified in the writings of Sieyès and other protagonists of the French Revolution. See Emmanuel Joseph Sieyès, *Qu'est-ce que le tiers état?* (Geneva: Droz, 1970), pp. 119–20, available in English in Emmanuel Joseph Sieyès, *Political Writings: Including the Debate Between Sieyès and Tom Paine in 1791*, ed. Michael Sonenscher (Indianapolis: Hackett, 2003). Sieyès was well aware of these ambiguities and tensions, and hoped that they might somehow be resolved by what he regards as the unifying capacities of the nation. These issues are treated in depth in Gérard Mairet, *Le Principe de souveraineté: Histoires et fondements du pouvoir moderne* (Paris: Gallimard, 1997), Part I; and Pierre Rosanvallon, *La Légitimité démocratique: Impartialité, réflexivité, proximité* (Paris: Seuil, 2008), available in English as *Democratic Legitimacy: Impartiality, Reflexivity, Proximity*, trans. Arthur Goldhammer (Princeton: Princeton University Press, 2011), Part III, chapter 1.

3 Giovanni Gentile, *Genesis and Structure of Society*, trans. H. S. Harris (Urbana: University of Illinois Press, 1960). For a critical evaluation of Gentile's theory of the mediated unity of citizen and state, see Richard Bellamy, *Modern Italian Social Theory: Ideology and Politics from Pareto to the Present* (Stanford: Stanford University Press, 1987), chapter 6.

4 Carl Schmitt, *Constitutional Theory* (Durham, NC: Duke University Press, 2008), origin-ally published in German in 1928, chapters 14–16, and Renato Cristi, 'Carl Schmitt on Sovereignty and Constituent Power', in David Dyzenhaus (ed.), *Law as Politics: Carl Schmitt's Critique of Liberalism* (Durham, NC: Duke University Press, 1998), pp. 179–93. The introduction (p. 17) makes the point that for Schmitt, democracy can only really be attained when a homogeneously constituted people opts for political substance over juridical form; he thinks this is the political reality that most liberals refuse to recognise. Although the sociological deficit in this approach is staggering, and Schmitt is generally regarded as an extremist, he is of great interest precisely because elem-ents of his thinking about the relations between liberalism/legality and democracy/legitimacy appear in more moderate and mainstream theories of modern politics.

5 For two very good analyses of the evolution of Schmitt's thought in historical con-text, see David Dyzenhaus, *Legality and Legitimacy: Carl Schmitt, Hans Kelsen, and Hermann Heller in Weimar* (Oxford: Oxford University Press, 1997); and Ellen Kennedy, *Constitutional Failure: Carl Schmitt in Weimar* (Chapel Hill: Duke University Press, 2004). The political foundation alluded to can be a state and indeed tends to be one in modern societies with secular structures of authority. This foundational role need not necessarily be performed by a state, however, since, in Schmitt's view, the idea of the state presupposes the concept of the political. The implication is that *political* conflict precedes the rise of the modern state, and political conflict will certainly survive the demise of this historically specific set of institutions. See the first sentence of Carl Schmitt, *Der Begriff des Politischen* (Berlin: Duncker & Humblot, 3rd edn, 1996), p. 20, available in English as *The Concept of the Political* (Chicago: University of Chicago Press, 1996).

6 Georg Wilhelm Friedrich Hegel, *Grundlinien der Philosophie des Rechts oder Naturrecht und Staatswissenschaft im Grundrisse*, ed. Eva Moldenhauer, Werke,

7 (Frankfurt: Suhrkamp, 1986), paragraph 258, pp. 399–404, available in English as *Elements of the Philosophy of Right*, trans. H. B. Nisbet (Cambridge: Cambridge University Press, 1991), pp. 275–81. Prior to Hegel, the terms civil society and the state are usually used synonymously by social contract philosophers from Hobbes to Kant. On this point see Norberto Bobbio, 'Gramsci and the Conception of Civil Society', in John Keane (ed.), *Civil Society and the State: New European Perspectives* (London and New York: Verso, 1988), pp. 73–99.

7 See Hegel, *Grundlinien*, Part III, available in English as *Philosophy of Right*; and Karl Marx, 'Contribution to the Critique of Hegel's *Philosophy of Right*: Introduction', in Robert C. Tucker (ed.), *The Marx-Engels Reader* (New York: Norton, 2nd edn, 1978), pp. 53–65. Just exactly how harmonious Hegel regards supposedly harmoniously mediated unity to be is a matter of some conjecture, given his appreciation of the realities of alienation and exploitation in civil society. On this point see Shlomo Avineri, *Hegel's Theory of the Modern State* (Cambridge: Cambridge University Press, 1972), chapters 7–9; and David James, *Hegel's Philosophy of Right: Subjectivity and Ethical Life* (London: Continuum, 2007), chapters 3–4.

8 In the case of Žižek, Hegelian influences are admittedly synthesised with Lacanian ones. See the essays collected in Slavoj Žižek, *The Sublime Object of Ideology* (London: Verso, 2nd edn, 2008); and Yannis Stavrakakis, *The Lacanian Left: Psychoanalysis, Theory, Politics* (Albany: State University of New York Press, 2007). Robyn Marasco traces Hegel's continued relevance in Robyn Marasco, *The Highway of Despair: Critical Theory After Hegel* (New York: Columbia University Press, 2015). The link between Hegel, dialectics and critical theory is brilliantly traced by Fredric Jameson, *Late Marxism: Adorno, or, The Persistence of the Dialectic* (London: Verso, 1990).

9 Jean-Marc Coicaud, *Legitimacy and Politics: A Contribution to the Study of Political Right and Political Responsibility*, trans. and ed. David Ames Curtis (Cambridge: Cambridge University Press, 2002), chapter 3. Theorists of communicative action might be inclined to say that the key question is not so much which kind of dialectic, but rather, what kind of reason structures the interactions between law, economy, and the state. This is a disagreement about the defining characteristics of mediation processes.

10 Georg Wilhelm Friedrich Hegel, *Phänomenologie des Geistes* (Stuttgart: Reclam, 1987), Prologue and Introduction, pp. 1–77, available in English as *Phenomenology of Spirit* (Oxford: Clarendon Press, 1979), pp. 1–57; and Theodor W. Adorno, *Drei Studien zu Hegel: Aspekte. Erfahrungsgehalt. Skoteinos oder Wie zu lesen sei* (Frankfurt: Suhrkamp, 1963), available in English as *Hegel: Three Studies* (Cambridge, MA: MIT Press, 1993).

11 Georg Simmel, 'Wie ist Gesellschaft möglich?', in *Soziologie: Untersuchungen über die Formen der Vergesellschaftung*, Gesamtausgabe, 11, ed. Otthein Rammstedt (Frankfurt: Suhrkamp, 1992 [1908]), pp. 42–62, available in English as 'How Is Society Possible?', in *On Individuality and Social Forms: Selected Writings*, ed. Donald N. Levine (Chicago: University of Chicago Press, 1971), pp. 6–22.

12 For a detailed account linking Simmel, Adorno, and systems theory to a re-articulation of critical theory, see Darrow Schecter, *Critical Theory in the Twenty-First Century* (New York: Bloomsbury, 2013), chapters 3–5. For an analysis of Simmel that emphasises his relevance for critical theory, see Henry Schermer and David Jary, *Form and Dialectic in Georg Simmel's Sociology: A New Interpretation* (Basingstoke: Palgrave Macmillan, 2013).

13 This would be a Young Hegelian position anticipating the Left Hegelian views of Marx and Stirner rather than a position Hegel explicitly defends. In the *Philosophy*

of Right Hegel regards the civil service (not *das Volk*) as a universal class with decisive legislative authority within the modern state. There is broad agreement between Weber and the mature Hegel on this point. On Left Hegelianism, see David McLellan, *The Young Hegelians and Karl Marx* (London: Macmillan, 1969); and Warren Breckman, *Marx, the Young Hegelians and the Origins of Radical Social Theory: Dethroning the Self* (Cambridge: Cambridge University Press, 1999). For a very good analysis of Weber's assessment of the role of the civil service in modern politics, see Reinhard Bendix, *Max Weber: An Intellectual Portrait* (London: Heinemann, 1960), chapters 12–13.

14 As stated at the outset of this chapter, the relations between national and international levels of legal jurisdiction and normative order are rapidly evolving and should not be located within exclusively or in some cases even predominantly national frameworks. On this point see Ulrich K. Preuß, 'Disconnecting Constitutions from Statehood: Is Global Constitutionalism a Promising Concept?', in Martin Loughlin and Petra Dobner (eds), *The Twilight of Constitutionalism?* (Oxford: Oxford University Press, 2010), pp. 23–46, at pp. 37–8.

15 The distinction between republican, positive liberty and liberal, negative liberty is defined and discussed in some detail by Isaiah Berlin in his famous 1958 essay 'Two Concepts of Liberty', in *The Proper Study of Mankind: An Anthology of Essays*, ed. Henry Hardy and Roger Hausheer (London: Pimlico, 1998), pp. 191–242. For an articulate defence of the compatibility of the liberal and republican positions, see Richard Bellamy, *Liberalism and Modern Society: An Historical Argument* (Cambridge: Polity, 1992).

16 Hegel, *Grundlinien*, Parts I and II, available in English as *Philosophy of Right*. Key in this context is his insistence on the transitions (he uses the word *Übergang*) from abstract private law to morality and from morality to ethical life.

17 See Quentin Skinner, 'The Sovereign State: A Genealogy', in Hent Kalmo and Quentin Skinner (eds), *Sovereignty in Fragments: The Past, Present and Future of a Contested Concept* (Cambridge: Cambridge University Press, 2010), pp. 26–46; and Neil MacCormick, 'Sovereignty and After', in Hent Kalmo and Quentin Skinner (eds), *Sovereignty in Fragments: The Past, Present and Future of a Contested Concept* (Cambridge: Cambridge University Press, 2010), pp. 151–68.

18 Alexis de Tocqueville, *L'Ancien Régime et la Révolution*, ed. J. P. Mayer (Paris: Gallimard, revised and corrected edn, 1967), chapters 1–2; Max Weber, *Staatssoziologie: Soziologie der rationalen Staatsanstalt und der modernen politischen Parteien und Parlamente*, ed. Johannes Winckelmann (Berlin: Duncker & Humblot, 2nd edn, 1966), a collection of articles written between 1913 and 1919, chapters 1–3, and Gianfranco Poggi, *The Development of the Modern State: A Sociological Introduction* (Stanford: Stanford University Press, 1978), chapters 2–4. Poggi remarks (p. 19) that feudal political obligation was organised in accordance with highly personal, vertically structured chains of traditional command.

19 There is no space here to enter into a lengthy account of the Reformation, but the differences between the Lutheran, Calvinist, and Anglo-Calvinist Reformations must certainly be borne in mind in any history of the formation of the modern state in Europe and beyond. For a reliable overview, see the introduction to John Witte, *Law and Protestantism: The Legal Teachings of the Lutheran Reformation* (Cambridge: Cambridge University Press, 2002), pp. 1–30. For a detailed and original interpretation of the religious background to the formation of the modern British state, see Steven C. A. Pincus, *1688: The First Modern Revolution* (New Haven: Yale University Press, 2009), Part II.

20 In some parts of Europe an unstable amalgam of this kind survived well into the second half of the nineteenth century. See Thornhill, *Sociology of Constitutions*, chapter 4.
21 For two recent examples see Owen Bowcott, 'Half of victims would think twice on going through courts again', *Guardian* (11 September 2015), p. 17; and Emily Dugan, 'Cruel court charge denies compensation to rape victim', *Independent* (28 October 2015), p. 1.
22 Harriet Sherwood, Anu Anand, Maeve Shearlaw, and Jonathan Franklin, 'UN women: 20 years on from summit in Beijing, equality remains a distant dream', *Guardian* (11 September 2015), p. 29. The work of Thomas Piketty provides a wealth of historical and empirical evidence to show that there is still much work to be done to achieve socio-economic equality. See Thomas Piketty, *Capital in the Twenty-First Century*, trans. Arthur Goldhammer (Cambridge, MA: The Belknap Press of Harvard University Press, 2014).
23 James Meek offers a devastating account of the close links between privatisation, outsourcing, inequality and the dismantling of the British state in *Private Island: Why Britain Now Belongs to Someone Else* (London: Verso, 2014). Meek's account is pertinently complemented by the empirical data provided by Stewart Lansley and Joanna Mack, *Breadline Britain: The Rise of Mass Poverty* (London: Oneworld, 2015), especially chapter 8.
24 The work of Wendy Brown does this very effectively. See Wendy Brown, *States of Injury: Power and Freedom in Late Modernity* (Princeton: Princeton University Press, 1995), chapters 2 and 7, *Edgework: Critical Essays on Knowledge and Politics* (Princeton: Princeton University Press, 2005), chapters 1, 3, and 6, and *Undoing the Demos: Neoliberalism's Stealth Revolution* (Cambridge, MA: MIT Press, 2015), chapters 4–6.
25 Jürgen Habermas raises similar questions in *Legitimationsprobleme im Spätkapitalismus* (Frankfurt: Suhrkamp, 1973), available in English as *Legitimation Crisis* (Boston: Beacon Press, 1975). Claus Offe revisits his own position in the debates on 'late capitalism' of the 1960s and 1970s in 'Erneute Lektüre: Die Strukturprobleme nach 33 Jahren', in *Strukturprobleme des kapitalistischen Staates: Aufsätze zur politischen Soziologie*, ed. Jens Borchert and Stephan Lessenich (Frankfurt: Campus-Verlag, revised new edn, 2006), pp. 181–96.
26 It may be somewhat misleading to invoke a general concept of reason to explain what happens in comprehensively differentiated fields such as science, art, law, economics, politics, education, health, and sport. From a systems-theoretical perspective it is more precise to say that a social system codes its operations in society according to a binary logic that facilitates intelligible communication within each particular system. An economic system exists through its codes (sometimes designated as ability to pay/inability to pay rather than, say, private/public); it does not exist as a fixed locus. This argument is developed by Dirk Baecker, *Form und Formen der Kommunikation* (Frankfurt: Suhrkamp, 2007). Baecker indicates that whilst one can observe sense, meaning, and communication in sociological terms, it is far more difficult to do so with reason. From a critical-theory perspective questions arise as to how systems are coded and if they can be re-coded to address systemic malfunctions and blind spots. The ability to pay may well be an economic issue that transcends national boundaries whilst also transgressing the boundaries between public and private. But this ability cannot be allowed to justify the destruction of natural and human resources. This point is made by Christoph Görg, *Gesellschaftliche Naturverhältnisse* (Münster: Westfälisches Dampfboot, 1999).

27 Joris Luyendijk makes this point with reference to the collapse of Lehman Brothers, the manifest failure of the financial system to regulate its own operations, and the simultaneous incapacity of political parties to pass legislation incentivising the financial system to reform itself, in *Swimming with Sharks: My Journey into the World of Bankers* (London: Guardian Books, 2015).

28 On this account, self-overcoming and solidarity are not mutually exclusive. On the contrary, they condition one another in a reciprocal manner summed up in the term emancipation. For a summary of first-generation views on these issues, see Darrow Schecter, *The History of the Left from Marx to the Present: Theoretical Perspectives* (London: Continuum, 2007), chapter 3.

29 Teubner, *Constitutional Fragments*, chapter 2. This possibility will be explored in detail in the section on societal constitutionalism in chapter 5 of the present book.

30 Hegel, *Grundlinien*, Part III, available in English as *Philosophy of Right*.

31 Karl Marx, 'Contribution to the Critique of Hegel's *Philosophy of Right*', in Robert C. Tucker (ed.), *The Marx-Engels Reader* (New York: Norton, 2nd edn, 1978), pp. 16–25, at p. 22. In this and other early writings Marx distinguishes between political emancipation, which culminates in the construction of the modern state, and human emancipation, which he sees as the goal of the revolution to come.

32 This notion of the strengthening of unity through a difference that is ultimately recuperated for unity is captured by the term *Aufhebung*, which is often translated in terms of a movement that simultaneously cancels as it preserves. On this point see Angelika Nuzzo, 'Dialectic as Logic of Transformative Processes', in Katerina Deligiorgi (ed.), *Hegel: New Directions* (Chesham: Acumen, 2006), pp. 85–103.

33 Karl Marx, 'The Civil War in France', in Robert Tucker (ed.), *The Marx Engels Reader* (New York: Norton, 1978), pp. 618–52, at p. 635. Kristin Ross delves into the political potential of the Paris Commune in *The Emergence of Social Space: Rimbaud and the Paris Commune* (London: Verso, 2008) and *Communal Luxury: The Political Imaginary of the Paris Commune* (London: Verso, 2015).

34 Marx, 'Contribution to the Critique of Hegel's *Philosophy of Right*: Introduction'.

35 Anarchists are amongst the few that consistently contest the necessity and rationality of the state. For the best and most comprehensive overview, see Peter H. Marshall, *Demanding the Impossible: A History of Anarchism* (London: HarperCollins, 1992).

36 Hegel, *Vorlesungen über die Philosophie der Geschichte*, Part IV, section 3, and *Grundlinien*, Part III.

37 If one reads the *Phenomenology* in conjunction with the *Philosophy of Right*, one notes a symmetry between Hegel's understanding of the richness of individual experience and his theorisation of the complexity of the modern state. He is doubtful that this mutually conditioning depth can be captured by the notion of a utilitarian, contractual outlook that reduces individual experience to a calculation of interest whilst reducing political obligation to a calculation of security. These issues are looked at by Mark C. Taylor, *Journeys to Selfhood: Hegel and Kierkegaard* (Berkeley: University of California Press, 1980) and by Robert B. Pippin, *After the Beautiful: Hegel and the Philosophy of Pictorial Modernism* (Chicago: University of Chicago Press, 2014).

38 The mediation of distance between individual citizens and public authority is therefore closely related to the terms 'strong' and 'weak' when applied to states. The supple, elastic institutional form characteristic of strong states mediates that distance whilst also respecting and preserving the thesis and antithesis that go into the synthesis of individual citizen and authority. On the particularities of strong and weak states, see Schecter, 'Historical Bloc'. The problems for Hegel and less

stringently dialectical thinkers begin at the point where institutional syntheses mediate more than two terms at once, such that institutional form is burdened with the task of creating some kind of unity out of a plurality of constitutional elements.

39 Despite the considerable differences that otherwise distinguish their respective positions, Hegel, Marx, Weber, Schmitt, and Habermas might all agree that mediation processes survive the passing of different state forms, but none of these thinkers are able to do so without relying on a foundational model. The outlines of a post-foundational model appropriate for twenty-first century realities can be glimpsed in the essays collected in Alberto Febbrajo and Gorm Harste (eds), *Law and Intersystemic Communication: Understanding 'Structural Coupling'* (Farnham: Ashgate, 2013).

40 For an analysis of the likely consequences of the Transatlantic Trade and Investment Partnership, see Serge Halimi, 'Grand Marché transatlantique: les puissants redessint le monde', *Le Monde Diplomatique* (June 2014), p. 11 and Raoul Marc Jennar, 'Cinquante états négotient en secret la libéralisation des services', *Le Monde Diplomatique* (September 2014), pp. 12–13.

41 Chapter 3 of Schecter, *Critical Theory in the Twenty-First Century*, analyses the concept of mediated non-identity in relation to those of mediated unity (Hegel), mediated disunity (Marx), and non-mediated non-identity (Heidegger). Whereas the political and epistemological implications of mediated non-identity are investigated with specific reference to Adorno in that book, this book focuses on the constitutional and sociological ramifications of the concept.

42 Global warming, flooding, the crisis of fossil fuels, and the erosion of the ozone layer, as well as a wide range of related phenomena, have heightened awareness of the extent to which science, technology, criteria guiding the disposal of waste, and other socially embedded practices render any neat separation between humanity and nature highly problematic. For an excellent analysis explaining how flooding is not always a 'natural disaster', and in fact can be better understood as a consequence of colonialism and human mismanagement, see Rohan D'Souza, *Drowned and Dammed: Colonial Capitalism and Flood Control in Eastern India* (Oxford: Oxford University Press, 2006).

43 David Hume, 'That Politics May Someday Be Reduced to a Science', in C. W. Hendel (ed.), *David Hume's Political Essays* (New York: The Liberal Arts Press, 1953), pp. 12–23.

44 Foucault remains the most brilliant critic of prevailing standards of truth in these matters. See Michel Foucault, *L'Archéologie du savoir* (Paris: Gallimard, 1969), available in English as *Archaeology of Knowledge*, trans. A. M. Sheridan Smith (London: Routledge, 2002).

45 John Locke, *Two Treatises of Government* (London: Dent, 1978), Book 2, chapters 7 and 9.

46 Leonard T. Hobhouse, *Liberalism* (London and New York: Oxford University Press, 1964), chapter 6; and John Rawls, *Political Liberalism* (New York: Columbia University Press, 1993), Lecture 5, pp. 173–211.

47 See chapter 2 of John Stuart Mill, *On Liberty*, ed. Gertrude Himmelfarb (London: Penguin, 1982 [1859]), pp. 78–113. The question of refugees, like that of the environment, is not going to go away in the manner of a transient problem or adjustment to the teething pains of a new governing coalition. See Amelia Gentleman, '"We feel like we are dying slowly": the horror of the Calais refugee camp', *Guardian* (4 November 2015), G2, pp. 6–11.

48 John Rawls, *A Theory of Justice* (Cambridge, MA: Harvard University Press, 1971), and 'Justice as fairness: political not metaphysical', *Philosophy & Public Affairs*, 14:3 (1985), 223–51, at 224.
49 M. Lazzarato, *Governing by Debt*, trans. Joshua David Jordan (Cambridge, MA: MIT Press, 2015); and Frédéric Lordon, *La Malfaçon: Monnaie européenne et souveraineté démocratique* (Paris: Les Liens qui libèrent, 2014).
50 The essays collected in Alberto Febbrajo and Francesco Gambino (eds), *Il diritto frammentato* (Milan: Giuffrè, 2013), clarify how these processes of auto-enforcement unfold in ways that undermine binary frameworks of form/essence, legality/legitimacy, authority/power, negative liberty/positive liberty.
51 Immanuel Kant, 'An Answer to the Question: What is Enlightenment?', trans. H. B. Nisbet, in *Kant's Political Writings*, ed. Hans Reiss (Cambridge: Cambridge University Press, 1970), pp. 54–60.
52 Immanuel Kant, 'On the Common Saying: "This May be True in Theory, but it Does not Apply in Practice"', in *Kant's Political Writings*, ed. Hans Reiss (Cambridge: Cambridge University Press, 1970); and Habermas, *Faktizität und Geltung*, pp. 231–2, available in English as *Between Facts and Norms*, pp. 188–9.
53 This point is expounded in more detail by Darrow Schecter, 'Liberalism and the limits of legal legitimacy: Kant and Habermas', *King's College Law Journal*, 16 (2005), 99–119.

2

Mediated unity in question: on the relation between law, politics, and other social systems in modern societies

The discussion in chapter 1 shows that two premises are often invoked to articulate the theoretical preconditions of modern democratic statehood. Whilst the mediated unity of the governors and the governed is normally taken to be the basis of rational political representation, overarching legal-political form is taken to be the foundation of democratic government and consensual normative integration. The epistemological and sociological critique of those premises is developed further in this chapter, in which the presumption of mediated unity and overarching legal-political form is contrasted with the FD of law, politics, and other social systems frequently observed in modern society. The stress on law and politics serves to examine the widespread belief that citizen access to the state via the law distinguishes democracies from other state forms. Questions are thereby raised about what is taken to be the inherently political-juridical bond obtaining between autonomous citizens and post-feudal government in a variety of states. This understanding of the centrality of politics is salient in the republican tradition from Robespierre in the eighteenth century to Pablo Iglesias and Jean-Luc Mélenchon today. Whilst Robespierre is known for his staunchly republican version of democracy and virtue, he is also closely associated with a highly centralised Jacobin approach to political organisation that links him in various ways to figures as disparate as Lenin and Hugo Chavez. The marked contrast between republican conceptions of the public good and the Jacobin conflation of high intensity politics with party politics is touched on at the end of this chapter. It is a contrast between two types of politics – public sphere/

civil society politics and party politics – that are nevertheless easily confused due to the close association of republicanism and Jacobinism in the highly influential French context. Divergences between these perspectives persist, despite the fact that disputes about the acceptable means to enact political ends and belief in the compact unity of the general will can be found in the books of representative thinkers from both camps. The tension is very much part of the controversial legacy of Gramsci, an essential figure of reference for Podemos and a number of other parties and movements around the world in search of alternative forms of state. Whilst Gramsci often discusses the project of building a counter-hegemony in civil society, his writings also contain numerous references to the need to follow the Jacobin and Leninist models of party organisation.[1]

One might ask in this context if liberalism in power is democratic for each individual citizen and all of the people of a modern state because liberal institutions successfully dispense with notions of the general will and 'the enemy within' repeatedly found in republican and other strong dialectical conceptions of democracy. The normative case in favour of liberalism will be even stronger if it can be demonstrated that this apparent impartiality is due to liberalism's consistent insistence on *juridical* and therefore neutral, rather than on *political* and therefore biased, means of conflict adjudication. If so, it might be said that liberal government is legitimate, and even truthful, to a certain extent. That question begs another, however, which is raised at the end of chapter 1. Might it in fact be the case that liberalism in power is hegemonic rather than genuinely truthful because of its capacity to transform a non-disclosed, formal theory of human essence into institutions that subtly privilege essentialist criteria of educational success, physical and mental health, normal gender difference, and desirable economic growth that are never really neutral (critique of existing patterns of mediation)?[2] If notions of neutrality, merit, and expertise can be shown to be problematic in this regard, it can be convincingly argued that access to schools and universities, health care, legal rights, and rewarding work is never really equal (critique of the currently prevailing protection of rights). Hence it becomes important to see where, exactly, the mediations between law, neutrality, and equality become strained in the everyday life of people in functionally differentiated societies. These preliminary remarks serve to highlight some of the ambiguities in the specifically liberal democratic instantiation of FD that will be examined in more detail in chapters 2–4. This is by no means a polemic directed at liberal democracy. Instead, the matter is stated in these terms to emphasise the links between broadly speaking liberal democratic institutions, a determinate conception of post-feudal statehood, and one historically documented model of FD that is often regarded as universal and uniquely suited to complex modern societies.[3] In keeping with the methodological desideratum of non-polemical critique, it will be argued in chapters 2–4 that what is referred to above as liberalism's capacity to transform a non-disclosed, formal theory of human essence into institutions that subtly privilege essentialist criteria is actually a flawed and misleading statement of the question at hand. It anthropomorphically credits liberalism with human powers to transform, manipulate, distort, and so on, with the result that a great deal of opposition to liberal democracy seems to be framed in terms of personal attacks and moralistic outcries. Ascertaining the extent to which one historically documented model of FD has eclipsed others is much more centrally at stake in the present work, even if, somewhat contradictorily, it will be useful throughout the book to investigate this issue by examining some of the recurrent inconsistencies in liberal democratic theory and practice. It is customarily repeated that the inherently political-juridical bond believed to characterise liberal democratic citizenship enables the people to make the laws that govern them, and to amend the laws that cease to meet with their consent. According to this account, democratic law is not imposed by elites in a top-down, vertically structured direction. On the contrary, the law is believed to develop according to a far more horizontally structured, civic dynamic, in which the citizens are the legislative protagonists in a twofold sense. In the first instance, they are protagonists in formal processes linking them to legally binding decisions with macro-level political authority in the guise of party political representation in parliaments and legislatures. In the second, they are at the heart of the more informal, cultural and institutional settings that are referred to at various points below in terms of political will formation. Chapter 1 makes clear that although this argument can be articulated in weak dialectical terms that highlight some of the glaring problems with strong dialectical accounts of legitimacy and sovereignty, the argument cannot dispense with some notion of mediated unity in order to do so. An effective deconstruction of that notion will therefore have major implications for the theory and practice of liberal democracy. The main point, however, is that it will also have major implications for the theory and practice of the reigning model of FD. The problem might not be liberal democracy, as such, but rather that this model of FD does not permit liberal democracy to make good on its most important theoretical and practical claims. One of these, most notably, is the claim that conflicts between divergent interests and values are adjudicated neutrally and therefore fairly. This point is easily obscured if one remains locked in a framework juxtaposing really democratic law made by the people with ostensibly democratic law imposed by elites. It may be the case that law functions in an entirely different way, that is, as a self-reproducing and differentiated social system that is paradoxically part of society and differentiated from it at the same time. The crucial issue then becomes that of ascertaining precisely how law and other social systems are differentiated.[4]

The immanent critique of the view that liberal democratic citizenship enables the people to make the laws that govern them would be incomplete and misleading if it did not also indicate the conditions under which such rigorously democratic norms of inclusion and integration might be institutionalised in actual practice. If one is going to analyse FD in relation to democracy, one must therefore show how, in Europe, North America, and elsewhere in the world, one main paradigm of FD, with some variations, has emerged as hegemonic, to the detriment of other possible models. Failing to do so will produce the singular impression that one must choose between hopelessly utopian democratic norms and epistemological realism – whatever that might actually mean – and that only the latter can seriously be expected to provide the basis of rational normative integration and public policy. If the process of FD is a sociological fact, differentiation nonetheless unfolds in a wide variety of historical contexts in which constitutional traditions and a range of other factors shape the kind of FD likely to emerge in any particular one. It may be the case that to an increasing extent the most relevant context is now global. This does not invalidate the argument that the currently hegemonic model did not emerge as a result of natural selection, demonstrably superior efficiency, or maximum democratic input. Hence other models are still possible that may be more efficient and democratic in both quantitative and qualitative terms. An accurate prognosis concerning an eventual transition in this regard can start with four preliminary hypotheses.

First, if the currently hegemonic model of FD did not emerge as a result of historical determinism or natural selection, it is unlikely that it managed to impose itself through force alone or through pervasive false consciousness. Broadly following Durkheim, one can say that during the various phases of its evolution in Europe and elsewhere, it helped indirectly to perform a number of essential tasks of governance by creating networks of interdependence and social solidarity.[5] To this extent one can draw parallels between the dominant paradigm of FD and the modern nation state, which, especially during the first three decades following 1945, enjoyed high levels of citizen approval whilst also performing key tasks of government in Europe and elsewhere. The current migratory, financial, political, climatic and other upheavals will surely induce major changes in modes of FD and statehood in the intermediate and long term. A key question then becomes the following: in what ways are the dominant modes of FD and statehood likely to be reformed in the short term, in anticipation of the more thorough changes to come?[6] One implication, second, is that de-differentiation offers no convincing answers to the manifest problems with the dominant modalities of differentiation and democratic statehood. It is highly doubtful that a de-differentiated society can coexist with a consistently and thoroughly democratic political system. The simple reason is that sociological differentiation and democratic complexity reflexively condition one another.[7] Nineteenth- and twentieth-century European history indicates that attempts by the state to de-differentiate society in an effort to produce compact unity and intensive consensus tend to lead to authoritarian, centralised solutions to problems that for the most part require de-centralised approaches.[8] A third hypothesis borne out by several contemporary examples of cumbersome technocratic management is that the large-scale implementation of privatisation, outsourcing, and related strategies to achieve de-centralisation and flexibility through crassly instrumental means will undermine the autonomy of the political system by imposing quantitative solutions to the problems of democratic deficits. These are usually complex problems related to choosing between qualitatively different kinds of steering and planning that demand efficient use of the institutional resources accrued from collective learning. In short, one must be clear about the kind of de-centralisation one is proposing in connection with democracy and FD.[9] If FD demands a certain degree of de-centralisation, it is important to remember that there are distinct ways through which the latter can be achieved. Supposed remedies that confuse corporate tax cuts with effective incentives to invest, or conflate de-regulation with enhanced consumer choice, may deepen rather than alleviate the problems at hand.[10] This is the crux, fourthly, for a book seeking to re-articulate critical theory by integrating historical analysis with select strands of legal, political, constitutional, and sociological theory. It is likely that the current crisis of democracy, which has been variously analysed in recent years in terms of 'post-democracy', 'a neoliberal fantasy', 'simulative democracy', 'apolitical democracy', 'democracies without democracy', 'political disaffection', 'the delayed crisis of democratic capitalism', 'after democracy', and so on, may actually be better understood as the crisis of a determinate instance of FD, rather than as a simple crisis of democracy as such.[11]

It is becoming increasingly clear that political discussions about the problems of democracy that do not simultaneously address sociological questions related to FD miss key aspects of the main issues at stake. Just as the welfare state in many countries has been progressively dismantled because it has come to be seen as a luxury to be abandoned in times of economic stagnation, there is a risk that a similar approach could be adopted in order to 'solve' the so-called crisis of democracy. This would be a passive revolution rather than a solution, however. Attempts to solve the current problems of democracy by reversing FD processes are likely to culminate in authoritarian populist experiments that may well hasten the demise of democratic institutions and rational political will formation. The dilemmas involved are considerable when one considers that it is not desirable or feasible to dismantle these processes. However, the palpable epistemological and organisational gains they promise will surely be offset if they are not accompanied by the appropriate regulation and corresponding norms of integration. As explained in chapter 1, until recently normative integration has been performed in several parts of the world, most notably in Europe and North America, by a broadly speaking liberal democratic state constituted as a monopoly on the legitimate use of force within a given territory, authorised to legislate in an unrivalled, rather than in an all-encompassing way. This particular state form is defined by a formal division of political powers and guided, in the main, by what is referred to in that chapter as the weak/formal model of legality–legitimacy dialectics. This prompts the question as to how best to understand the constitutional framework within which differentiation now unfolds and is likely to progress in the near future.

It would be misleading to describe the main paradigm of FD as simply capitalist or liberal democratic. As suggested above, one must try to discern the outlines of the constellation within which liberal democratic governance, the key institutions of post-feudal statehood, and one specific model of FD mutually condition one another. There is probably no single conceptual term that can effectively capture the polyvalent logic of the processes structuring the unfolding of FD in the period from the Industrial Revolution until 1945, or from 1945 to the end of the Cold War in 1989. There is certainly no single categorisation capable of accurately capturing the predominant logic defining the period from 1989 until today: neoliberalism, globalisation, bio-political governance, modernisation, transnational constitutionalism, and the like only describe part of the story. Moreover, in the absence of an overarching legal-political form to unify state and civil society, the applicability of the term 'democratic' to social systems with relatively weak coupling to the political system may well be limited. Certain parts of Scandinavia at distinct historical moments offer notable exceptions to that general tendency in the sense that Scandinavian countries may have at times managed to reconcile FD and state authority without unduly privileging specific social systems or particular systemic interests.[12] Yet it could be objected that the main features of the Scandinavian model, which at times have been replicated to a certain extent in Scotland and elsewhere, are better analysed in terms of social democracy and corporatism rather than as stringent FD. Once again one seems to be confronted with the unenviable and ominously undemocratic choice between utopian norms and epistemological realism. Late capitalism, trade regime, welfare state capitalism, democratic capitalism, accumulation regime, and bio-political regime are some of the designations that have been used to try to capture something fundamental about the dynamics between economics, politics, law, religion, scientific research, digital communication, international relations, and globalisation in the post-Cold War world. None of them do justice to the complexity and contingency involved. At present, there appears to be little in the way of macro-political initiative that is not shaped by calculations of economic growth and strategies of accumulation. Wrangles over budgets, immense difficulties in regulating and taxing financial transactions, disputes over natural resources, and a host of other conflicts therefore suggest that the currently dominant paradigm of FD is an ambiguous one marked by inconsistencies and countervailing tendencies that amalgamate austerity and extravagance with frugality and waste.[13] Its obscurities are complicated further by the presence of simultaneously overlapping and hybrid legal orders that synthesise diverse aspects of public, private, international, administrative, transnational, and other kinds of law.[14] It is moreover a model in which anti-hierarchical and de-centralised republican tendencies compete with a marked proclivity, inherited from past practice dating back to Roman Law and Canonical Law, to de-centralise almost exclusively through private contract or, in more updated terms, through privatisation. This kind of appropriation can lead to transparency deficits and the informal hegemony of financial markets, services industries, insurance companies, rating agencies, and consultancy firms.[15] One is confronted with an ensemble of contradictory regimes, each of which is governed by contrasting codes and imperatives. The crux, however, is that it is possible to provide convincing historical evidence in support of the claim that modern statehood helped establish a propitious framework for the unfolding of differentiation processes in certain parts of the world. It is much less clear, going forward into the twenty-first century, what multiple effects differentiation processes will have on the enabling conditions of late modern statehood. The appropriate dialectical methodology is as yet discernible only in bare outline. One must bear in mind that if modern state building was and in essential respects remains rooted in territorial entities, FD tends to work according to a de-territorialised dialectic that is relatively unconcerned with the integrity of national boundaries.[16]

The point about the presence of simultaneously overlapping and hybrid legal orders highlights some of the key questions involved when thinking about and evaluating the different present and possible future instantiations of FD: de-centralisation steered by private accumulation strategies will certainly produce a very different set of outcomes than de-centralisation steered by intra-systemic, and, where possible, inter-systemic communication and democratic decision-making. In the first case, inequality in several senses is sure to be entrenched by the immense difficulties encountered when trying to exercise any meaningful degree of accountability. Decision-making will inevitably boil down to decisionism exacerbated by insidious power differentials, resulting in a reversion to archaic decision by personal command combined with some of the more anonymous modes of coerced integration frequently observed in late modern societies.[17] In the second case it is reasonable to suppose that the norms linking decision-making processes with actual outcomes are marked by dialogue and compromise. Disagreement and conflict will continue to exist. One would expect that a society characterised by extensive differentiation is going to be intensively pluralist in interests and outlooks, and not one in which the preconditions of liberty are known in advance from a supposedly pre-political private sphere of naturally legitimate exchange (chapter 1). In this context it might be objected that it is too simplistic and in any case arbitrary to contrast the personal power of decision-makers operative in existing hierarchies with the shared decision-making authority characteristic of the non-instrumental mediation and substantive justice towards which differentiation might one day evolve. It could also be pointed out that whilst autocratic power may not be democratic or rational, it is attached to a specific person and is therefore wielded transparently. The response is that whilst constitutions almost always cast a somewhat hypothetical glance at possible future scenarios, the history of post-feudal statehood is not hypothetical. It conclusively demonstrates that the exercise of political power is made more predictable and less prone to arbitrary excess and bureaucratic manipulation when political power is constitutionally limited, divided, and, crucially, shared. Such institutional arrangements have enabled liberal democratic states to perform better than rival state forms in concrete ways that make the reality of qualitative differences tangible rather than speculative. The historical importance of the mediating role played by law in this regard is unquestionable, but also easy to misconstrue. *Mediation* is part of the reason why the *differentiation* of law and politics is the precondition of individual autonomy enjoyed as rights of citizenship within the liberal democratic version of FD. The question thereby raised is the extent to which the effective exercise of rights also depends on the specific kind of mediated non-identity instituted between law, politics, and other social systems, and this, in turn, is related to the specific kinds of de-centralisation that may be available in any particular socio-historical context. This is a difficult but important question, given that the fusion of law and politics, like their hermetic separation, must be detrimental to both systemic autonomy and individual autonomy. An uncritical acceptance of the premises of the mediated unity paradigm can lead to two principal misunderstandings concerning the mediating role often attributed to the liberal democratic state. The state does not represent the middle ground between the fusion of law and politics and the separation of law and politics. Nor is it the case that whilst law is the form, politics is the content of democratic statehood. Whilst a certain degree of contingency may be unavoidable, the impact contingency has on individual lives will therefore vary in accordance with the structure of inter-systemic mediations prevailing in any particular time and place, and this, in turn, is a constitutional question in the widest sense. In this way it can be argued that the constitution provides a key way of interpreting the relations between statehood and FD at any particular historical juncture. Drawing together the reflections on statehood and FD developed thus far, one can say that differentiation propels a dynamic of coupling, un-coupling, and re-coupling of social systems, and that this is a dynamic that proceeds without a structuring centre. It is therefore possible to speak of de-centralisation in several senses, none of which unconditionally mean privatisation or personal control of collective resources.[18]

It has already been noted at several junctures that, whilst modern state-hood and FD tend in many cases to signal an institutional shift away from rigidly stratified orders based on naturalised categories of obligation and subordination, there is nothing inherently egalitarian about differentiation processes. It is therefore important to be as clear as possible about *how* post-traditional societies distinguish their systemic operations. Stated slightly differently, much depends on the principles and practices according to which discrete social systems of knowledge and communication are coded. The specific ways in which systems are coded has an impact on the kinds of reflexivity they develop and also influences the quality of the communication they enjoy with neighbouring systems. Naturalistic justifications for centralised command and personal control can creep back in if legal, economic, political, and other systems have timeless properties ascribed to them or are dogmatically defined in terms of which problems they are or are not allowed to address. This point is made at the outset of this chapter when it is noted that violations against what is supposed to be neutral epistemological form in educational, health, legal, and economic matters will contribute to violations of rights of equal access if naturalist assumptions of inherent individualist competitive steering are allowed to be substituted for democratic practices of allocation and inclusion. FD can be checked and even reversed through de-differentiation of the kind observed in several authoritarian states in Europe during the interwar period of the twentieth century, and, to a more consensual extent, in states marked by corporatist compromise after 1945 in Europe and elsewhere. In a parallel vein, many of the potentially anti-hierarchical tendencies accompanying FD can be neutralised or offset by arbitrarily re-politicising rather than respecting the mediated non-identity of law, politics, and other social systems. The ongoing European refugee crisis indicates that it is possible to re-classify people on the basis of gender, country of origin, religion, level of education, level of income, ethnicity, or other criteria, instead of recognising them as bearers of universal human rights.[19] The specific ways in which rights can be deployed thus plays a highly important role in shaping how emergent and evolving FD actually functions in relation to pre-existing patterns of statehood, power, patronage, and hierarchy. Given that there is nothing natural or inevitable about the consolidation of the currently hegemonic version of FD, it is reasonable to think that alternatives can still be tested and evaluated, lest modern democratic choice revert to timeless order and traditional command. The possibility of feasible alternatives is examined in chapter 5. The current chapter explores the reasons why it is imprecise to say that social systems are fully differentiated or definitively de-coupled from one another. The fact that it is possible at times to de-differentiate and at others to re-politicise confirms the point sketched in chapter 1, that is, that systems are mediated by a de-centred dialectic characterised by a certain degree of paradox, contingency, and mediated non-identity. Instead of boundless differentiation and infinite fragmentation, differentiation is often accompanied by notable instances of systemic re-coupling. Whilst it might be erroneous to depict these links anthropomorphically as alliances, it would be similarly anthropomorphic to suppose that systems exist in isolation and regard their respective environments as potentially hostile invaders. They are not analogous to the individual states comprising what is still sometimes referred to as the international state system.[20]

Statehood and FD in the twenty-first century: can sociological and political modernity still be reconciled via law and the state?

From Durkheim and Weber to Parsons and Luhmann, it might be said that FD is one of the defining characteristics of sociological modernity.[21] Pinpointing the defining characteristics of political modernity is both easier and more difficult. It is easy to cite the Glorious, American, and French Revolutions as fundamental reference points. But is there a process analogous to *differentiation* that is demonstrably unfolding in the same way? Bearing in mind the continual rescinding of restrictions on political participation, it seems that ever-widening *inclusion*, secured through vertical, territorially based representation, accountability, and rights, is a consistently recurring theme in political modernity. The theoretical and practical difficulties begin when considering what dialectical principle of unity, if any, might be able simultaneously to sustain processes of differentiation and inclusion. One can imagine states, constitutions, rights, laws, political parties, and representative institutions without substantive democracy. But state legitimacy in most parts of Europe,

North America, and elsewhere depends on the capacity of the state to reconcile sociological realities with democratic norms of accountability, participation, the division of powers, and full inclusivity without discrimination on
the basis of race, health, religion, income, gender, class, and so on. From
Kant to Rawls and Habermas, then, a range of thinkers regard the central
challenge of political modernity to consist in consolidating formal guarantees
of accountability and participation with a vibrant public sphere and decidedly
non-plebiscitary/populist approaches to public will formation. Habermas, in
particular, is acutely aware that consolidation in this sense cannot ignore the
ongoing transition from feudal stratification, which is hierarchical and vertically
structured, to modern FD, which is potentially more flexible, and in principle
amenable to a far greater degree of horizontally structured social dynamics.[22]
Public will formation, in turn, embraces an extensive network of organisations
and institutions featuring the mass media, the production and reception of
art, schools and universities, the relations between scientific communities
and non-expert opinion, sport, religion, health, and the diverse dimensions
of civil society. These include the culture of daily life, historical memory, and
coming to terms with individual and collective trauma. In evaluating the extent
to which law and politics have become differentiated in any specific context,
one is therefore implicitly posing the following questions: to what extent can
sociological and political modernity continue to be reconciled via law and the
state, and is it possible to harmonise substantive practices of democracy with
institutional pluralism and an independent judiciary capable of safeguarding
individual rights?[23]

Like other observers, J. A. G. Griffith notes that it is at times necessary
to strengthen democracy by limiting executive prerogative in matters of secondary legislation and other instances where government ministries and
administrative agencies are able to usurp parliamentary legislative authority.
The judiciary can protect minorities and other groups of people from the possible effects of secondary legislation that proposes or implies major *political* interventions in social processes such as economic exchange, scientific
research, or access to education. The courts thus anticipate potential threats
to individuals, and, where successful, indirectly uphold the legislative process
by protecting human rights. In such instances the courts play an active role
in fortifying democracy by buttressing the legislative authority of the state
constitution against the power, often abused by the executive, to make laws
via extra-legislative means. This shows, first, that not all instances of politicisation are synonymous with democratisation: the differences between the
promulgation of executive decisions and deliberative legislative authority
denote distinct uses of the term 'political', and imply very different models of
democracy. Needless to say, both models continue to coexist within the same

constitutional framework. There can be little doubt about the combined forces of governing parties and state executives in abetting contemporary populism. In some countries the *Rechtsstaat* has ceded to an authoritarian *Parteienstaat* in which the injunction that parties must govern without annexing key parts of the state is openly flouted. There is historical precedent for the collapse of parliamentary democracies shortly after this kind of transition. At the same time, however, the coexistence of these markedly different dynamics under the common banner of democracy also raises questions concerning a possible re-coupling of legislative and judicial functions that is relevant to the argument about FD, social systems, and social statehood sketched in this book. It highlights, second, that the processes of public political will formation are delicate and susceptible to manipulation on the part of government ministries, informally powerful groups, and the media.[24]

The more ambitious claim about social statehood just alluded to, which needs more empirical evidence than is provided here, is that judicial authority, which is normally not directly legislative, can at times stimulate a potentially legislative faculty on the part of economic, scientific, educational, and other social systems in an effort to develop their respective self-steering capacities. Although this tendency towards qualified self-steering can be observed on a broad transnational basis in organisations such as the World Trade Organization (WTO) and institutions like the European Union (EU), it is not as yet clear how far advanced it is with regard to social-systemic self-steering. But it is one possible future direction for FD, especially in light of the manifest failure of many states in the contemporary world to efficiently guide the social systems operative within their territories. This incompetence has much more to do with complexity and overburdened states than it does with malice, megalomania, or conspiracies. Governing parties and ministries within nation states are not responsive enough to the particular kinds of knowledge required for the functioning of specific social systems. At the same time, the institutions of transnational governance entrusted with the task of guiding systems on a global scale cannot sufficiently cope, either. FD is going to continue apace and will need the steering provided by a new kind of statehood. Optimally, it will be a form of self-steering that is attuned to the needs and creative capacities of neighbouring systems. This issue raises questions that are taken up below and in subsequent chapters: under what patterns of FD does politicisation contribute to democratisation, and, on the contrary, under which ones does politicisation potentially de-stabilise democracy through the evident mismanagement of social systems?[25]

Politicisation is no more synonymous with democratisation than decentralisation is automatically synonymous with qualitatively enhanced citizen autonomy or participation. Politicisation may democratise if it nurtures institutions promoting rational modes of inclusion directed by rights-based claims that can be enforced by judicial knowledge and procedural transparency. It may instead have a de-stabilising effect when it demonstrably stimulates populist threats to democracy of the kind recently seen with Erdogan, Orban, Modi, Trump, Le Pen, Kurz, and many others. Historical evolution and constitutional design may well be more informative in this regard than the usual catalogue of theoretical categories and concepts such as *pouvoir constituant/pouvoir constitué*, public/private, state/civil society, democracy/liberalism, and system/lifeworld. There is quite clearly the need for an inter-systemic mediating dialectic elastic enough to strengthen and intensify democratisation in some systems, whilst limiting and restricting politicisation, understood as party political mismanagement and ministerial neglect of systemic functions, in others. The chances of this happening may seem very slim, and the confusion pervasive, given that the meanings of the terms political and democracy are contingent on whether they are being applied to the executive, legislative, or judicial dimensions of liberal democratic statehood. Within the liberal democratic paradigm, a democratised executive sounds adventurist and irresponsible. Many may object that the idea was tested only very briefly during the Paris Commune and in isolated cases during the Spanish Civil War. Others may say that a democratised judiciary inevitably means a politicised judiciary, and that the latter is surely a formula for dictatorship. By extension, a democratised economy would seem to have to mean something like single party political control and command central planning, in other words something inherently unwieldy, inefficient, and badly out of line with real prices and consumer demand.

The picture looks very different if one disentangles the liberal democratic understanding of the separation of powers from liberal democratic assumptions about the ways in which the FD of society must work. These assumptions generally proceed from premises that tend to naturalise certain socio-political boundaries whilst also positing existing divisions as normal or somehow simply given rather than dialectically produced through social evolutionary and historical processes that can be understood and reformed. Chapter 3 discusses the possibility of a paradigm shift in this regard by distinguishing between politically constituted statehood and socially constituted statehood. In anticipation of that discussion, it is worth cautioning against any exaggeration of the differences between them; the possibility of social statehood is implied by politically constituted statehood and entails a more extensive and openly debated constitutionalisation of the latter. This is borne out by the fact that to some extent politically constituted states already do strengthen and intensify democratisation in some systems whilst limiting and restricting politicisation in others. It was just remarked that the judiciaries of strong states protect

diverse kinds of people from the possible adverse effects of secondary legislation politicising the operations of discrete social processes. That observation
underscores the point that although functionally differentiated, social systems
are also mediated. Indeed, this mediation has been the task of politically
constituted modern states since their inception. Structuring and regulating
mediation processes will be the task of socially constituted statehood, too,
should it manage to emerge and demonstrate its viability. The need for a transition in this direction has in any case become manifest. It is certainly accurate
to speak of dysfunctional FD when governments threaten to rate university
courses in accordance with the likely salaries a given degree result will supposedly guarantee, as has recently happened in Great Britain.[26] It might seem
exaggerated to analyse this and other phenomena as evidence in support of
the somewhat bolder claim that what is widely taken to be democratic statehood has in important respects also become dysfunctional in many countries.
This would imply that a number of ostensibly established and stable nation
states are in fact in crisis. This is not really an exaggeration, however. One can
examine the Brexit debacle as well as the Trump election campaign and presi-
dency in this light. The more centrally relevant point for the discussion at hand
is that critical social research in this field must examine theories and practices
of statehood in conjunction with theories and practices of FD.

Systems have their own sense and are governed by unique modes of reasoning and knowledge. These particularities are described and analysed by
sociologists in terms of codes and other symbolic media of communication.
The epistemological content of a given social-systemic code is distorted – and
the functioning of that system demonstrably impaired – if a single overriding
logic of governance prevails, and a uniform model of inter-systemic mediation
is imposed. Imposing a uniform model in this regard can only be accomplished
by ignoring system specificity. The result is that inter-systemic communication
is then shunted into pre-established channels that conform to that logic. In
this context, prevailing is not really mediating, or, stated slightly differently,
it is mediating according to a decidedly instrumental mode of reason that
does not so much mediate as it coercively integrates. Stated differently again,
there is no way that a single overriding logic of governance can do justice to
the distinct judicial and legislative functions operative within each system. It
is moreover not necessarily the case that the legislative and judicial functions
observable in one social system have direct equivalents in others. What is
appropriate for any given system will of course change over time; re-coding
will become urgent as society evolves. It is therefore imperative to develop
the critique of instrumental reason in a decidedly sociological direction. In
order to do this convincingly it will be necessary to avoid the tendency to see
instrumental reason at work everywhere and in equal measure in all aspects

of social life. One sometimes finds this approach in some of the works of first-generation critical theory. It is also implausible that instrumental reason is neatly confined to what Habermas and others refer to in very generic terms as the system, however. An effective sociological critique of instrumental reason must therefore not only uncover the links between dysfunctional mediation, the mismanagement of individual social systems, and coercive integration. It has to do this whilst also investigating how systems are currently steered by codes that are susceptible to re-coding by an informed citizenry broadly educated in the rigours of collective self-management.

The history of politically constituted statehood demonstrates that the judiciary must sometimes buttress the legislature in order to maintain a democratic separation of state powers. That history also indicates that interventions in the economy and other fields are sometimes necessary in order to maintain a democratic separation of social systems, or to establish and maintain what political philosophers from Aristotle and Machiavelli to Montesquieu used to refer to as mixed constitutions.[27] Hence it would be wrong to suppose that systems develop independently of states (it is the qualitative kind of statehood that matters), or that instrumental reason is the downfall of self-regulating systems that would otherwise coexist in peaceful isolation had they not been manipulated by intrusive state interventions in the sphere of naturally legitimate exchange (defenders of this claim often attribute self-steering capacities to markets that the latter clearly do not possess). To repeat, social systems communicate with one another and are mediated. Third-generation critical theorists adopting a sociological approach to these issues endeavour to ascertain if the mediations are knowledge-enhancing and conducive to self-steering for the systems in question, or if the mediations tend to be authoritarian and dirigiste. Socially constituted statehood will remain skeletal, and the risk of a slide from the legal state to the party state will remain acute, as long as state executives, in alliance with aggregates of private power, continue to perform the key functions required to steer inter-systemic mediation. This problem can be addressed with a two-pronged argument. It needs to be shown that social systems really do coexist in a relation of mediated non-identity, such that the task of non-coercive inter-systemic mediation is by definition highly intricate and interdisciplinary. It must also be shown that epistemological and aesthetic concepts and practices can make important contributions in a war of position between the legislative and judicial dimensions of inter-systemic mediation against the executive and decisionistic ones. The second section of chapter 4 develops this argument by looking at epistemological and aesthetic considerations about the reality of conceptual and institutional form. It is not fanciful to assert that epistemology and aesthetics have a continuing role to play in fostering the emergence of the model of social statehood already contained in the currently hegemonic one. Critical philosophy and aesthetic resistance will thus continue to de-legitimate abuses of power and the negligent enforcement of rights precisely because they are related to and are involved in processes of inter-systemic mediation. They may be far less visible in this regard than the primary legal, political, and economic systems. But their links with the educational system certainly are visible, thus raising the possibility of a new constellation of systemic coexistence in which mediated non-identity becomes an operative organisational and communicative principle.

One may ask what is constitutional about all this. The simple answer for the time being, which illustrates the continuity between politically constituted and socially constituted statehood, is the factual evidence and normative demand that political authority be divided, shared, and held accountable. If this were not the case, it would be pointless to distinguish between power and authority, and even more difficult than it already is to discern between politicisation and democratisation. The importance of the distinction between power and authority is obviously not limited to the exercise of political power and democratic authority. One can go further and argue that dividing power, sharing power, and making it optimally accountable within each social system is the key to enhancing the self-steering capacities of that system. In *The Labour Constitution*, Ruth Dukes effectively shows how modern industrial economic systems need to produce laws capable of steering the labour process without relying on the party political control of the economy that one normally associates with nationalised (social democracy) or centrally planned (socialist and communist) economies. It is worth recalling that (a) modern economic systems have been compelled to develop this capacity as a result of market failure and the de-stabilising effects of monopoly capitalism, and that (b) party political control of the economy can just as easily be employed to privatise, outsource, and de-regulate. Her research examines the ideas of Hugo Sinzheimer, Otto Kahn-Freund, and constitutional provisions for industrial democracy in the Weimar Republic and well beyond.[28]

David Graeber notes that it is entirely plausible to regard democracy as a project and an ongoing global movement embracing all aspects of daily life, rather than a political technique for securing the transfer of legitimate power from one government to the next through parliamentary elections.[29] Hence whilst for Graeber politicisation and democratisation are closely related and mutually reinforcing, Niklas Luhmann regards politicisation external to the political system to be an impediment to the functioning of the political system and neighbouring social systems as well. One could insert Habermas and Rawls as intermediate positions between these two 'extremes'. From the standpoint adopted in chapter 5 of this book, however, it seems pressing to ask how one might reconceptualise the mediated relation between social systems, so that one can protect standards of objectivity in science, academic research, news reporting, and other fields without, as a consequence, having to fetishise very biased notions of efficiency, growth, and productivity in the economic system. In a related vein, there is no compelling contemporary political or sociological claim capable of illustrating why the protection of individual and minority rights inevitably requires the unassailable protection of private interests in matters related to job security and housing, the provision of health care and education, the safeguarding of natural resources, and a wide variety of other issues. It does not follow from the right not to have one's phone tapped that the provision of collective services such as health, housing, transport, and education must be de-regulated in ways that preserve established patterns, thereby privileging a few big firms and marginalising alternative ways of thinking and living.[30]

Arguments linking the defence of privacy and human rights with demands for de-regulation, privatisation, and outsourcing lack plausibility. Contrary to their own intentions, in many cases they illustrate that social systems across nations and states have been functionally differentiated in historically discernible ways that have evident repercussions for prevailing understandings and practices of de-centralisation, democratisation, politicisation, and political will formation, as well as for the delineation of systemic boundaries and the validity of a wide variety of rights claims. Moreover, it can also be shown that distinct models of FD are revealing in terms of the ways in which economic, political, and cultural elites are established and evolve within national and international contexts.[31] Private property, like freedom of conscience and expression, played a major role in the safeguarding of individual liberty against arbitrary government intervention in seventeenth- to nineteenth-century Europe and other parts of the globe; the introduction of judicial review is an important part of that historical narrative. British intellectual and political history from John Milton and J. S. Mill to H. L. A. Hart and beyond provides substantial evidence for this claim. But it must also be recalled that private property and the rule of law, conventionally conceived, effectively performed these tasks during an historical epoch in which electoral rights of suffrage and political rights of participation and accountability were drastically circumscribed according to differences of gender, race, and class that are not compatible with universal human rights or norms of juridical consistency.[32]

The dialectic of systemic specificity (differentiation) and political democracy (inclusion) therefore needs re-thinking in the light of the profoundly changed national and international context in which social processes and communication unfold today. Attempts to reconcile political and sociological modernity that do not make this conceptual effort will fail in institutional practice. In anticipation of the line of inquiry to be followed in chapters 4 and 5, it is worth noting the contrast between synthetic plasticity of the kind implied by the concept of mediated unity, on the one hand, and the managerial prerogative to 'add' or clumsily assimilate sociological realities to what are sometimes taken to be unshakeable, pre-existing meta-political foundations such as *the nation's state*, on the other. This contrast is especially glaring when the nation's state is regarded to be the protective shell of a non-negotiable ethnic essence or fundamentalist doctrine.[33] It was perhaps possible to add in this metaphorical sense of stretching or extending when, in a first historical instance, restrictions on rights of suffrage were rescinded, and then, in a second instance, when social rights of welfare were comprehensively introduced in Europe after 1945. The ongoing neoliberal restructuration of the welfare state since the late 1970s suggests that what can be added can also be subtracted.[34] The more pressing point is that the quantitative constitutional paradigm of adding rights to (burdening) or subtracting rights from (streamlining) the state will have to cede place to another one if there is to be a re-thinking of the dynamics between social communication and normative integration/inclusion that is relevant today. Once again, however, the question remains: will that constitutional paradigm shift consolidate the liberal democratic state or demand fundamental, compositional changes in statehood, bearing in mind the challenges posed by FD? There is no simple or obvious answer to this question. It is likely that the monopoly on the legitimate use of force and the separation of powers will be preserved for the foreseeable future. Hybrid legalities are already challenging existing practices of unrivalled legislative authority.[35]

Moreover, if the weak/formal model of legality-legitimacy dialectics associated with liberal democracy is decidedly less susceptible to authoritarian interpretations than its strong dialectical counterpart, it is nonetheless situated within the mediated unity paradigm of statehood. The previous chapter shows that one cannot presuppose the existence of the requisite amount and degree of formal elasticity needed to generate mediated unity within nation states. From an Italian or German standpoint it is certainly plausible to argue that one of the key conditions of stability after 1945 was the transfer of authority from the nation state to international bodies, thus relieving the state in these countries from tasks it tried to handle according to the dictates of strong dialectical foundations in the interwar period. From a contemporary Greek perspective, however, it would seem that this transfer of power has actually made it almost impossible for the state to enjoy any meaningful degree of autonomy or legislative integrity. Greek citizens might very reasonably protest that unless all countries are subject to the same rules, human rights and juridical norms cannot be applied in a uniform, consistent manner. A perspective that pits the Germans against the Greeks fails to consider the point about simultaneously overlapping and hybrid legal orders that synthesise diverse legal registers. It is no longer axiomatic that international treaties between geographically specific nation states establish legal orders enjoying precedence over transnational orders responding to de-territorialised, inter-systemic communication. These developments demand a fresh look at the links between the specific kind of centralisation needed to consolidate modern statehood, and the codes that steer social-systemic *autopoiesis*.[36]

In chapter 1 it is noted that one of the fundamental conditions of legitimate and stable statehood, as opposed to governance by play of competing aggregates of privately organised centres of power, is the enforcement of the unrivalled power of the state in key areas of jurisdiction, such as taxation, the military, and the courts, in the sense that there can be no rival powers vying for control of tax collection, public security, or the administration of justice, lest there be a state within the state. But from the perspective of the liberal democratic nation state, there must also not be an all-out politicisation of taxation, defence, justice, or other areas of social life such as medical research, religious affiliation, or the labour process. This is because in these areas, specific kinds of competence or matters of individual conscience are at least as relevant as notions of unqualified inclusivity based on the model of universal citizenship. One thinks, for example, of the possible effects of tying rates of tax to party membership. To date, the capacity of the liberal democratic state to enact all-inclusive citizenship thus depends on being relieved of excessive demands that are likely to strain its capacity to apply power and enforce the law according to objective standards that do not privilege, discriminate, or unduly compensate for lack of the requisite competence and/or relevantly coded information. Liberal democrats are wont to argue that sacrificing objective standards in these matters is tantamount to diluting juridical neutrality with informal notions of solidarity, sympathy, and revenge, and that this, in turn, would be requital rather than rational justice. Moreover, it is believed by many who defend this line of argument that an excessive hybridisation of closely observed legal norm and informal social solidarity would undermine the rule of law by asking the courts to adjudicate cases in a determinate way before the cases actually come to court. Strictly speaking, in other words, one might say that there can be no such thing as 'class justice' that is distinct from extra-legal prejudice or outright revenge, since the very notion entails a political decision to outlaw economic inequality *prior* to the exchange processes that produce unequal results for the affected parties. The recurring argument is that the subjection of economic processes to political criteria undermines impartial justice at the same time that it violates the right to private property and prevents economic growth.[37]

Somewhat polemically, it might therefore be said that the Cold War was won because one side had developed a model of statehood far more attuned to the demands of sociological modernity than the other side, thus raising the question as to whether the victorious model of statehood is still modern enough today. Within the framework established by this particular paradigm of FD, the only way to retain the uncompromisingly legal dimension of justice whilst also respecting individual autonomy and stimulating the economy is rigorously to restrict the political dimension of both law and the economy. In constitutional terms, the rule of law is entrusted with the task of achieving this restriction by rendering political intervention rightful in the precise sense that interventions *proceed* according to rights-based *procedures*. These procedures can be regarded as means that entertain an ambiguous relation with the ends and projected outcomes to which they are linked in ways that are both contingent and causal. At this point, the relation between democracy/ politics and law/rights in most liberal democratic states becomes highly intricate and to a certain extent paradoxical. If it has already been shown that one cannot posit a mediated unity between citizens, governments, and states via law, it is nonetheless misleading to distinguish categorically between democratic processes and law-making processes. The dilemma can be framed as follows: if the law is democratic, it is necessarily politicised rather than consistently neutral; if the law is autopoietic, rather than democratic, questions are raised as regards the legitimacy of the law. If democratic institutions presuppose and reproduce *unity* through representation, the implementation of rights requires determinate *differentiations and divisions* such as, most notably, the division of powers. This point goes some of the way towards elucidating why one must carefully qualify the statement that what distinguishes democracies from other political forms is the privileged access to the state enjoyed by the citizens of democracies: citizens have markedly differentiated access to the state because the state is itself marked by variegated points of entry. Points of access and entry, that is, of inclusion, thus depend on historically evolved patterns of statehood and FD. The kinds of available access to the legislature are qualitatively different to the kinds of available access to the judiciary and executive. The need to qualify the terms of democratic inclusivity is accentuated further when one observes that (a) some social systems appear to be more tenuously coupled with the state than other systems, and that (b) the same system may have a very different relation to the state from one country to the next. This becomes clear when comparing the NHS in Britain with the health care system in the United States, for example. Moreover, in some cases it might be more accurate to say that a given social system is closely coupled to the political system, but barely coupled to the state. Under these conditions, the role of the liberal democratic state in a globalised world society remains an open question at this juncture. Stating the matter thus raises questions about the extent to which some of the most important reflexive institutional achievements of political modernity, such as the division of powers within the state, the relatively predictable application of centralised political power, and the positivisation of juridical procedure, may be jeopardised by the manifestly centrifugal tendencies of sociological modernity. Foreshadowing the discussion in chapter 5, a provisional solution might be identifiable if FD can be gently and intelligently reformed so that key social systems acquire elements of the reflexivity ushered in by political modernity in relation to the state, such as the division of powers. One can imagine, in other words, a constitution for the economic system that sets up a system of checks and balances between the decisions taken in the banking, private financial, and public financial (treasury) sub-systems. If designed properly, this would be far more conducive to investment and price stability than a tax on financial transactions.[38] FD is itself in many ways an important achievement of sociological modernity and not, intrinsically, a threat to democracy or individual autonomy. In this context one is reminded of the thesis that 'epistemological critique is social critique and vice versa'. Adorno's statement is still very relevant to the project of developing new ways of thinking about collective learning and the resources it generates for addressing social problems. A great deal might be gained if social systems manage to teach the institutions of political modernity to respond to the so-called crisis of democracy in more resolutely de-centralised, flexible, and participatory ways than has been the case up until now. As indicated earlier in this chapter, it is likely that the problems of democracy or post-democracy, as it is sometimes called, may actually be better understood as a crisis of a determinate instance of FD, than as a crisis of democracy.[39]

Politicisation as democratisation? Reconsidering the ostensible primacy of politics in democratic thought and practice

The liberal democratic instantiation of FD suggests that the only feasible way to think about law and justice in relation to social class and the economy is in terms of the equal opportunity to compete for what are widely considered to be the best jobs, complemented by very modest levels of redistribution that can be rescinded if the economy slumps. If this premise holds, the only realistic way to think about law and justice in relation to citizenship and politics is in terms of the formal separation of powers and the freedom of press, assembly, and information. According to this logic, one must think of law and politics in terms of political rights that must not be permitted to infringe upon economic rights of property and exchange. It is thereby declared that this is the best way to maintain impartial justice across the systemic fields of economic exchange and political decision, and to adhere to the injunction that the state may enforce unrivalled, not all-encompassing power. Otherwise, it is frequently claimed, one runs the risk that modern power will cease to be articulated in an iterative, juridical form, and therefore become irrational, prejudicial, and unpredictable.[40] From this standpoint, it would seem that any attempt to bring about substantial economic or political reform can only be accomplished by re-suturing the legal to the economic system in order to achieve socio-economic equality, as Lenin had envisioned, or by re-fusing law and politics in what would inevitably be a highly centralised, authoritarian state of the kind envisioned by Carl Schmitt and other thinkers of what one might designate as the 'integrity of the political'.[41] In both cases, whether that of re-suturing or re-fusing, the liberal democratic version of the rule of law is sacrificed to dogma. It is sacrificed to the dogma of class equality, in the first instance, and jettisoned in favour of unquestioned state authority to legislate and protect the primacy of properly political concerns against the lowly material interests of society, in the second.[42] Although both approaches are objectionably authoritarian, they each in their own way raise a valid question, which can be formulated as follows: what is the role of politics and instances of politicisation in a liberal democracy, once one disallows the integrity of politics and dismisses the legislative pre-eminence of the state? If it is constitutionally decreed that the only way to maintain impartial justice across systemic fields is by preventing political rights from infringing substantially upon economic as well as a wide variety of other rights, then one has a constitution that allows for a very partial politicisation of rights rather than anything that Schmitt, Arendt, Castoriadis, Lefort, and many others would recognise as political in the strong sense of the term, or as republican democracy.[43] In response to the obvious problems with the positions of Schmitt and ostensibly left interpretations of his work, a number of prominent philosophers suggest that late modern societies should embrace the formal separation of legal, political, and economic systems in order to avoid the catastrophic consequences of strong dialectical models of unity and the authoritarian centralisation they usually bring. In order to distinguish their views from liberal democratic positions on the questions of properly political action, formal justice, and participatory democracy, however, these thinkers add, each in their own distinct way, that late modern societies should simultaneously concentrate on fostering an extra-juridical civic culture of informal justice, republican virtue, and non-populist political will formation. They reckon that the outlines of this culture can be imagined and spontaneously cultivated as public sphere vigilance, activism in civil society, hospitality, friendship, and cosmopolitanism.[44]

It would perhaps be tempting to contrast the defence of the expressly liberal version of FD and the role of law within it, on the one hand, with both the celebration of the dangers of politics and evident glorification of the state in Schmitt, as well as the strident anti-liberalism of several prominent high profile university figures, on the other. The defence of the liberal democratic vision of FD is more coherent and ultimately more convincing than academically radical appeals to the communist hypothesis, revolutionary populism, or the multitude.[45] It is in fact that version of FD which has always been hegemonic, apart from brief social democratic interludes, and that needs to be dialectically and sociologically critiqued in immanent, not absolute terms. The task of formulating that critique is aided by two factors. Like the strong dialectical model associated with the integrity of politics, the weak dialectical model associated with liberalism also relies on a dialectical argument about mediations to sustain its central claims about legality, legitimacy, representation, and democracy. The society implied by the more formally circumscribed model is conceptually closer, in terms of FD and proposed mediations, to the normative ideal of a self-governing society, than any of the oppressive Jacobin alternatives that would flow from strong dialectics in these matters. Although there are fundamental differences between Schmitt and the academic radicals, they all occupy positions well within the continuum between more liberal/less democratic and more democratic/less liberal sketched at the end of chapter 1. The more important point in terms of facts and norms is the following: if FD is a sociological fact confirmed by comparative historical analysis, there are different ways of contesting the hegemonic version without demanding a return (or a projected great leap forward) to right and left invocations of organic unity. As hinted earlier, there is little point in attempting to reverse differentiation processes in the name of a new subject-object of history or a revolutionary state. One needs instead to think about how the normative frameworks accompanying differentiation processes can be reformed at a time when the currently hegemonic model of FD has for the most part ceased to be an adequate vehicle for collective learning or a stimulus for systemic reflexivity. The symptoms of this inability to adapt and flexibly to adjust have become strikingly visible on several fronts. The enforcement of non-enforcement in the guise of austerity has become every bit as dogmatic and, in places like Greece, as economically ineffective as the former ideologies of state socialism. Authoritarian populism is a de-stabilising threat across Europe and many other parts of the world. The Snowden affair and the Panama Papers scandal provide ample evidence of the extent to which states around the globe are undermined by private centres of power and information that those states nonetheless feel obliged to protect for largely economic reasons. Health, environmental, and migration crises pose equally formidable challenges to the contemporary constitution of statehood and FD.[46]

These remarks condense a key historical point made in chapters 1 and 2 of this book, and anticipate one of its main conclusions: the centralisation and simultaneous tripartite division of political power, on the one hand, and the positivisation of law, on the other, are fundamental conditions of modern statehood. Statehood paves the way for the rapid unfolding of FD observed in the run-up to the Industrial Revolution and the subsequent course of its ongoing aftermath. Depending on the country in question, these centralising dynamics can be justifiably credited with having created the preconditions for scientific discoveries, economic growth, the independence of legal authority from political power, the emancipation of aesthetic reason from religious tradition and political instrumentalisation, formal equality between genders and races, and many other of the palpable gains of sociological modernity. In the second decade of the twenty-first century it has become questionable if the centralist logic of legal positivisation and ethnic or republican notions of territorial statehood can still provide an adequate framework for normatively regulating the expansion of differentiation in ways that stimulate the productive capacities of science, economics, aesthetics, education, the media, and so on. If the term 'regime collisions' (Fischer-Lescano and Teubner) captures something essential about the hybrid nature of the constitution of states and social systems today, 'the dark side of functional differentiation' (Kjaer, Teubner, and Febbrajo) indicates what is at stake in the search for a reformed normative framework.[47]

The hypothesis sketched here and developed more fully in chapter 5 is that the productive capacities of science, economics, education, health, aesthetics, and other social systems were spectacularly enhanced in Europe and North America with the help of the foundation provided by political modernity. The institutional framework provided by political modernity and often associated with the seventeenth- and eighteenth-century revolutions performed these tasks with remarkable efficiency when the productive potential of incipiently differentiated social systems was manifestly in need of explicitly quantitative stimulation. Polemics against liberal democracy often ignore the fact that privatisation and anti-mercantilist initiatives in favour of free trade have at times played an important role in providing this stimulus.[48] The dark side of FD becomes visible when the need for quantitative expansion develops into a need for qualitative communication between systems – not undiminished differentiation and expansion, or abrupt shifts from privatisation to nationalisation and back again – and the modes of transition to that shift are barred by outdated constitutional norms, blocked by sclerotic institutions, and impeded by the recycling of failed 'remedies' that were appropriate for earlier stages in the dialectic of political and sociological modernities.[49]

This chapter concludes with a brief look at how the problematic relation between politicisation and democratisation within the currently hegemonic

model of FD sheds light on some of the obstacles facing an eventually possible reconfiguration of the dialectic of statehood and FD. Might the normative
dimension of late modern, increasingly post-territorial statehood now be conceived in de-centralist terms that can better synchronise with the de facto de-
centralisation of late modern FD? If so, normative integration could progress
from its territorial-constitutional origins towards a possible social-systemic
constitutional future, in which national boundaries will surely play a very different role than they did in the heroic period of state formation, when geographical boundaries, sovereignty, and the consolidation of the nation state
were interlocking processes. At that point human rights would no longer be
dependent on accidents of territorial/naturalist point of origin.[50]

There is a marked tendency for the people of North American and Western
European societies to think of politics, citizenship, and democracy as the
domain of the state. Yet the state does not rule in favour of politics against
the economy, nor does it rule in favour of the economy against politics. The
state is meant to guarantee that the space between political authority, economic efficiency, artistic originality and vision, scientific validity, freedom of
information, religious affiliation, educational standards, and so on is neither
collapsed nor widened so far as to amount to a complete separation; one can
say that the state denotes a dynamic set of relationships between institutions, and, perhaps most importantly, that the state mediates. It will cease
to do so impartially, however, if law is beholden to politics or any other single
field of endeavour. If this happens, there is likely to be a reversion to the re-
suturing/re-fusing dynamics characteristic of twentieth-century political reaction in interwar Europe. The implications for prevailing notions of citizenship
and democracy have yet fully to be developed for three main reasons. First,
it has proven to be extremely difficult for societies that define themselves as
democratic to give up on the idea that there is an organic bond between the
people and the law that distinguishes democracy from other political forms.
Second, it has proven to be equally arduous for democratic societies to part
with the notion that impartial mediation is somehow intrinsically linked with
enforcing a clear demarcation between a naturally legitimate private sphere
of exchange and a public authority empowered to adjudicate between trading
partners without privileging any one of them, as if that authority was a monolithic entity, somehow standing above or outside individual acts of exchange in
the manner of a referee. This preoccupation normally leads to a dichotomous
juxtaposition of the prerogatives of the abstract individual, closely associated
with the private law of the free market, and demand for public regulation
of market dysfunctions, associated with nationalisation, ponderous bureau-
cracy, and therewith, by extension, an increasingly overburdened state that
appears inefficient and in need of spending cuts. That is, third, the impression

persists that whereas economic exchange flows horizontally and consensually, political steering must necessarily be vertical and hierarchical. If Luhmann and others are correct, this characterisation may have been true of stratified societies, but it does not provide an accurate description of modern societies. It is now far more accurate to think of law, politics, economics, education, media, scientific research, health, and the like as social systems engaged in horizontally flowing communication and different kinds of lateral exchange.[51] It can therefore be very plausibly argued that the most pertinent problems of FD and post-territorial statehood concern the possibilities of co-ordinating and thereby democratising inter-systemic communication. If this can be accomplished, one would then have a society governed by a plurality of horizontal steering instances tailored to the specificities of distinct systemic codes. How might it be possible to re-imagine democracy without the stratified, pyramidal image of a privileged connection between law and politics that begins below, with 'the people', and culminates above, in the supposed law-giving authority of the sovereign state?

Historical research indicates that the liberal democratic state may consider itself to be confronted with excessive political demands if it is constantly called upon to respect criteria of equality that do not square with the disparities in relevant competence that are likely to arise when system-specific fields of endeavour require unique kinds of training and knowledge that are patently not evenly distributed, and in any case not congruent with the unqualified inclusivity that defines citizenship. Just as the state cannot demand of a civil servant that he act as a medical doctor or journalist, the state cannot function like a state if it is asked to correct the decisions of judges according to their projected popularity or unpopularity with democratic (or quite possibly undemocratic) majorities. Safeguarding the judiciary from electoral pressure and populist sanction enables modern states, to considerably varying degrees depending on the historical evolution of the particular state in question, to detach considerations of justice from fairly random opinions about differences in personal income, religious faith, ethnic background, and a variety of other factors that in principle bear no relation to the enforcement of impersonal juridical norms. Judges have to be able to make what might turn out to be unpopular decisions without fearing dismissal or populist backlash; to this extent they depend on responsible communication of information by the mass media within a generalised democratic culture of political will formation characterised by pluralism, tolerance, and mutual respect. It is therefore crucially important that judges do not have to make extravagant promises in order to be elected or appointed, and it is imperative that they are free to interpret the law without being obliged to toe a party line or committing themselves to a given religion whilst doing so. When constitutional provisions do not adequately guide the differentiation of law, politics, and other social systems, political parties or coalitions of allied parties representing a variety of societal interests have repeatedly tried to colonise state institutions and wield them against their party political competitors and even, in some cases, against the rest of society. If successful, the colonisation process can lead to the establishment of a wide array of left and right corporatist substitutes for states, that is, what one can designate as unstable states, with all that corporatism implies in terms of electoral corruption, political responsiveness to interest groups rather than equality of citizenship, un-accountable executive power to the detriment of legislative authority, and, in extreme cases such as fascism and state socialism, neutralisation of the judiciary. In this light, one can see why, both in terms of sociological relevance and normative integration, the partial politicisation of rights offers distinct advantages over decidedly more integral conceptions of the political. This brings the discussion to a few final observations relating to the emphasis above on safeguarding the judiciary and the evident need to guide differentiation processes.

Habermas's work on the early modern European public sphere indicates that there may well have been an historical moment when a privileged relation between law and politics did in fact exist. In terms of the argument developed in this chapter, however, it is very interesting to note that the nexus was sustained by informal networks and residually feudal loyalties and interests that were neither very liberal nor democratic in any real sense. This observation relates to the point made earlier, namely that private property and a very specific instantiation of the rule of law mediated between extremely well situated elites in the public sphere, parliament, and the state executive, at a time when electoral rights of suffrage and political rights of participation and accountability were drastically circumscribed. In the aftermath of 1848 and the struggles accompanying the gradual rescinding of restrictions on electoral participation thereafter, some elites feared that the idea of democracy in practice might well mean something approaching mob rule, radical redistribution, and the end of correct standards in all professions. There were and are other, far more rational and progressive reasons to divide and share political power, some of which have been touched on in the preceding pages. The implementation of impersonal juridical norms has been an important factor in ensuring that legislation on equal pay, gay rights, environmental protection, disabled access, child safety, and a wide variety of other issues is enforced without consideration of extraneous criteria that are not relevant to the systemically specific logic governing valid decisions in the matter at hand. As soon as democracy in practice evolves beyond the literal notion of majority rule, so as to reconcile majority rule with minority rights, the tension between systemic specificity and democratic decision-making enters into a qualitatively new phase. One is able to redefine the criteria informing decisions about inclusion in fundamental ways, depending on how FD is institutionalised in any given context. Today there is a great deal of evidence to suggest that the context is transnational and functional.

Constitutional design enables judges to interpret the law without being obliged to toe a party line or commit themselves to a given religion whilst doing so. Comparable constitutional design should enable hospital patients to receive treatment regardless of income, sexual preference, race, religion, country of origin, or similar criteria, since none of those factors figure in what it takes to heal an illness. Even according to the strictest health systemic coding criteria, ability to pay/inability to pay is irrelevant to the health and wellbeing of any given patient. Similarly, the deciding factor regarding student applications for access to places on university courses must be their academic and civic portfolios rather than personal income or family wealth. If there is environmental justice and an even application of human rights, it will be possible for all inhalers of air – global humanity – to enjoy fresh air regardless of where they happen to be born. Examples capable of consolidating the argument can be multiplied in a number of directions. The crux of the matter at this stage in the argument developed here is this: key elements of transnational statehood will have to be devolved upon citizens with rights pertaining to specific systemic functions and re-designed codes in order to ensure that the spaces between political authority and other dimensions of statehood are neither collapsed nor widened to a state of complete fragmentation.

Notes

1 See Pablo Iglesias Turrión, *Disputar la democracia: Política para tiempos de crisis* (Madrid: Akal, 2014), pp. 40–9; Darrow Schecter, 'Gramsci's unorthodox Marxism: political ambiguity and sociological relevance', *Modern Italy*, 15 (2010), 145–59; and the chapters collected in Mark McNally (ed.), *Antonio Gramsci*, Explorations in Contemporary Political Thought (Ashgate: Palgrave Macmillan, 2015). Paul Mason discusses the Gramscian dimension of the June 2017 parliamentary elections in Paul Mason, 'Corbyn's victory was not supposed to happen: but to disrupt logic is the first step in defeating Britain's ruling elite', *Guardian* (13 June 2017), G2, pp. 10–11.

2 This theme is examined in detail in Darrow Schecter, *Beyond Hegemony: Towards a New Philosophy of Political Legitimacy* (Manchester: Manchester University Press, 2005).

3 These links are analysed and subjected to a thorough critique by Christoph Menke in *Kritik der Rechte* (Berlin: Suhrkamp, 2015).

4 Joseph Raz, *The Authority of Law: Essays on Law and Morality* (Oxford: Clarendon Press, 1979), chapter 1; John Rawls, *The Law of Peoples, with 'The idea of public reason revisited'* (Cambridge, MA: Harvard University Press, 1999), pp. 121–8, and pp. 131–48; and Anders Esmark, 'Systems and Sovereignty: A Systems Theoretical

Look at the Transformation of Sovereignty', in Mathias Albert and Lena Hilkermeier (eds), *Observing International Relations: Niklas Luhmann and World Politics* (London: Routledge, 2004), pp. 121–41.

5 Emile Durkheim, *De la division du travail social* (Paris: Presses universitaires du France, 4th edn, 1996 [1893]), available in English as *The Division of Labor in Society* (New York: Free Press, 1933), chapters 5–7. Whereas many thinkers focus on the alienating aspects of differentiation and division, Durkheim is one of the first to see the normative and integrative potential of such processes.

6 One should not completely discount the possibility that reactionary forces of the kind currently mobilising in Austria, Poland, Turkey, and elsewhere will attempt to restore order on a more authoritarian and less differentiated basis. For the Turkish case see Umut Sahverdi, 'Transformations in the Turkish Educational System in Relation to the Islamic Turn in Turkish Statehood' (D.Phil, University of Sussex, forthcoming).

7 Habermas makes a strong case for this position. See Vol. II, chapter 7 of Habermas, *Theorie des kommunikativen Handelns*, available in English as *The Theory of Communicative Action*, in which he cites the sociology of Talcott Parsons as a key influence on the development of his own argument. For a more recent (and cautious) assessment of the dialectic of differentiation and democracy, see Christian Joerges, 'A New Alliance of De-Legalisation and Legal Formalism? Reflections on the Response to the Social Deficit of the European Integration Project', in Hauke Brunkhorst (ed.), *Demokratie in der Weltgesellschaft*, Soziale Welt: Sonderband, 18 (Baden-Baden: Nomos, 2009), pp. 437–50.

8 The relation between democracy and complexity is taken up from a number of standpoints by the authors in Seyla Benhabib (ed.), *Democracy and Difference: Contesting the Boundaries of the Political* (Princeton: Princeton University Press, 1996). The point about problems that require de-centralised solutions rather than simply privatised ones touches upon basic ambiguities in liberalism and Marxism. It is an issue for liberalism in that whilst there is no overarching juridical-political bond between the individual citizen and post-feudal authority, it might be argued that there is a potentially unifying bond that is torn between its public, juridical-political dimensions and its private, juridical-contractual dimensions. Marx spots this problem in his early writings on Hegel, and draws pertinent conclusions in his more mature reflections on the Paris Commune. The assumed primacy of the private sphere is a source of conflict, waged by some elites in the name of liberalism and freedom, which survives well into the twenty-first century in the guise of rampant inequality and planned precariousness. See Thomas Piketty, *Le Capital au XXIᵉ siècle* (Paris: Seuil, 2013), available in English as *Capital*, Part III, to name just one prominent articulation of this perspective. In a parallel vein, state socialism (Marxism in power) declined as a result of privileging the centralised, authoritarian rule of one-party states, established in the name of class democracy, at the expense of the libertarian aspirations of the Paris Commune and the soviets that flourished in Turin, Budapest, Berlin, Munich, St Petersburg, and elsewhere in the immediate aftermath of World War I. The twin failures of liberal democracy and state socialism highlight what is at stake when assessing the current dilemmas of social democracy. For an excellent analysis of this thorny issue see Gerassimos Moschonas, *In the Name of Social Democracy: The Great Transformation, 1945 to the Present*, trans. Gregory Elliott (London: Verso, revised and updated edn, 2002), Part III.

9 Nick Srnicek and Alex Williams, *Inventing the Future: Postcapitalism and a World Without Work* (London: Verso Books, 2015), chapters 2–3; and Kathi Weeks, *The Problem with Work: Feminism, Marxism, Antiwork Politics, and Postwork Imaginaries* (Durham, NC: Duke University Press, 2011), chapter 5.

10 George Monbiot, *How Did We Get into This Mess? Politics, Equality, Nature* (London: Verso, 2016); and Yanis Varoufakis, *And the Weak Suffer What They Must? Europe, Austerity and the Threat to Global Stability* (London: The Bodley Head, 2016).

11 Crouch, *Post-Democracy*, chapters 5–6; Dean, *Democracy and Other Neoliberal Fantasies*, chapters 1–3; Ingolfur Blühdorn, *Simulative Demokratie: Neue Politik nach der postdemokratischen Wende* (Berlin: Suhrkamp, 2013), pp. 264–81; Michelsen and Walter (eds), *Unpolitische Demokratie*, chapters 1 and 8; Massimo L. Salvadori, *Democrazie senza democrazia* (Bari: Laterza, 2009), chapter 8; Wolfgang Merkel and Marcus Spittler, 'Disaffection or Changes in European Democracies?', in Ludolfo Paramio (ed.), *Desafección política y gobernabilidad: el reto político* (Madrid: Marcial Pons, 2015), pp. 61–105; Wolfgang Streeck, *Gekaufte Zeit: Die vertagte Krise des demokratischen Kapitalismus*, Frankfurter Adorno-Vorlesungen, 2012 (Berlin: Suhrkamp, 2013), available in English as *Buying Time: The Delayed Crisis of Democratic Capitalism*, trans. Patrick Camiller and David Fernbach (London: Verso, 2nd edn, 2017), chapter 3; and Emmanuel Todd, *Après la démocratie* (Paris: Gallimard, 2008), chapter 6. Although the arguments deployed by these authors are generally very strong and convincing in a number of ways, the relation between FD and democracy is rarely explored in any detail. If one does not discuss various possible models of FD, it may well seem that 'the people' are intrinsically privately oriented or simply too benighted to translate the 'lofty' ideals of democracy into actual practice. A conclusion of this kind would amount to a retreat to the a-historical psychologism of Pareto, Mosca, and Michels.

12 Kitschelt, *Transformation*, chapters 1–2; Sheri Berman, *The Primacy of Politics: Social Democracy and the Making of Europe's Twentieth Century* (Cambridge: Cambridge University Press, 2006), chapter 7.

13 Michael T. Klare, *The Race for What's Left: The Global Scramble for the World's Last Resources* (New York: Metropolitan Books, 2012).

14 Alain Supiot, 'The Territorial Inscription of Laws', in Gralf-Peter Calliess, Andreas Fischer-Lescano, Dan Wielsch, and Peer Zumbansen (eds), *Soziologische Jurisprudenz: Festschrift für Gunther Teubner zum 65. Geburtstag am 30. April 2009* (Berlin: de Gruyter, 2009), pp. 375–93.

15 Carlos de Cabo Martin, *Pensamiento crítico, constitucionalismo crítico* (Madrid: Trotta, 2014), pp. 12, 48, 63; and Brunkhorst, *Critical Theory of Legal Revolutions*, chapter 3.

16 This state of affairs is aptly described by Andreas Fischer-Lescano and Gunther Teubner as a collision of regimes, or *Regime-Kollisionen*, as they say in their already cited brilliant work of this title. The transnational, as distinct from international dimension has recently been fruitfully developed further by Möller, *Formwandel der Verfassung*.

17 Thomas Wirtz, 'Entscheidung: Niklas Luhmann und Carl Schmitt', in Albrecht Koschorke and Cornelia Vismann (eds), *Widerstände der Systemtheorie: Kulturtheoretische Analysen zum Werk von Niklas Luhmann* (Berlin: Akademie Verlag, 1999), pp. 175–97; and John Paterson, 'The Precautionary Principle: Practical Reason, Regulatory Decision-Making and Judicial Review in the Context of Functional Differentiation', in Andreas Philippopoulos-Mihalopoulos (ed.), *Law and Ecology: New Environmental Foundations* (Abingdon: Routledge, 2011), pp. 83–104.

18 Fischer-Lescano and Teubner, *Regime-Kollisionen*, p. 64.

19 These issues are treated with sophistication and nuance in James Hampshire, *The Politics of Immigration: Contradictions of the Liberal State* (Cambridge: Polity, 2013), chapter 6. The question of human rights and territorial borders is cogently

addressed by Dennis Broeders, 'The new digital borders of Europe', *International Sociology*, 22:1 (2007), 71–92.

20 This point is forcefully made by Teubner, *Constitutional Fragments*, and in his essays collected in *Critical Theory and Legal Autopoiesis*.

21 Niklas Luhmann, *Soziologische Aufklärung 4: Beiträge zur funktionalen Differenzierung der Gesellschaft* (Wiesbaden: VS Verlag für Sozialwissenschaften, 4th edn, 2009 [1987]), Part II, chapter 5.

22 Habermas, *Faktizität und Geltung*, available in English as *Between Facts and Norms*, chapter 2. Perhaps the most famous statement linking the legal system's capacity to function properly to a far wider set of constitutional arrangements is Charles de Secondat Montesquieu, *L'Esprit des lois* (Paris: Gallimard, 1992 [1748]), available in English as *The Spirit of the Laws* (Cambridge: Cambridge University Press, 1989). See in particular Book 1, chapter 11, on the separation of powers in Britain, and A. V. Dicey's praise of the rule of law in A. V. Dicey, *Introduction to the Study of the Law of the Constitution* (London: Macmillan, 8th edn, 1931 [1885]), pp. xxxvii–xlviii. Dicey's main ideas are expounded with clarity by Hilaire Barnett, *Constitutional & Administrative Law* (London: Cavendish, 5th edn, 2004), chapters 4 and 7.

23 These questions are taken up with flair by the contributors to Catriona McKinnon and Iain Hampsher-Monk (eds), *The Demands of Citizenship* (London: Continuum, 2000), Part II. See also Drucilla Cornell, *The Philosophy of the Limit* (London: Routledge, 1992), chapters 1 and 5.

24 J. A. G. Griffith, *The Politics of the Judiciary* (Glasgow: Fontana/Collins, 1977), Part II, chapter 4, and Brunkhorst, *Critical Theory of Legal Revolutions*, pp. 54–6 and 132–5. On the case of the media, see Christian Fuchs, *Digital Demagogue: Authoritarian Capitalism in the Age of Trump and Twitter* (London: Pluto, 2018). Chapter 2 is very adept at linking the analyses of the crisis of democracy in the interwar period found in the writings of Horkheimer, Neumann, and Pollock with contemporary phenomena pointing towards a possible crisis of democratic institutions today.

25 Griffith, *Politics of the Judiciary*, pp. 290–303.

26 In a related vein, it is entirely possible to regard entrenched socio-economic inequality in the twenty-first century as a phenomenon related to dysfunctional FD. This is far more plausible than explaining social inequality in terms of the unequal distribution of natural talents, or to see it as a spontaneous response to unpredictable market demand.

27 The conclusion of chapter 3 provides a brief discussion of mixed constitutions in classical and early modern political theory, and shows how the concerns of ancient, Renaissance, and early modern thinkers come up in new guises in the writings of Gramsci and Luhmann. The notion of the mixed constitution provides a reminder that although the explicit theorisation of social systems and societal constitutions is comparatively recent, it can very plausibly be argued that constitutional thinking has always been social to a significant extent. The conclusion of this book returns to this point and develops some of the implications.

28 Ruth Dukes, *The Labour Constitution: The Enduring Idea of Labour Law* (Oxford: Oxford University Press, 2014), chapter 2.

29 See David Graeber, *The Democracy Project: A History, a Crisis, a Movement* (London: Penguin Books, 2014), chapter 5.

30 Meek, *Private Island*, chapters 2–3.

31 John Scott, 'Modes of Power and Reconceptualization of Elites', in Michael Savage and Karel Williams (eds), *Remembering Elites* (Oxford: Wiley-Blackwell, 2008), pp. 27–43.

32 H. T. Dickinson, *Liberty and Property: Political Ideology in Eighteenth-Century Britain* (London: Methuen, 1977), chapters 3–4 and 6; and Razmig Keucheyan, 'Périssables démocraties', *Le Monde Diplomatique* (April 2015), p. 3, and *Hémisphère gauche: Une cartographie des nouvelles pensées critiques* (Paris: La Découverte, 2010), available in English as *The Left Hemisphere: Mapping Critical Theory Today*, trans. Gregory Elliott (London: Verso, 2013), chapter 5.

33 This foundation can be conceived of in terms of the organisational disciplinary techniques employed by a dominant ethnic group that agrees to tolerate added ethnic elements as long as they do not aspire to challenge the founding group/creed. One might regard the current refugee crisis as an example of an unwillingness or fear to try to integrate new and comparatively unknown ethnic elements into what is still considered to be a national norm, and, by extension, the basis of state authority. For an analysis, see the essays collected in Ferran Requejo and Camil Ungureanu, *Democracy, Law and Religious Pluralism in Europe: Secularism and Post-Secularism* (London: Routledge, 2015).

34 Florian Schui, *Austerity: The Great Failure* (New Haven: Yale University Press, 2014), introduction and chapters 2–3.

35 Poul F. Kjaer, 'Law and Order within and beyond National Configurations', in Poul F. Kjaer, Gunther Teubner, and Alberto Febbrajo (eds), *The Financial Crisis in Constitutional Perspective: The Dark Side of Functional Differentiation* (Oxford: Hart, 2011), pp. 395–430; and Martti Koskenniemi, 'Legal Fragmentation(s): An Essay on Fluidity and Form', in Gralf-Peter Calliess, Andreas Fischer-Lescano, Dan Wielsch, and Peer Zumbansen (eds), *Soziologische Jurisprudenz: Festschrift für Gunther Teubner zum 65. Geburtstag* (Berlin: De Gruyter, 2009), pp. 795–810.

36 Philippopoulos-Mihalopoulos, *Niklas Luhmann*, chapter 3; and Martin Loughlin, *Sword and Scales: An Examination of the Relationship between Law and Politics* (Oxford: Hart, 2000). On page 21 Loughlin remarks that if twentieth-century European history is characterised by the rise of totalitarian states, the twenty-first century seems to be marked by states undermined by international authorities and interests. These are two closely related but also very distinct reasons for state failure in the last one hundred years.

37 Kant supplements his defence of private property with the insistence that whilst there can be moral politicians, there cannot be political moralists. In his view it is fortunate if a politician happens to have an acute sense of duty, but one cannot legally enjoin moral behaviour with political means without thereby sacrificing the autonomy of the law and the dignity of individual choice in ethical matters. See Immanuel Kant, 'Appendix to "Perpetual Peace" ', in *Kant's Political Writings*, ed. Hans Reiss (Cambridge: Cambridge University Press, 1970), pp. 116–30; Joseph Raz, *The Morality of Freedom* (Oxford: Clarendon, 1986), chapter 1; and Barnett, *Constitutional & Administrative Law*, chapter 5.

38 Sarah Banet-Weiser and Manuel Castells, 'Economy is Culture', in Manuel Castells (ed.), *Another Economy is Possible: Culture and Economy in a Time of Crisis* (Cambridge: Polity, 2017), pp. 4–33; and Ann Pettifor, *The Production of Money: How to Break the Power of Bankers* (London: Verso, 2017), chapter 7.

39 For a comprehensive discussion of the challenges of collective learning, see Joseph E. Stiglitz and Bruce C. Greenwald, *Creating a Learning Society: A New Paradigm for Development and Social Progress*, Kenneth J Arrow Lecture Series at Columbia University, 1 (New York: Columbia University Press, 2014).

40 Tom Bingham, *The Rule of Law* (London: Allen Lane, 2010), chapters 3, 6, and 12; Andrew Le Sueur, Maurice Sunkin, and Jo Eric Khushal Murkens, *Public Law: Text,*

Cases, and Materials (Oxford: Oxford University Press, 2010), Part I, chapters 3–4, and Geoffrey Rivlin, *Understanding the Law* (Oxford: Oxford University Press, 3rd edn, 2004), pp. 46–8.

41 Gentile and Schmitt can be interpreted as thinkers who locate the authenticity of the political in the integrity of the state. There are other, more agonistic and pluralist ways of thinking about the primacy of politics. Arendt, for example, defends a decidedly non-statist approach to understanding the irreducibility of political concerns to material interests, technological rationality, or administrative imperatives. See Hannah Arendt, *The Human Condition* (Chicago: University of Chicago Press, 1958), Part III on 'Action'.

42 Schmitt constantly bemoans the tendency for parliamentary democracy to degenerate into a series of petty negotiations about how to divide the nation's wealth. See Carl Schmitt, *Legalität und Legitimität* (Berlin: Duncker & Humblot, 5th edn, 1993), pp. 15, 27–8, 31, 40, 57, 61, and 90, available in English as *Legality and Legitimacy*, trans. and ed. Jeffrey Seitzer and with an introduction by John P. McCormick (Durham, NC and London: Duke University Press, 2004), pp. 10–11, 25–7, 30–1, 41, 58–9, 61–2, 92–3.

43 In this context, Adorno's invocation of solidarity with metaphysics in the moment of its demise looks less like a 'melancholy science' than a prescient comment on the wider demise of mediated unity in all of its manifestations, including, in this case, that between law, government, and politics in what was meant to have been the democratic state. See the last sentence of Adorno, *Negative Dialectics*. Also see Gillian Rose, *The Melancholy Science: An Introduction to the Thoughts of Theodor W. Adorno* (London: Macmillan, 1978); Arendt, *The Human Condition*, section 3; Cornelius Castoriadis, *L'Institution imaginaire de la société* (Paris: Seuil, 1975), available in English as *The Imaginary Institution of Society* (Cambridge: Polity, 1987), Part II; and Claude Lefort, 'Les Droits de l'homme ne sont pas une politique', *Le Débat*, 16 (2000), 36–55.

44 For a good example of this line of thinking which playfully challenges Schmitt's friend–enemy polemics, see Jacques Derrida, *Politiques de l'amitié, suivi de L'Oreille de Heidegger* (Paris: Galilée, 1994), available in English as *Politics of Friendship* (London: Verso, 1997); and A. J. P. Thomson, *Deconstruction and Democracy: Derrida's Politics of Friendship* (London: Continuum, 2005). Hauke Brunkhorst and Piet Strydom examine the political and epistemological facets of cosmopolitanism in Hauke Brunkhorst, 'Some Conceptual and Structural Problems of Global Cosmopolitanism', in Anastasia Marinopoulou (ed.), *Cosmopolitan Modernity* (Oxford: Peter Lang, 2015), pp. 19–71, and Piet Strydom, 'Cosmopolitanization and the Prospects of a Cosmopolitan Modernity', in Anastasia Marinopoulou (ed.), *Cosmopolitan Modernity* (Oxford: Peter Lang, 2015), pp. 73–100. For some time now Chantal Mouffe has been contesting the conflation of populism with anti-democratic authoritarianism. She regards Schmitt as a promising source of ideas for left-wing political projects. See Chantal Mouffe, *The Challenge of Carl Schmitt* (London: Verso, 1999), and her more recent statements in the media in support of Podemos.

45 Emblematic, in this regard, is Alain Badiou, 'The communist hypothesis', *New Left Review*, 49: January–February (2008), 29–42. The collective revolutionary subjectivity of the multitude can be seen as Michael Hardt and Toni Negri's answer to what is sometimes referred to as the end of the working class and the death of socialism. See Michael Hardt and Antonio Negri, *Empire* (Cambridge, MA: Harvard University Press, 2000); Andre Gorz, *Farewell to the Working Class: An Essay on Post-Industrial Socialism*, trans. Michael Sonenscher (London: Pluto, 1987); and Alain Touraine, *L'Après-socialisme* (Paris: B. Grasset, 1980).

46 Monbiot, *How Did We Get into This Mess?*; Helena Smith, 'Everything that Tsipras was promised was a fairytale', *Guardian* (10 May 2016), p. 21; Edward Snowden, 'Governments can reduce our dignity to that of tagged animals', *Guardian* (3 May 2016), G2, pp. 6–9; and Geoffroy de Lagasnerie, *L'Art de la révolte: Snowden, Assange, Manning* (Paris: Fayard, 2015).

47 Fischer-Lescano and Teubner, *Regime-Kollisionen*, chapter 5; and Poul F. Kjaer, Gunther Teubner, and Alberto Febbrajo (eds), *The Financial Crisis in Constitutional Perspective: The Dark Side of Functional Differentiation* (Oxford: Hart, 2011), chapters 1–2.

48 Sandra Halperin, 'Modernity and the embedding of economic expansion', *European Journal of Social Theory*, 19:2 (2016), 172–90.

49 Whilst failed remedies such as different variants of mercantilism are recycled, other approaches, such as those broadly associated with Keynesianism, are prematurely written off as irrevocably failed. See Halperin, 'Modernity', pp. 172–3, and Gerassimos Moschonas, 'Reforming Europe, Renewing Social Democracy? The PES, the Debt Crisis, and the Euro-Parties', in David J. Bailey, Jean-Michel de Waele, Fabien Escalona, and Mathieu Vieira (eds), *European Social Democracy during the Global Economic Crisis: Renovation or Resignation?* (Manchester: Manchester University Press, 2014), pp. 252–69.

50 Although somewhat speculative, it can be argued that when human rights are defined in terms of specific systemic functions instead of abstract ruminations about human nature, rights will acquire some of the iterative and appellative dignity that is currently bestowed on procedure with greater generosity than it is upon individual citizens. For a more detailed exposition of this view, see Jan Winczorek, 'Making Law Together? On Some Intersystemic Conditions of Judicial Cooperation', in Alberto Febbrajo and Gorm Harste, *Law and Intersystemic Communication: Understanding 'Structural Coupling'* (Farnham: Ashgate, 2013), pp. 229–53.

51 It has been rightly remarked that Luhmann is somewhat contradictory in this regard. In many instances his analyses of social systems and FD invoke a thoroughly horizontal model of communication that is interrupted by systemic boundaries. In other words, he seems to retreat from the implications that follow from his own analysis for the nation state and the role of states in international affairs more generally. See Tanya Hitzel-Cassagnes, 'Paradoxien im Organisationsbereich: Global Governance', in Marc Amstutz and Andreas Fischer-Lescano (eds), *Kritische Systemtheorie: Zur Evolution einer normativen Theorie* (Bielefeld: Transcript, 2013), pp. 149–72, at pp. 165–6; and Niklas Luhmann, *Die Politik der Gesellschaft* (Frankfurt: Suhrkamp, 2000), pp. 97 and 221–5.

3

Functional differentiation *and* mediated unity in question: looming constitutional conflicts between the de-centralist logic of functional differentiation and the bio-political steering of austerity and global governance

It has been seen so far that the theoretical premises informing prevailing accounts of modern statehood and political representation have become susceptible to comprehensive critique and deconstruction. This is not to argue that states no longer exist or have ceased to be important actors in domestic and international politics. In many parts of the world, the territorially demarcated nation state quite manifestly has existed since the demise of feudalism. It continues to play a major role, with residual feudal characteristics in some cases, in planning and co-ordinating the operations of key social systems such as law, health, economics, transport, housing, education, politics, and the system of scientific and scholarly research. Whilst these operations retain a recognisably territorial inflection, it can be shown that there is nothing inherently national about law, health, economics, transport, and so on, and certainly nothing inherently national about science and knowledge. Luhmann, Rudolf Stichweh and other systems theorists are in fact convinced that over time, national particularities bound up with state building tend to become notably less marked than extra-territorial systemic specificity bound up with sociological coding.[1] Like FD, modern state building is an ongoing historical process in many parts of the world, and a key issue in political sociology. In terms of facts and norms, then, statehood and FD provide the best framework for thinking about normative integration in ways that do not appeal to moral abstraction or rely on passive acceptance of existing institutions. That is why the tensions between some of the de-centralising tendencies of late modern FD and a number of the more coercively centripetal dynamics observable in conjunction with austerity and global governance – largely the remit of international agencies functioning like non-elected state executives at this juncture – are potentially of great theoretical and practical interest. Difficult questions are thereby raised about the real authority of elected state legislatures in the twenty-first century, thus prompting related questions about the best way to understand informal structures of social conflict, political compromise, party policy, and party electoral strategy. Formal and informal structures in this sense help constitute the conditions of statehood within nationally defined territories. National states encounter the dynamic unfolding of FD worldwide, which they help shape and which states in turn are shaped by. There are notable discrepancies between the national and territorial dimensions of statehood, on the one hand, and the social-systemic dimensions of statehood, on the other. They highlight some of the issues involved when assessing the extent to which social power (collective) develops the reflexive capacity (learning) to evolve in self-limiting and self-reforming directions normally associated almost exclusively with the political constitutions of territorially defined modern nation states. This issue is discussed below in terms of the distinction between politically and socially constituted statehood. Whilst the sociological dimension of statehood can be studied in a variety of ways, the approach adopted here focuses on the constitutional implications of social-systemic differentiation. In this book, the term constitutional is employed in a much broader sense than the restrictively conventional notion implied by a written document stating founding principles. The concept of constitutive constitutionalism thus denotes relations of formal juridical-political authority as well as informal operative power cutting across public/private inter-systemic boundaries.[2]

It has already been seen that constituent power is no longer feasible as a unified essence that enacts the political primacy of popular sovereignty through democratic law and government. Moreover, it has been suggested that constituent power might one day be conceived in terms of federated social systems rather than as geographical regions structured according to the hierarchical logic of centres and peripheries. In addition, it has been established that systems are too complex to be managed exclusively from a foundation that in principle might function like a traditionally conceived state, that is, like an ensemble of public institutions equipped and authorised to apply power in an unrivalled way. A traditionally conceived state entrusted with this mediating task would have to apply power evenly between systems, and this, of course, would be impossible due to their incommensurable codes. Formulating the matter thus already shifts the main frame of reference from politically constituted statehood, based on territorial integrity and the unrivalled application of power across public and private spheres, to socially constituted statehood, based on FD and non-territorial, system-specific coding. We are still a long way from a decisive transition in this regard; until that time comes it is very likely that federalism will continue to be widely thought of in regional and geographical, rather than in social-systemic, terms. However, there is a great deal of evidence to suggest that the current historical conjunction approximates a transitional stage pointing beyond conventional territorial statehood. The constant reconfiguration of digital public spaces and virtual geographies is one of several factors pointing in this direction.[3] The danger here is that in some cases it may be more like a regressive transition to neo-feudal rule by private aggregates of power, bureaucratic hierarchy, and decisionism, than a step beyond politically constituted statehood to socially constituted statehood. One need only consider what the imposition of austerity does to the margins of political alternatives. Hence there are several radically juxtaposed and competing visions regarding the constitution, in several senses, of twenty-first-century world society. Moreover, the lines of conflict between these visions are drawn in ways that are not always particularly well illuminated by party political elections and official diplomatic negotiations between what continue to look like rival nation states. It is therefore advisable to begin thinking about hybrid models capable of indicating how certain aspects of modern, politically constituted statehood overlap and intermesh with certain aspects of late modern, post-statist, socially constituted statehood. Although this might appear somewhat speculative, it helps illustrate some of the points of convergence/continuity and divergence/transition between what are too often taken to be distinct periods in the evolution of statehood and FD. This comparison will hopefully help test the hypothesis that whilst some elements of post-feudal modern statehood will be transformed and carried forward into post-territorial, post-national statehood, other elements of modern statehood may pass into desuetude in the course of that process. It is even possible that residual feudal elements will persist in the twenty-first century and find ways of coexisting with socially constituted statehood.

One likely objection can be immediately anticipated: how is statehood possible without relying on the modern state as its foundation? The short answer, which will be developed in some detail below, can be summarised as follows: according to a line of argument often associated with certain strands of early modern republicanism and social contract theory, it is frequently supposed that liberal democracies are founded on intensive, deliberative citizen participation resulting in an exit from the state of nature, thus producing consensual compromise and fundamental agreement about the bases of the state. As a corollary of far more recent provenance, it is conceded that in reality, elections and in some cases plebiscites come about as close to an inclusive and consensual agreement in these crucial matters of founding principles as one can do under conditions of mass democracy. Weber's analysis of these phenomena continues to be an essential point of reference in this regard.[4] In any case, an historically far more accurate account of power and compromise than the one conjured up by the consensual social contract is provided by the model of private parties concluding contracts within states, or what loosely pass for states, on the one hand, and elites within states acting in a manner analogous to private parties when concluding international treaties with the elites of other states, on the other.[5] It is this particular model of highly antagonistic and competitive statehood that has forcefully contributed to the very specific form of FD that is under examination in this chapter and the next one. It is a model of statehood characterised in notable cases by the erosion of the very notion of the *state of law* by the de facto *legalisation* of ad hoc measures through extra-parliamentary channels. It is true that inter-systemic communication may be characterised as somewhat inchoate as yet. By contrast, there are well organised informal networks of communication linking government ministries, CEOs, specific think tanks, rating agencies, high profile social media personalities, key figures at central banks and big commercial news services and so on, which take part in the planning of official political agendas, national budgets, military interventions, and flows of information. These networks effectively sidestep public scrutiny and elude political accountability. A paradigm of statehood so deeply imbued with privately negotiated contractual bargaining may in theory be committed to politically neutral differentiation and mediation. In practice, however, as will be seen in the analysis of neoliberalism offered below and in the next chapter, it is a paradigm that often yields to the pressures of highly selective, decisionistic de-differentiation. This becomes abundantly clear when measures such as bank bailouts or interference in academic autonomy are deemed to be necessary means to deal with financial crises, information leaks affecting national security, and other instances in which the preconditions of liberal democratic government are called into question.[6] When this occurs on a major scale, ostensibly democratic statehood, in the sense of legislative constitutive authority, can dispense with public political will formation and recognisable citizen input into the legislative process. Under these conditions, it is not exaggerated to say that it is possible to have a formally democratic state without significant democratic content. One could go further by observing the – modern rather than ancient – Greek example and concluding that the key institutions of international governance insist that democratic content be minimised when the demands of democracy and austerity clash. It might be asked whether this was not always a likely theoretical and practical scenario from the moment the mediated unity paradigm was convincingly challenged by the FD paradigm, that is, from the moment it became widely accepted that legal regulation and/or political democratisation of the economic system violates the principle of systemic integrity? Here it is important to be analytically clear, since there are notable differences between arguments for private property and minimally regulated markets, on the one hand, and arguments for FD and systemic specificity, on the other. These differences can easily become obscured if one assumes that the de-centralist implications of FD and systemic specificity are naturally complemented by austerity and minimally regulated markets. It can, on the contrary, be shown that austerity and de-regulation can lead to a partial re-annexation of the economic and legal systems by a political system coerced to function in line with exogenous imperatives. This typically happens when the election outcomes in a given national political system are rendered practically inconsequential by the plans of global governance agencies. The existing neoliberal hegemony is reinforced when arguments for fiscal responsibility, constitutionally guaranteed balanced budgets, the need for more flexible employment contracts, and system-specific integrity are conflated, thus promoting a model of statehood that consistently elevates privately negotiated deals to the status of government policy. The extent to which this is the case in any given situation will of course depend on distinct patterns of state formation and the party political composition of specific governments. But it is striking to note that social democratic and republican attempts to regulate trade or experiment with alternative models of FD are often denounced as infringements on rights that tamper with founding political principles and agreements.[7]

The option of legalisation rather than political legislation with democratic consensus has been recently taken on a large scale in the bailouts following the financial crisis of 2007–2008. Extra-parliamentary legalisation strategies are not simply synonymous with conspiracies or timeless elite rule. They are better explained in terms of the partial politicisation of rights in conjunction with a unique instance of statehood first arising in early modern Europe.[8] An analysis of the prerogative of selective de-differentiation as a privilege that persists despite the rule of law and the separation of powers sheds light on some of the idiosyncrasies both of this model of statehood and the particular version of FD that it sustains. Constitutional flaws of this kind are typically excused as the best possible responses to contingency, risk, and other factors that supposedly make residual decisionism regrettable but inevitable. The fact that one is not talking about matters beyond human control or impervious to accountability becomes strikingly apparent when analysing the forces and interests opposed to the transition from conventional political statehood to transnational social statehood that has seemingly foundered with the advent of neoliberalism and the twin crises of the welfare state and social democracy. It will be seen in chapter 5 that the arguments for social statehood are not intended to turn back the clock in order to resurrect social democratic welfarism. At this stage it will suffice to note that some of these nationalist and conservative forces would prefer a regression to neo-feudal rule by ruling clique and arbitrary fiat. Although feudal authority demonstrably did not exist in places like the United States, Trump now seems determined to interpret the concept of the legal state in ways that undermine the autonomy of the American legal system from other social systems operating in the United States. If he proceeds as he seems to intend, his version of neoliberalism will unfold as a constant exercise in selective de-differentiation.[9]

It is obvious for historical, political, and semantic reasons that statehood is bound up with states. It is, however, not at all obvious whether some of the key synthesising and unifying capacities of states, analysed in chapters 1 and 2 in terms of the weak and strong dialectics of mediated unity, can be gradually conferred upon social systems in ways that maximise transparency, accountability, and citizen participation in decision-making. A series of very creative social, political, and cultural interventions will be required to accomplish such extensive and innovative qualitative democratic change. There is clearly a great deal at stake, since failure in this regard is likely to intensify the already widespread sensation that states today are too weak to prevent offshore tax evasion effectively, to say nothing of managing inter-systemic communication. In order to solve problems relating to the haphazard dispersion of feudal power, states needed to develop unifying capacities enabling them to mediate between private and public spheres from an epistemologically privileged political centre. By contrast, social systems need to be highly responsive to a plurality of social-systemic neighbours without relying on a central mediating instance, thus obliging them to communicate with each other in ways that are still insufficiently understood at present. History suggests that if strong states used to enjoy at least modest steering capabilities enabling them effectively to reconcile opposing interests and values, this may have been because they were designed to be formally and positively centralised in the senses explained in chapters 1–2, without being too intrusive in the process. It might therefore be said that until very recently, strong states have managed somehow to produce a degree of centralised authority without resorting to authoritarian syntheses. The qualification as strong in relation to states, in other words, really means synthetically nimble, rather than militarily powerful or politically disciplined. From a sociological perspective, however, it would be more accurate to say that strong states and positively centralised authority have always been, to a considerable extent, a vital political resource developed by society in response to a wide variety of historically evolving challenges.[10] Taking the British example and looking back at the years between the end of World War II and the first Thatcher government in 1979 in admittedly very theoretical terms for the moment, this delicately achieved equilibrium looks like a feat of considerable dialectical elasticity and political resourcefulness. Perhaps most worryingly, it also appears to have been a compromise of temporally limited viability. In this light, it seems difficult to overestimate the importance of finding the right historical and conceptual frameworks for assessing what remains of the synthetic reconciling capacities of the state, and what is in the process of developing in terms of social-systemic autonomy and inter-systemic co-ordination.[11]

When evenly applied, consistently distributed power can be seen as a legal-political resource. The normative challenges posed by the need to apply power evenly across de-centred and dispersed social systems are therefore staggering; it might even be argued that one simply cannot do this because of their incommensurable codes. In response, it has been noted that they exhibit varying degrees of capacity for self-limitation and self-reform. But contemporary social systems also seem to be resistant to steering, and unresponsive to political criteria of justice and accountability. This is likely to be the case as long as systems are forced to work within a model of political statehood characterised by pervasive private contract, ubiquitous legalisation, and authoritarian re-coupling of the kind delivered by austerity. It remains to be seen if this unresponsiveness can be explained in terms of communicative problems stemming from the discrepancies between social-systemic codes (system-specific) and politically constituted meta-codes (putatively unifying and overarching), such as what is still often taken to be natural nationhood. As Gramsci, Foucault, and many others show, power in modern society is de-centred and capillary. Accountability, transparency, legitimacy, and participation will prove to be difficult as long as the dispersal of power is not adequately reflected in suitably de-centralised organs of social-systemic authority.[12]

Some observers might be reluctant to see these phenomena in terms of the discrepant logics of territorial states conserving regional power bases and of global systems developing recognisably constitutional properties irrespective of geographical location. It is nonetheless relatively uncontroversial to say that at least during the decades following World War II in Western Europe, the tensions between these countervailing forces underpinned a relatively stable constellation that has become fragile in the wake of neoliberalism and the currently prevailing model of globalisation. Some experts might regard austerity and proposals to make labour markets more flexible as an unfortunate but necessary response to excessive government spending during these years. It is certainly the case that many centre and centre-right political parties claim that international financial markets will not tolerate profligate governments or burgeoning welfare states. What is clear is that there has been an extensive re-structuring of government expenditure, labour markets, and welfare states since the end of the Cold War and, in a related vein, individual attitudes about household debt, personal responsibility for material security, and so on have also changed.[13] One can attempt to ascertain whether the citizens of democracies are now less inclined to vote for centre-left and left parties than they had been in the recent past, or whether they are less inclined to join or stay in unions, or whether they feel more or less solidaristic towards their fellow citizens than they once did. But it might be the case that the conditions of statehood have actually changed in barely perceptible but important ways without electoral sanction or political consultation during the historical period in question. It is likely that the way many modern states are actually constituted has been changed, thus raising questions about the different ways in which it is possible to alter the constitution of a state, some of which are clearly more consensual and deliberative than others. For example, it is possible to modify the political system, which in principle is democratically controlled, via access from the economic system, which, under the current institutionalisation of statehood and FD, largely is not.[14] If one actively re-structures the battery of citizens' rights without modifying the codes guiding discrete social systems accordingly, for example, one has in effect altered the mediations between systems, and thereby reformed the constitution in the extended sense used here. What the term 'accordingly' might mean in practice would have to be debated and resolved with a collective decision involving all affected citizens, rather than negotiated in private through treaties or elite committees. One immediately thinks, for example, of constitutional amendments adopted by the EU that outlaw deficit spending within individual member states. Such measures drastically reduce the scope for political choice, and by extension, significantly curtail citizens' rights. In view of the implications, ostensible changes in voting behaviour or patterns of union membership will only yield a very partial view of a considerably larger picture.[15]

The need to adapt and improve the co-ordinating functions of statehood has not abated with the crisis of nation-state authority accompanying globalisation and what is sometimes referred to as post-democracy; if anything this need has become manifestly more acute. Although the indispensability of statehood will clearly outlive the eventual demise of several paradigmatic state institutions, the conditions of statehood in the twenty-first century differ considerably from those obtaining during the crucial years of state formation in Europe and elsewhere.[16] The dilemma can be summarised as follows: states appear to have forfeited a considerable proportion of their ability to plan in predictable and efficient ways; social systems continue to work within the constraints of politically constituted statehood and are not (as yet) self-steering. The main point in this regard is that the transfer of steering functions from states to social systems has been underway for some time now, just as, somewhat paradoxically, the ongoing process of state formation coexists with the ongoing unfolding of FD. The proliferation of rights-based disputes and rights-based discourses can be seen as a confirmation of this incipient transfer of responsibilities.

In the early stages of state formation the right of suffrage was the paradigmatic right of political inclusion. Suffrage eventually evolved from limited, strictly qualified suffrage, based on property ownership, income, and education, to universal suffrage and unrestricted political inclusion. Political inclusion was complemented (and in some cases preceded) by diverse instances of state-regulated socio-economic inclusion which could be seen to fill out and complete political citizenship. Today, there is a lively debate as to whether this continued proliferation clearly signals a move towards society-centred statehood, or if it is really more like *political outsourcing* by the state. Rather than helping to try to solve the social conflicts in which it is enmeshed, the contemporary state often displays a marked tendency to foist its problems onto individuals, organisations, and social systems. The complexity of this matter comes into focus when one considers that although evenly applied, consistently distributed power can be seen as a legal-political resource, the boundaries between the legal and political systems are often blurred in the state.[17] There are no uninterrupted linear transitions from modern states to functionally differentiated societies. In fact, statehood and FD co-evolve. What is evolving, however, is the reflexive capacity of society to explain its own operations to itself. Shifting the paradigm within which we conceptualise autonomy and emancipation from a (political) state-centred one to a (social) society-centred one is marked by class conflict, but also by social-systemic conflicts of the most variegated kind. These, in turn, become intelligible in terms of a wide variety of rights claims which include a familiar array of divisions on lines of gender, race, and religion. But they are also accompanied by less spectacularly visible divergences about the criteria defining prevailing standards of economic growth, educational achievement, aesthetic value, equal access to information, and legal validity.[18] The normative and integrative features of society-centred statehood are as yet somewhat difficult to ascertain in view of the continued prevalence of state-centred perspectives, which privilege the supposed communicative superiority of political parties and state executives over social systems and movements.[19] The importance of analysing the normative and regulative aspects of this incipient transition to society-centred statehood thus comes sharply into focus. Several distinct scenarios are conceivable. The possibilities range from the currently hegemonic version, marked by financial austerity, political outsourcing, economic privatisation, and so on, to the societal constitutionalist model outlined in chapter 5. In anticipation of that discussion, an analysis of the currently hegemonic model is offered in this chapter and the next.

Re-thinking democracy: politically constituted and socially constituted statehood

Several of the phenomena accompanying globalisation, a number of which have intensified since the end of the Cold War, raise major questions about current instantiations of statehood and the future capacity of the liberal democratic state to co-ordinate social systems in ways that square with the guiding principles of political modernity and citizenship. Such principles include unrestricted inclusion with regard to gender, race, disability, sexual preference, and related factors, the greatest possible transparency and accountability of political power, and legitimacy based on rational political will formation. Any model of globalisation that carelessly sheds these principles in practice is likely to be both crisis-ridden and chronically undemocratic. Can key state institutions, for example government ministries, be adapted to become better equipped to plan the workings of the diverse social systems of which they are nominally in charge? This would be one way to re-organise and prolong the evolution of politically constituted late modern statehood.[20] Failure in this regard is likely to spawn large-scale protests against what are rightly or wrongly perceived to be the illegitimate and dysfunctional encroachments of the state on the cultural life of the nation or unwarranted interventions in society on the part of the forces of global governance, such as the Troika and the WTO.[21] If key state institutions eventually do fail, it will be imperative to develop various approaches to post-statist statehood capable of offering new solutions to questions regarding the re-coupling and flexible guiding of social-systemic operations. Chapters 1 and 2 of this book are centrally concerned with a critique of the premises of mediated unity and overarching legal-political form in relation to modern statehood, democratic legitimacy, and political modernity. It will be seen in this chapter and the next that existing patterns of FD are susceptible to an analogous critique. Just as it is clearly the case that the nation state has existed since feudalism and continues to play a role in the attempted planning and co-ordinating of key social systems, the dynamics of FD continue apace. The immanent critique of FD in chapters 3 and 4 is therefore directed at the particular ways in which FD has been instantiated until now, and is emphatically not directed at the mere fact of social-systemic differentiation as such. On the contrary, it has been stated at several junctures that a great deal depends on the specific ways in which FD is institutionalised. In normative principle and actual practice, FD holds out the possibility of providing the libertarian ideal of free flows of information and steadfastly horizontal social organisation with a new constitutional framework and a new model of post-statist statehood. Taken together, these reforms could make a substantial contribution towards dismantling hierarchy and the diverse instances of entrenched social inequality that are rarely adequately addressed by the separation of powers and rights of party political affiliation and trade union membership. It is easy to overlook the fact that, although progressive with respect to the localistic and personalist structures of feudal politics, formal political equality bestows a largely defensive quality on demands for greater socio-economic inclusion that often makes those demands seem like insolent offences against common sense. This observation brings us to an important juncture in *Critical Theory and Sociological Theory*. It is the space where one may begin to make meaningful analytical distinctions between politically constituted statehood, social democracy, post-democratic constitutionalisation, and socially constituted statehood. These distinctions will inform the arguments developed in the pages to follow.

Chapters 1–2 articulate six hypotheses pertaining to the dialectics of mediated unity in relation to modern statehood. Chapters 3–5 articulate a series of related hypotheses, building on the initial ones, pertaining to the dialectics of mediated non-identity in relation to late modern, social statehood (the terms social statehood and socially constituted statehood will be used interchangeably). The six hypotheses outlined in chapters 1–2 are thus important for the overall argument and must be borne in mind going forward. It is therefore useful to repeat them here in some detail before moving on. The first two chapters show, first, that what is often assumed to be the current crisis of democracy must also be understood as the crisis of a determinate instance of FD, nurtured by a specific form of state, rather than as a crisis affecting democracy *tout court* in its purported validity for all times and places. Writing in the *Guardian* in October 2016, Larry Elliot discusses the assumptions often made by 'the people who run the global economy'. If his analysis in this article is accurate, the IMF, World Bank, and other organisations of global governance play a leading role in steering a social system that in liberal democratic principle is meant to be self-directing and spontaneously responsive to supply and demand. By focusing on democracy and the state without simultaneously analysing the distinguishing features of the dominant model of FD, in other words, it is easy to come to the conclusion that democracy is failing and that statehood in some generic sense is now beyond repair. The distinction between politically and socially constituted statehood is intended to prevent such generalisations from obscuring the discrete issues under consideration. The next two chapters articulate the thesis that the difference between political statehood and post-statist social statehood is not that between form and essence or form and content. As will become especially clear in chapter 4, it is a distinction that draws comparisons between two different but very unequally available forms of statehood. It would otherwise be very inviting to think of political statehood as formal statehood, whilst thinking of social statehood as essential statehood based on the foundation of an essential, meta-signifying subject. The premises of that foundation are deconstructed in earlier chapters. The allusion to very unequal availability refers to the contrast between the currently hegemonic model of form (political statehood) and the societal constitutionalist model of form that is its most promising rival, in light of the crisis of political statehood and the possible regression to a semi-feudal model of 'populist democracy' that forfeits the most important gains of political modernity.[22]

Second, it is signalled that it is as yet unclear how citizens in the twenty-first century, appropriately re-organised as an updated *pouvoir constituant*, might provide FD with a normative framework capable of enhancing its qualitatively productive and anti-hierarchical dimensions, whilst also reining in the centrifugal, potentially destructive tendencies of FD that Gunther Teubner and others have identified as its 'dark side'. Third, it is demonstrated that the determinate instance of FD in question was and continues to be decisively nurtured by a historically *specific form of state*. It is that state, in turn, that actively contributes to the consolidation of the *currently hegemonic variant of FD*. The fact that the theoretical premises underpinning that version of statehood have become doubtful highlights some of the looming conflicts alluded to in the title of this chapter. Fourth, it is explained that even though this form of state can be very broadly characterised as liberal democratic, one must bear in mind that there are considerable differences between the evolutionary trajectories of individual liberal democratic states, just as, by extension, there are considerable differences between the electoral trajectories of liberal democratic parties. The interwar period of the previous century indicates that liberal democracies can and sometimes do experience crises in the guises of fascism and, to a markedly less dramatic extent, different kinds of authoritarian and consensual corporatism. A significant part of that story is intermittent recourse to different variants of legalisation/*Verrechtlichung*, as well as religious, military, and executive abuses of power. The more important point for the moment is that although there are liberal democratic parties and liberal democratic states, and although there are socialist parties and there have been state socialist states, to date there is no such thing as a FD party or a FD state. The latter imply sociological categories of analysis that are difficult to apply to the frameworks of analysis bequeathed by political modernity. FD is an intrinsic part of the constitution of late modern world society; it plays a role that can be broadly compared to the function played by the notion of the mixed constitution in thinkers like Aristotle, Machiavelli, and Montesquieu. This point will be elaborated towards the end of this chapter. Parties and states are essential analytical components of the state-centred methodological framework for the study of a practice of statehood that simultaneously presupposes the *separation* of state and society as well as the mediated unity of state and society via law, government, and, in more general terms, democracy. In the previous chapter one facet of this issue is discussed in terms of the ambiguity surrounding the distinction, which is not always consistently maintained, between the political system and the state in Luhmann and in the writings of a number of other systems theorists.[23]

In some cases, such as that of Great Britain, the territorially demarcated nation state managed for centuries to provide an adequate regulatory framework for social systems. In retrospect, it can be argued that the trajectory of relative regulatory success peaked in the decades immediately following World War II. Until the Thatcher years, at any rate, and the transition from corporatism to neoliberalism, class conflict in Britain was mitigated through corporatist compromise and comprehensive provision of welfare rights. At that time, extensive nationalisation of industry and the expansion of the welfare state were lauded by some as inclusive social democratic planning and criticised by others as pernicious public interference in the self-governing logic of the private sphere. From a systems-theoretical perspective, however, fundamentally important issues related to the dynamics of differentiation are misconstrued if society is thought to start where government and public policy seem to leave off. It is not difficult to see that a naturalist or in some cases quasi-geographical conception of boundaries inspires this sociologically naïve belief.[24] Whilst the liberal component of what remains of mainstream liberal democratic thought tends to cling to the illusion of the separation of state and society, the democratic component often seems to hanker after their unity.[25] Unorthodox thinkers from Tocqueville and Simmel to Arendt and Castoriadis see that the liberal separation of state and society is as improbable as their mediated unity in representative democracy. It is far more plausible to argue that there are exceptional, revolutionary moments that shed new light on the very terms in which separation and unity are normally understood.[26]

The essential qualifying remark in this regard is that in marked contrast to almost all other forms of state, the liberal democratic state is internally differentiated by the separation of powers and other instances of checks and balances. In addition, this particular instantiation of political authority relies on a vibrant public sphere and is committed to rational, rather than populist or autocratic, political will formation. As the young Habermas notes in relation to Kant's critique of Hobbes, liberal democracy endeavours to make consensus rather than power or strategic calculation the basis of legitimacy. How plausible is this project today? One can begin thinking about a tentative answer by invoking Marx in a way that many Marxists sceptical of Habermas might oppose, namely by endorsing the dictum that society only takes on collective tasks for whose realisation the material conditions are ripe. One can continue by enlisting Luhmann in a way that Habermas might not agree with, to wit, by arguing that today the term material really refers to FD and constitutions in the extended sense.[27] Like most other forms of state, then, liberal democracy attempts to constitute society politically, but it does so as the closest known equivalent to what would be a FD state without a FD party, and as such, discloses the real possibility of post-statist, functionally differentiated social statehood. It is too often and far too casually remarked that capitalism continually readjusts its modes of production and consumption in step with a continually changing social reality. But it is rarely observed that the affinities and congruities between liberal democratic statehood and the sociological realities of FD constitute the matrix of a form of governance that has been dominant for some time now. Point four of six is therefore worth expounding in some detail. It is distinctly possible that the liberal democratic state form is 'constitutionally closer' to society than the vast majority of its predecessors in the West and elsewhere. Far from being the culminating point in a movement towards 'the end of history', the liberal democratic state was and remains a transitional state with continually unfolding potential that will either be forfeited by neoliberalism or realised by some form of socially constituted statehood – there is no going back to liberal democracy and the early model of politically constituted statehood associated with the Glorious Revolution, the eighteenth-century revolutions, and their somewhat belated sequels. It might be appealing for the sake of simplicity to say that parties and states in their existing instantiations either will have to go or will have to be substantially reconstituted if democracy is to be rescued from its manifestly undemocratic plebiscitary and populist instantiations in many parts of the globe today. Alternatively, it could be argued that FD will have to go or be substantially re-constitutionalised so as to rescue it from some of its uncontrollably expansionist dynamics.

When stated so baldly, this is a misleading and markedly un-dialectical juxtaposition. It is not merely the case that there are no uninterrupted linear transitions from modern states to functionally differentiated societies. Previous chapters make clear that some form of statehood will accompany us into the coming decades and that FD is a permanent feature of sociological modernity. Attempts to reverse it have failed in the past and are almost certain to fail if attempted in the future. Just as the debates about the demise of democracy should be reformulated as debates about the future of FD, debates about the future of FD will have to be informed by critical constitutional theory, lest they stagnate into purely descriptive exercises in evolutionary accounts of conflict and change. Parties and states in their current forms *are* undergoing profound transformation (they are in fact 'going', as regards the manifestations in which we once knew them), just as, in a related vein, differentiation processes are responding to subtle pushes towards constitutionalisation. Chapter 5 provides substantial evidence for the claim that, however inchoate at present, contemporary examples of societal constitutionalism pose subtle, but potentially far-reaching, challenges to existing patterns of FD.[28]

Fifth, despite the differences between the constitutional trajectories of individual liberal democratic parties and states, and speaking in ideal-typical terms, one can discern a number of the defining features distinguishing liberal democratic legality/legitimacy and power dynamics from those obtaining in dynastic empires, absolute monarchies, fascist dictatorships, and authoritarian state socialist regimes. In somewhat more nuanced terms with acute contemporary relevance, one can also discern a number of the defining features distinguishing the legality/legitimacy and power dynamics obtaining in liberal democratic states before and after the ascendance of the bio-political policies nominally associated with the governments of Thatcher, Reagan, and Kohl. Far too little research has been done on the silent structural transformation that was initiated in this phase of post-war European history. The volte-face of the Mitterrand government shortly after coming to power in May 1981 can be seen as a turning point in the transition from liberal democracy and political government to neoliberalism and global governance anticipated with remarkable prescience by Foucault.[29] In this period one can detect parallels between the attenuated synthesising and unifying capacities of states, which had once given them a modest ability to plan in predictable ways, and a clear decline in electoral fortunes of left variants of social democracy, reduced implementation of Keynesian techniques for stimulating investment and consumer demand, the reversal of comprehensive welfare provision, and the erosion of trade union influence on governments and policy.

Whilst the parallels quite clearly affect the margins of manoeuvre that Bernie Sanders, Jeremy Corbyn, and other social democratic party leaders can rely on, they also highlight a more general point about the simultaneous de-politicisation and populist mobilisation observable in neoliberal democracies today.[30] Writing in 1983, Perry Anderson criticises social democratic and

Euro-communist parties for failing to elaborate a plausible 'transition beyond capitalist democracy to a socialist democracy'.[31] From the perspective developed here, however, there are major questions raised when characterising discrete social systems as capitalist, socialist, or anything else so broad, generic, and manifestly at odds with the specific codes of particular systems. The question is not really whether there can be socialist education, for example, instead of capitalist education. The guiding assumption underlying this idea is that the working class, organised as a political party, seizes the state, and then institutes socialist (according to which definition?) education, science, sport, aesthetics, law, and so on. Staying with the example of education, the more pertinent questions might be how to re-code educational processes in ways that challenge narrow notions of merit, competence, and selection, and how to guide the interaction between social systems. As is well known, Luhmann is usually either reticent or pessimistic about the issues of re-coding and constitutional inter-systemic guidance. His reflections nonetheless offer fruitful points of departure for the formulation of a less rigidly articulated version of systems theory than his own.[32]

The point about the paradoxical dialectics of simultaneous de-politicisation and mobilisation is closely related to the issue concerning the specific ways in which law is functionally differentiated from politics within the framework of an historically specific form of state. It is observed that one is dealing with a form of political statehood constituted according to the instrumental logic guiding private parties concluding contracts within states, as well as states acting in a manner analogous to private parties when concluding international treaties. The predominantly strategic and instrumental nature of the European debates surrounding Brexit offers an interesting case in point. One must therefore bear in mind that there are a plurality of possible ways of differentiating law and politics, politics and economics, economics and law, and so on, and that some of these will not necessarily produce a constellation in which politicisation results in populist mobilisation that engenders official demands to privatise as the only way to de-centralise and to de-politicise as the only way to safeguard an independent judiciary and the rights of individuals. Schmitt may well have been an important figure in terms of raising the question of the status of 'the political' in liberal democracies. The more pertinent question concerns the dynamics of differentiation, and that, in turn, is a dialectical and constitutional question rather than a question about the pristine integrity of authentic politics. Neoliberal governance can be seen as part of a project to reshape and reform informally what Franz Neumann refers to in 1937 as the structure of political compromise.[33] The difference between the context of his reflections and the situation today is that the re-structuring in question is being launched both within and beyond the territorial borders of the state. Sixth,

it seems that one of the main objectives of this passive revolution is to liberate determinate social systems from the constraints of formal constitutional
control and political accountability to which they were subjected during the
historical period of viable political statehood. In this case it is not simply a matter of privatisation, since what is in question are the very processes through
which law, politics, economics, and other social systems are *mediated*. The
introduction of this book explains why a dialectical understanding of mediation
is needed in order to assess the possibilities for a transition from politically to
socially constituted statehood. Critically evaluating the intensity of the mediation processes enables observers to assess the quality of the 'constituent
closeness' alluded to above in relation to liberal democratic statehood. Part of
what a critical evaluation entails is examining the extent to which notions of a
founding 'constituent power' must now cede place to a more nuanced conception of social communication and different possible modes of inter-systemic
proximity. This shift of emphasis is indispensable in an era in which collective subjects and unified foundations have become deeply problematic, thus
making society potentially the space in which the fraught tensions between
class inequality, FD, and the possibility of non-punitive justice might be openly
negotiated by a democratically organised citizenry. Hegel and Gramsci are
important precursors to contemporary debates on this topic. Both clearly see
that the state does not stand outside and above society, but provides, on the
contrary, the legal and extra-legal framework for the reproduction of a wide
variety of social relations and transactions. Gramsci's conception of the integral state as including both civil society and political society can be compared
with the thesis that constitutions address juridical questions of legality, as
well as socio-economic, political, cultural, and linguistic questions of common
sense, power, and legitimacy. Indeed, it is certainly possible to develop the
theory of the integral state into a theory of the integral constitution.[34]

Governing by debt: on the emerging
transnational historical bloc and
post-democratic constitutionalisation
through rights regimes

As the terminological affinities between liberal democracy and neoliberalism
strongly imply, neoliberal institutions rely on their liberal democratic predecessors, especially as regards an avowed commitment to the rule of law and the
enforcement of the division of powers. Depending on the national context,
however, neoliberal policies can also work in opposition to some of the main

tenets of liberal democracy. These divergences can be analysed in terms of bio-political intrusion into the private sphere, dogmatism in matters related to austerity, and many other patently illiberal policies that surely would have been anathema to J. S. Mill, Isaiah Berlin, John Rawls, Ronald Dworkin, and many other liberal and liberal democratic thinkers. Pervasive surveillance and severe curtailment of rights protecting access to the free circulation of information highlight the stakes involved when assessing the long-term impact of the practices uncovered by WikiLeaks and other instances of insidiously ubiquitous governance in neoliberal regimes. Serge Halimi and Pierre Rimbert point out that in the autumn of 2016, Manuel Valls's government attempted to outlaw a union demonstration in France for the first time in decades, noting also that large sectors of the press have been pressured by newspaper owners and shareholders to make such prohibitions seem normal and necessary.[35] There are thus acute tensions between the liberal democratic instantiation of the modern state and the neoliberal assault on key dimensions of modern statehood. These attacks are related to the point made at the end of the previous section, namely that the term 'neoliberal' is misleading precisely because the project does not consist in an attempt to return modern states in Europe and elsewhere to their liberal founding principles. In many instances it can be seen as an attempt to re-form society in order to enforce a specific model of FD and achieve notable cases of selective de-differentiation. At the present historical juncture, however, enforcing existing patterns of differentiation may only be feasible by dispensing with paradigmatic liberal democratic liberties, thereby jeopardising some of the most important conquests of political modernity.[36]

One can investigate neoliberal policies to re-form society as attempts to patch up and maintain a decidedly instrumental version of legitimacy. In other words, they arise neither as a fortuitous concatenation of random events nor as the result of a conspiracy. They take shape instead as loosely co-ordinated plans, that is, as a series of formal decisions and informal agreements. Whether one is looking at the initiatives of the IMF, WTO, European Central Bank, Federal Reserve, or other similar agencies, these decisions are responses to the problems of social integration and systemic malfunction that ensue when the particular patterns of differentiation demanded by systemic specificity are formalised and coded in determinate ways that clash with the logic of democratic inclusion.[37] Crucial disagreements in this field can thus be seen to turn on two main issues. First, there is the question about the extent to which systems really are autopoietic, and the extent to which they are steered and indeed need distinct kinds of steering, depending on the system in question. One is then confronted with the qualitatively different scenarios implied by distinct models of steering, and, by extension, distinct models of statehood and constitutional legitimacy. These models range from globalised governance controlled by the IMF, WTO, European Central Bank, Federal Reserve, and the like to a highly de-centralised version managed by appropriately educated and trained citizens. Hybrid models are also possible. This first question thus raises many related queries about the qualitative differences between natural-biological, social, and other kinds of systems. Theoretical and institutional errors are likely to result if social systems are assumed to have properties that are really only proper to biological systems.[38] Second, there is the related question as to whether social systems – especially political, legal, educational, and economic systems – would function better if unencumbered by the claims of democratic inclusivity, or if, on the contrary, enhanced democratic inclusivity might make systems more flexible and adaptable to spontaneously arising problems in their respective environments and quicker in reaction to unforeseen possibilities for inter-systemic communication. The second question asks citizens to think about what the term 'better' actually means in relation to the functioning of specific social systems and what the term 'appropriately' means in relation to education and training. The representatives of systems-theoretical orthodoxy and neoliberal intransigence are likely to protest and claim that these questions pit unwieldy radical democracy against the mandatory FD of educational and political systems. It can be objected that within the currently hegemonic model of statehood and FD, the de facto divorce between education and citizenship professionalises politics whilst nurturing decidedly populist versions of democracy. It amounts to training for key positions in the IMF, European Central Bank, and related organisations for the well-placed, the right to participate in generalised competition for increasingly precarious jobs all the way down the scale of pay and prestige for the less well-placed, and highly ineffectual channels of political redress in the face of steadily increasing socio-economic inequality for almost everybody. Thus the second question also implicitly asks whether the democratic claims under consideration have to be formulated as rights claims in order to be intelligible to states and social systems. If this hypothesis concerning the intelligibility of rights claims can be shown to be true, it would effectively reinforce the argument that state crises and systemic malfunctions arise in part as a result of closed, relatively unresponsive decision-making circuits, and as a result, too, of the inadequate co-ordination of social communication related to scientific, health, educational, housing, and environmental concerns. A related and somewhat more complex hypothesis that needs extensive verification is that states read rights claims in more general and diffuse ways than social systems do. It can be provisionally countered that in comparison to social systems, states can at least read rights claims: social systems are still underdeveloped in this regard. More specifically, as regards individual state forms, liberal democratic states have been by far the most successful ones in performing this objective of juridical legibility precisely because of their constitutional design (internal differentiation/separation of powers), maintaining what is previously referred to in this chapter as liberal democratic proximity to society. Proximity in this sense facilitates a superior model of communication between states and society than that observed in all other known rival models of legitimate order. Formulating the matter in these terms highlights the dangers and urgent tasks of the epoch Colin Crouch and others designate as post-democratic.[39]

The neoliberal project threatens to further undermine the mediated proximity characteristic of politically constituted statehood in its liberal democratic instantiation. It attempts to reduce the richness and complexity of society to an inventory of investments with objectively measurable outcomes. In so doing, it coercively imposes the codes of profit/loss and ability to pay/inability to pay on social systems that would clearly function better according to different, more elastic codes respecting systemic specificity and system-specific knowledge. The fact that states read rights claims in *general and diffuse* ways has prompted the neoliberal state to try to constitute society as a competition directed by *quantitative* metrics of excellence, innovation, and consumer satisfaction, in which everyone has equal rights to compete. Under these conditions, proximity cedes to fairly arbitrary fluctuations between an oppressively immediate and an unresponsive state. This has led, in British higher education and higher education elsewhere, to a notable commercialisation and homogenisation on the supply side, and a pervasive sense of insecurity and dissatisfaction on the demand side. One observes dysfunctional communication between markets, which are said to respond to demand rather than to shape or direct it, and clients, who are supposedly endowed with rational free will and individual autonomy. The inadequacies embedded in these assumptions point to phenomena beyond the educational sphere. To the extent that poorly regulated markets are dysfunctional, rights of access and inclusion are diluted and largely defensive. These parallels between dysfunctional communication and flawed mediation raise major questions about the relations between power and knowledge today. They shed light on a situation in which the readability of rights claims does not merely help integrate and protect. Rights can also be used by the neoliberal state to monitor and, crucially, predict the likely preferences of individuals whose citizenship has been steered in a palpably commercial direction.[40]

Returning to the point that states can at least read rights claims, one is struck by the potential of social systems to do this, if, that is, they can be re-coded in more careful alignment with system-specific knowledge. One would be close to realising something approaching Adorno's partially elaborated notion that non-instrumental knowledge, both sensuous and cognitive, may hold the key to non-coerced integration. According to most mainstream systems-theoretical approaches, systems currently read communications from neighbouring systems as irritations. Neighbouring systems harbour reservoirs of knowledge that remain inaccessible to each other due to the incomprehension stemming from their mutually incommensurable codes. They are speaking different languages, such that non-infringement seemingly represents the most developed evolutionary stage of inter-systemic communication. But is it really utopian to believe that economic systems will be better able to expand and diversify if they communicate with educational systems on a qualitatively enhanced communicative model vis-à-vis the non-infringement model of reciprocal indifference and guarded distance? Similar questions can be posed with regard to relations between scientific research and health, scientific research and environment, and, perhaps of particular relevance and urgency, law and environment.[41]

Although chapter 4 focuses on the question of which patterns of FD currently prevail and why, it is worth mentioning here that the logic of democratic inclusion constantly changes as different societies evolve and store diverse experiences of collective learning. It is also worth noting that some of the integration problems connected with the specific instance of liberal democratic instrumental legitimacy discussed here are obscured when the *legal* formalisation of systemic specificity is deemed to be naturally spontaneous or inherently private, that is, when it is assumed to be neutral and *apolitical*. Re-articulating the critique of instrumental reason as a critique of instrumental legitimacy offers a promising way of renewing contemporary critical theory. It does so to the extent that it anticipates the main claims of romantic, ontological, and predominantly aesthetic critiques of instrumental reason, and outmanoeuvres those critiques with sociological theory and historical detail. That is an important step towards the renewal of critical theory insofar as it challenges the thesis that only the theory of communicative action offers a plausible alternative to romantic, Hegelian-Marxist, ontological, and aesthetic critiques of instrumental reason.[42] The compatibility between the currently hegemonic model of FD and paradigmatic liberal democratic norms of political constitutionalism is becoming increasingly uneasy. Evidence in support of this claim is provided by more and more extensive reliance on coercive measures typified by the aforementioned examples of surveillance, restrictions on flows of information, and infringements of other liberties that would have been taken as unassailable rights in the heyday of liberal democracy. One is witnessing a breakdown in hegemony in an historical period in which hegemony is no longer exercised as a function of dominant and subordinate cultures.[43]

These developments are complicated further by the questions raised by the collection of what is sometimes referred to as 'big data' and other instances of algorithmic control of everyday life by multinational corporations. It is no longer speculative to believe that juridical, educational, investment, sanitary, and related decisions directly affecting the lives of millions of citizens will be made according to the codes furnished by software packages developed by private law firms and other enterprises and sold to various government ministries. Neoliberal regimes can thus be seen to alter the structure of mediations between social systems, and to do so in many cases without official alteration of formal constitutional law. During the liberal democratic phase of political statehood, associated with the conquest of universal franchise, and the broadly speaking social democratic phase of political statehood, associated with more extensive rights of inclusion and the welfare state, government ministries retain formal control of the administration of the major systemic functions. This changes in the late 1970s and early 1980s, however, in ways that anticipate the widespread shift to algorithmic decision-making and government outsourcing that is rampant today. In consonance with the previous warning against linear accounts of historical progression, one must bear in mind that there was and continues to be overlap between these phases of rights regime formation and evolution. It can be said that, in different ways, liberal and social democratic statehood belong to what John Gerard Ruggie refers to as the 'embedded liberalism' or 'ordo-liberalism' of the political-economic order established through the Bretton Woods agreement and the General Agreement on Tariffs and Trade (GATT) that followed World War II. In marked contrast to the TTIP and Comprehensive Economic and Trade Agreement treaties, however, the Bretton Woods and GATT treaties did not envisage the possibility of corporations suing governments for interfering with potential profits, or employers deciding between themselves, across international boundaries, what legal wages should be (a flagrant case of selective systemic de-differentiation). It is therefore fair to ask if the embedded liberalism of the post-war period has evolved, in the period following 1989, in the direction of an embedded neoliberalism, without, however, a corresponding change in the appropriate safeguards of accountability, transparency, and citizen participation. If so, it is possible to speak of a transition from markets embedded within states (Hegel) to states subjected to the needs of markets (Hayek). This will not come as a revelation to anyone who has witnessed the changes in the real preconditions of political statehood that have marked world society since the end of the Cold War.[44]

It might seem as if the need for the sacrifices and austerity demanded by market-embedded states is the inevitable outcome of excessive government spending during the unusual conditions reigning during the *trente glorieuses*, and a prerequisite for strategic advantage in what appears to be an increasingly global and competitive world. Stated in these terms, relinquishing freedoms and passively accepting one model of FD can easily look like a rational compromise and pragmatic accommodation to the palpable facts of twenty-first-century reality. To do so, however, is to discount the idea that there might be new ways of thinking about and enacting political change that activate late modern society's collective learning and realise its normative potential to achieve innovative forms of non-coercive integration and inclusion. It also conveniently ignores one of the most fertile tensions in systems theory: FD individuates social systems, whilst also making them qualitatively more dependent on one another, thus making the modalities of their mediations a crucial question. Negotiating dependence without recourse to centralisation raises the question of de-centred, post-statist mediation, and therewith the re-organisation of collectively binding decision-making within and across social systems. The need for this kind of reform is tangible. It holds out the possibility of politics beyond redistribution and recognition, and enables observers to consider the mediated non-identity of state and political system anew. In anticipation of the argument developed in the next chapter, it is probable that under certain constitutional arrangements and institutional mediations, FD is largely synonymous with de-politicisation and privatisation, reason is largely tantamount to instrumental reason, and politics is usually a matter of populism, plebiscites, and passive revolutions. Populism is best studied in political, sociological, and constitutional terms and not, in the first instance, as a matter of psychological predisposition or an alleged propensity towards mass hysteria on the part of ostensibly uncultivated voters. In conclusion, it seems uncontroversial to say that neoliberalism marks the latest reactionary departure from the metaphorical proximity between the key institutions of liberal democracy, modern statehood, and society. Extensive reliance on *Verrechtlichung*, bank bailouts, and other examples of selective de-differentiation provide convincing empirical examples. One way to articulate this argument historically is by saying that whilst the first wave against liberal democracy and proximity of accountability materialises within the framework of the nation state in centralist guise as fascism, the second wave does so in bio-political and technocratic guise as international governance. At this stage, however, there is no way to repristinate earlier forms of legitimacy. Paul Mason and Wolfgang Streeck articulate two very different, but nonetheless convincing, ways of making this case.[45]

At this juncture it is not clear where neoliberal parties and governments stand in relation to public political will formation or, judging from the Brexit and Trump debacles, to populism. Liberal democracies need civic education and other notable components of public political will formation beyond the predictable rituals of party political competition. The viability of liberal democratic politics is therefore contingent upon a specific version of modern statehood and a specific version of FD. It is not clear that either will survive into the second half of this century.[46] This observation raises questions about the defining features of the state in question and, in the longer term, the likely forms of statehood to follow the eventual demise of that state. The original features of the modern, politically constituted state are analysed in preceding chapters in terms of (a) the philosophical presupposition of the validity of weak dialectical models of mediated unity in matters of representation and normative inclusion; (b) an ideological commitment to the principle of overarching legal-political form, sharing a number of common traits with certain strands of republicanism and other democratic models of legitimacy; (c) the juridical presupposition of unrivalled, as opposed to all-inclusive enforcement of collectively binding decisions; (d) the epistemological presupposition of knowledge of the preconditions of liberty, acquired through consensual interaction in a naturally legitimate sphere of communication and exchange already emancipated from illegitimate political intrusion; and (e) the normative presupposition of unqualified political inclusivity, based on the idea of unqualified citizenship, designated as democracy. Chapters 1 and 2 thereby prepare the ground for considering how one might be clear and specific about what distinguishes the existing model of FD from others, and, importantly, how one might be clear and specific about the ways in which neoliberalism attempts to preserve the existing model of FD through illiberal means. That discussion also implicitly asks if we may currently be witnessing a forlorn attempt to return to a halcyon age of national unity that probably never really existed, and most certainly cannot be conjured up in the era of globalisation. A central point made in defence of this interpretation of the historical process and constitutional evolution is that the mediated unity of citizens, law, governments, and states has never obtained to a significant extent, not even – perilously, for liberal democrats – in the weak dialectical mode. It is remarked in this regard that it is really more accurate to speak of the partial politicisation of rights than it is to speak of mediated unity or overarching legal-political form. This observation prompts a few concluding reflections on the ways in which partially politicised rights regimes, initially established within nation-state contexts, are slowly becoming a global, rather than a merely international, phenomenon.

One must first qualify the claim that the current crisis of democracy is more accurately understood as the crisis of a particular instantiation of FD than as a crisis of democracy. The claim implies that not all crises of democracy are crises of FD and, conversely, that not all crises of FD are crises of democracy. How can one disentangle issues that appear to be irrevocably intertwined? One can start by noting that some of the great works of intellectual history and political sociology suggest that the study of modern politics and constitutional compromise should really begin with a comparison of the divergent logics of liberalism/individual freedom and democracy/socio-economic equality.

This argument is sometimes articulated in terms of likely conflict rather than possible compromise. In Schmitt's work, the postulate becomes a defence of non-egalitarian democracy, with all of the authoritarian connotations that his *völkische* critique of liberalism entails.[47] He is one of many notable figures to disregard the irreducibility of sociological modernity to political modernity, to conflate issues pertaining to territorial sovereignty with issues pertaining to an historically specific conception of democracy, and largely to ignore the implications of FD for the dialectics of inclusion and exclusion. The pertinent points raised by the preceding pages in this regard can be summarised as follows: there is no going back to a politically constituted society based on the (ostensible) foundation of mediated unity. Consequently, global humanity may come to enjoy a highly democratic version of FD, or it will be forced to live with moderately democratic or, equally plausibly, minimally democratic versions of FD, such as the one currently proposed in a neoliberal framework. The question of the kind of constitutional framing global FD may eventually acquire is therefore the constitutional question of the coming decades. It is possible to face it without recourse either to Schmitt or, at the other extreme, to Rousseau's notion that egalitarian democracy can only be practised in small, relatively homogeneous city-states such as Geneva.[48]

It is worth recalling in this context that Aristotle identifies monarchies, aristocracies, and democracies as the three main constitutional forms of political community. Aristotle and a number of other thinkers then and since, however, think that one rarely encounters pure states or uni-logical constitutions. Instead, according to this view, strong states tend to amalgamate select dimensions of monarchical, aristocratic, and/or democratic constitutions. This is why Aristotle and many of his followers favour what he refers to as a mixed constitution. More important, perhaps, in terms of his impact and continuing legacy, is his theorem that each constitutional form exhibits definite tendencies linked to universal traits in human nature that emerge in relation to the number of people wielding authority. He submits that monarchies evolve towards tyrannies, aristocracies become oligarchic, and democracies, in turn, succumb to the temptations of mob rule, and usually mutate into tyrannies that eventually engender calls for more democracy. Montesquieu modifies and refines this model by arguing that republics tend to evolve in either a democratic or an aristocratic direction, and that republics tend to coexist with monarchies and despotisms. The author of *The Spirit of the Laws* adds that each particular constitutional form is animated, so to speak, by a guiding principle that directs social action and political ambition. Republics thrive or perish according to their success in producing virtuous citizens in the specific sense that they pursue expressly public and political visions of freedom. Whilst monarchies need to cultivate a widespread sense of the importance of rank and honour, tyrannies must isolate individual citizens and perpetuate an atmosphere of fear and mutual suspicion among them. Montesquieu suggests that the number of people wielding authority is less important than constitutional design, climate, and the informal registers of cohesion and solidarity institutionalised in customs, habits, and the spirit informing the letter of the law.[49]

These and other thinkers demonstrate acute sensibility for the reality that the relations between state forms, legal systems, political culture, and modalities of social inclusion and exclusion are constitutional relations in the widest sense. Contemporary global history indicates that neoliberalism and global governance may pose insurmountable problems for the ideal of a mixed constitution, the institutional compromise between liberal freedoms and democratic norms, the welfare state, and in a perhaps more speculative vein, for social democracy. Rather than synthesising, mediating, and planning, states are increasingly forced to buy shares in enterprises in order to have a say in how they are managed. In many cases this means that they act in accordance with the logic of competitive global markets rather than in terms of the wellbeing of the citizens residing in those territories where the enterprises are located. States were once responsible for industrial policy that was either approved or rejected by the public; they now consult experts to devise strategic portfolios. Public approval matters little in an epoch in which states are empowered to do little more than authorise spending cuts compliant with the rigours of austerity as these are defined by the organisations of global governance. Under these circumstances, it is more accurate to speak of the state as an historical bloc of private actors and public authorities than in the ways that Hegel, Schmitt, Habermas, or even Colin Crouch, David Held, or Chantal Mouffe do. Gramsci intuits this development with his theory of the integral state with redefined roles for civil society, political society, and the economy. It is interesting in this regard that thinkers such as Gramsci and Luhmann, with such divergent positions on so many issues, seem to agree on one fundamental point. It may be that it is now sociologically and historically more accurate to think in terms of historical blocs and integral states, or political systems and functionally differentiated legal systems, than it is to think in terms of mediated unity, nation states, public and private, or liberalism and democracy.[50]

Notes

1 Rudolf Stichweh, *Die Weltgesellschaft: Soziologische Analysen* (Frankfurt: Suhrkamp, 2000), chapter 1.
2 A broadly similar approach can be found in Joel I. Colón-Ríos, *Weak Constitutionalism: Democratic Legitimacy and the Question of Constituent Power* (London: Routledge,

2012). The question of constituent power raised in the title of Colón's work is key in terms of re-thinking statehood and democracy in the light of FD, globalisation, and the demise of the paradigm of mediated unity.

3 On this point see David M. Berry, *Critical Theory and the Digital*, Critical Theory and Contemporary Society (New York: Bloomsbury, 2014), chapters 3 and 8; and Graeme Kirkpatrick, *Computer Games and the Social Imaginary* (Cambridge: Polity, 2013), chapter 4.

4 For a detailed discussion linking Weber with Habermas and Luhmann see Darrow Schecter, *The Critique of Instrumental Reason from Weber to Habermas* (London: Continuum, 2010), chapters 1 and 6.

5 Thomas Piketty, 'Global treaties have to be about more than trade', *Guardian* (17 November 2016), p. 39; and George Monbiot, 'TTIP may be dead, but a worse trade deal is coming', *Guardian* (7 September 2017), p. 29.

6 Tania Lieckweg, *Das Recht der Weltgesellschaft: Systemtheoretische Perspektiven auf die Globalisierung des Rechts am Beispiel der Lex Mercatoria* (Stuttgart: Lucius & Lucius, 2003), chapter 3; and William Davies, *The Limits of Neoliberalism: Authority, Sovereignty and the Logic of Competition*, Theory, Culture & Society (London: SAGE, 2014). Davies goes so far as to say that rather than working in sync with the FD of political and economic systems, neoliberalism seeks to replace politics with economics (p. 4).

7 Luhmann and others adduce good reasons to think that FD is an integral part of sociological modernity. The question of *how* social systems are differentiated then takes on great significance when it comes to assessing the balance between *Verrechtlichung* and democratic legal process. Orthodox systems theory forfeits a great deal of explanatory plausibility if it can be shown that the formation of systems and their respective environments is about as 'natural' as the supposed exit from the state of nature is spontaneous and unanimous. This issue is taken up by Nicole Deitelhoff and Jens Steffek in the introduction to Nicole Deitelhoff and Jens Steffek, *Was bleibt vom Staat? Demokratie, Recht und Verfassung im globalen Zeitalter*, Staatlichkeit im Wandel (Frankfurt: Campus-Verlag, 2009), pp. 7–34. Several of the chapters in this excellent volume address the phenomenon of *Verrechtlichung*.

8 Perez Zagorin notes that this period of state building is also one of revolution. See Perez Zagorin, *Rebels and Rulers, 1500–1660 Vol. 1, Society, States and Early Modern Revolution: Agrarian and Urban Rebellions* (Cambridge: Cambridge University Press, 1982), and *Rebels and Rulers, 1500–1660 Vol. 2, Provincial Rebellion: Revolutionary Civil Wars, 1560–1660* (Cambridge: Cambridge University Press, 1982).

9 There are good grounds for thinking that it is simplistic to blame Trump or think that the constitutional order in the United States was finely tuned until he came along. David Rudenstine shows that for the past seventy years, the Supreme Court has failed to challenge the executive on key issues. See David Rudenstine, *The Age of Deference: The Supreme Court, National Security, and the Constitutional Order* (New York: Oxford University Press, 2016).

10 From a specifically systems-theoretical sociological perspective, society's capacity to develop political resources like positive law and strong states is contingent upon a kind of division of labour between legal, political, and economic systems, such that no single system is overburdened with extraneous steering imperatives. On this account, FD ensures social stability, but can only do so by being relatively unresponsive to substantive demands for justice, equality, and legitimacy that transgress the formal limits on such claims imposed by this division of labour. Critical systems theorists are thus confronted with the problem of developing a theory

of politics that retains FD without passively accepting some of its conservative implications.

11 There is considerable debate as to whether this elasticity observable in historically strong states is best explicable in terms of constitutional design, felicitous evolution, colonial resources that are no longer accessible, or in terms of hegemonic relations within nationally organised states that have been de-stabilised by global forces. It is likely that a combination of all these factors and others is at work in shaping the present constellation of compromises, conflicts, and changing social-systemic boundaries in contemporary society. On this question see Richard Bellamy, *Political Constitutionalism: A Republican Defence of the Constitutionality of Democracy* (Cambridge: Cambridge University Press, 2007).

12 On this issue see Jean Clam, 'What is Modern Power?', in Chris Thornhill and Michael King (eds), *Luhmann on Law and Politics: Critical Appraisals and Applications* (Oxford: Hart, 2006), pp. 142–62.

13 Florence Sutcliffe-Braithwaite, 'Neo-liberalism and morality in the making of Thatcherite social policy', *The Historical Journal*, 55:2 (2012), 497–520.

14 Mark I. Vail, *Recasting Welfare Capitalism: Economic Adjustment in Contemporary France and Germany* (Philadelphia: Temple University Press, 2010), chapter 5.

15 Stephen Gill, 'Constitutionalizing inequality and the clash of globalizations', *International Studies Review*, 4:2 (2002), 47–65. Social democratic parties and trade unions played a major role in maintaining political stability in post-war Western Europe. It is as yet unclear if their ability to contribute to steering and planning has been attenuated by global economic forces, or if the sociological proximity between citizens, social democratic parties, and trade unions has been attenuated by the erosion of the social-cultural milieu cementing adhesion to those types of institutions. If one accepts Thomas Piketty's thesis that inequality has become more entrenched, it may be the case that there have been subtle qualitative changes in the ways that parties and unions interact with key state institutions. On this point see Piketty, *Le Capital au XXIe siècle*, chapter 2, and Moschonas, *In the Name of Social Democracy*, chapter 9.

16 For the case of the post-colonial Commonwealth states, see Hakeem O. Yusuf, *Colonial and Post-Colonial Constitutionalism in the Commonwealth: Peace, Order and Good Government* (London: Routledge, 2014).

17 Simon Jenkins analyses this phenomenon in relation to debates about triggering article 50 of the Lisbon Treaty. In his estimation, in the absence of clear parliamentary leadership from May's government, the judiciary is being drawn into the legislative process. See his 'The supreme court is doing MPs' dirty work for them on article 50', *Guardian* (8 December 2016), p. 39.

18 Ingeborg Maus anticipates several contemporary manifestations of this ambiguity in her *Rechtstheorie und politische Theorie im Industriekapitalismus* (Munich: Fink, 1986), chapter 10.

19 The communicative superiority in question assumes the *separation* of state and society as well as the mediated unity of state and society via law and government (please see the discussion of this incoherence further on in this chapter). Saskia Sassen discusses a number of the issues involved in these debates in terms of the 'embedded statism' (p. 102) characteristic of many studies of historical change. These tend to offer naturalistic evolutionary perspectives on historical transitions, despite a professed adherence to sociological methodology. See Saskia Sassen, *A Sociology of Globalization* (New York: W. W. Norton, 2007), pp. 102–4; James C. Scott, *Seeing Like a State: How Certain Schemes to Improve the Human Condition have Failed* (New Haven: Yale University Press, 1998), chapter 1;

and Susan L. Woodward, *The Ideology of Failed States: Why Intervention Fails* (Cambridge: Cambridge University Press, 2017), chapters 4–6.

20 Individual government ministries within states no longer have the resources that once enabled them, albeit to admittedly quite varying extents, to respond to the needs of discrete social systems such as health, education, transport, energy and so on. Emmanuel Macron, the French minister of Finance under François Hollande until September 2016 (elected president in April 2017), concedes that the current model of ministerial responsibility has been stretched to its outermost limit. See his remarks in the preface to Yann Algan and Thomas Cazenave, *L'Etat en mode start-up: Le Nouvel Age de l'action publique, préface d'Emmanuel Macron* (Paris: Eyrolles, 2016), pp. 7–10. The enormity of the challenges involved comes into focus when one considers that there are far more social systems than there are government ministries. A cursory look at the chapters of *L'Etat en mode start-up* indicates that the extra-territorial boundaries of social systems compound the problem of democratic legitimacy.

21 See Varoufakis, *Global Minotaur*, pp. 155–9; Seumas Milne, *The Revenge of History: The Battle for the Twenty-First Century* (London: Verso, 2012), pp. 155–67; and David Marsh, *Europe's Deadlock: How the Euro Crisis Could Be Solved – and Why It Won't Happen* (New Haven: Yale University Press, 2016), chapters 6–8.

22 Larry Elliot, 'As Kim and Lagarde talk, a fresh crisis brews', *Guardian* (10 October 2016), p. 22. For an analysis of the potential consequences of the triumph of the democratic populist model, see Paul K. Jones, *Critical Theory and Demagogic Populism*, Critical Theory and Contemporary Society (Manchester: Manchester University Press, forthcoming) and Robert Samuels, *Psychoanalyzing the Left and Right after Donald Trump* (New York: Palgrave Macmillan, 2016).

23 Niklas Luhmann, 'Der Wohlfahrtsstaat zwischen Evolution und Rationalität', in *Soziologische Aufklärung 4: Beiträge zur funktionalen Differenzierung der Gesellschaft* (Wiesbaden: VS Verlag für Sozialwissenschaften, 2009 [1983]), pp. 108–20.

24 Georg Simmel uncannily anticipates the systems-theoretical understanding of differentiation in 'Wie ist Gesellschaft möglich?'. Citing a work of sociological theory from 1908 emphasises the historical overlap between state building and FD, thus reinforcing the point that these processes have been intertwined and will continue to condition each other to some extent for the foreseeable future.

25 This point emerged very clearly in the French presidential elections of April 2017 and the positions variously assumed by Fillon, Macron, and Mélenchon. It is very interesting to note how poorly Hamon fared, given that his proposals did not appeal to notions of separation or unity. For an analysis, see Michel Offerle, 'Les Partis meurent longtemps', *Le Monde* (31 May 2017), p. 20.

26 On this point see Andreas Kalyvas, *Democracy and the Politics of the Extraordinary: Max Weber, Carl Schmitt, and Hannah Arendt* (Cambridge: Cambridge University Press, 2008), Part II of which focuses on the possibility of constitutional utopianism in Schmitt and beyond.

27 Habermas, *Strukturwandel*, pp. 178–209, available in English as *Structural Transformation*, pp. 102–29.

28 The works already cited by Thornhill, Brunkhorst, Fischer-Lescano, Teubner, and especially Möller offer very good examples of critical constitutional theory. Also see Martti Koskenniemi, 'Hegemonic Regimes', in Margaret Young (ed.), *Regime Interaction in International Law: Facing Fragmentation* (Cambridge: Cambridge University Press, 2012), pp. 305–24; and Hans-Jürgen Bieling, 'Die Konstitutionalisierung der Weltwirtschaft als Prozess hegemonialer Verstaatlichung', in Sonja Buckel and

Andreas Fischer-Lescano (eds), *Hegemonie gepanzert mit Zwang: Zivilgesellschaft und Politik im Staatsverständnis Antonio Gramscis* (Baden-Baden: Nomos, 2007), pp. 143–60.

29 Michel Foucault, *Naissance de la biopolitique: Cours au Collège de France, 1978–1979*, ed. Michel Senellart, sous la dir. de François Ewald et Alessandro Fontana (Paris: Gallimard Seuil, 2004), pp. 105–33, available in English as *The Birth of Biopolitics: Lectures at the College de France, 1978–1979*, trans. Graham Burchell (Basingstoke: Palgrave Macmillan, 2008), pp. 101–28. In this set of lectures Foucault focuses on the ordo-liberal hegemony of the West German social market economy in the decades following World War II. His analysis indicates that post-war West German politics was pre-defined by a determinate model of economic growth. For a more general discussion of Foucault on neoliberalism, see Geoffroy de Lagasnerie, *La Dernière Leçon de Michel Foucault: Sur le néolibéralisme, la théorie et la politique* ([Paris]: Fayard, 2012). On a more stringently historical account it can be argued that, strictly speaking, liberalism was probably politically irrelevant by about 1914. See George Dangerfield, *The Strange Death of Liberal England* (London: Constable, 1936).

30 Richard Seymour, *Corbyn: The Strange Rebirth of Radical Politics* (London: Verso, 2016), chapter 3; and Armin Schäfer, 'Liberalization, Inequality and Democracy's Discontent', in Armin Schäfer and Wolfgang Streeck (eds), *Politics in the Age of Austerity* (Cambridge: Polity, 2013), pp. 169–95.

31 See Perry Anderson, *In the Tracks of Historical Materialism* (London: Verso, 1983), p. 27.

32 See Niklas Luhmann and Karl-Eberhard Schorr, *Reflexionsprobleme im Erziehungssystem* (Stuttgart: Klett-Cotta, 1979), Part III, and Niklas Luhmann, *Das Erziehungssystem der Gesellschaft*, ed. Dieter Lenzen (Frankfurt: Suhrkamp, 2002), chapter 5. For a far more flexible approach to educational systems that shows that re-coding of this and other systems is possible, see the essays collected in Heinz Sünker, Dieter Timmermann, and Fritz-Ulrich Kolbe (eds), *Bildung, Gesellschaft, soziale Ungleichheit: Internationale Beiträge zur Bildungssoziologie und Bildungstheorie* (Frankfurt: Suhrkamp-Taschenbuch-Verlag, 1994).

33 Franz L. Neumann, 'The Change in the Function of Law in Modern Society', in William E. Scheuerman (ed.), *The Rule of Law under Siege: Selected Essays of Franz L. Neumann and Otto Kirchheimer* (Berkeley: University of California Press, 1996 [1937]), pp. 101–41. For an analysis of Neumann's legal theory in conjunction with the claims of critical theory, see Scheuermann's excellent *Between the Norm and the Exception*. This book includes an analysis of the ideas of Schmitt, Kirchheimer, Heller, and the juridical and constitutional dimensions of the collapse of Weimar democracy.

34 On this topic see Schecter, 'Gramsci's unorthodox Marxism' and 'Historical Bloc'.

35 See Serge Halimi and Pierre Rimbert, 'Information sous contrôle', *Le Monde Diplomatique* (July 2016), pp. 12–13. For a more detailed look at the politics of information, see Lagasnerie, *L'Art de la révolte*.

36 Möller, 'Struggles for Law', pp. 305–6; and Dieter Kerwer, 'Governance in a World Society: The Perspective of Systems Theory', in Matthias Albert and Lena Hilkermeier (eds), *Observing International Relations: Niklas Luhmann and World Politics* (London: Routledge & Kegan, 2004), pp. 197–203.

37 It is important to bear in mind that there are many instances in which public political will formation can take shape as a critique of the WTO and similar organisations. See Paul Statham and Hans-Jörg Trenz, *The Politicization of Europe: Contesting the Constitution in the Mass Media* (Abingdon: Routledge, 2013), pp. 21–5.

38 It is clear to Humberto Maturana and Francisco Varela, for example, two of the key figures in the development of systems theory, that biological systems do not function in ways that are directly analogous to social systems. See their *Autopoiesis and Cognition: The Realization of the Living* (Dordrecht: Reidel, 1980).
39 Crouch, *Post-Democracy*, chapter 5.
40 For the case of training, see Henry A. Giroux, *Neoliberalism's War on Higher Education* (Chicago: Haymarket Books, 2014), chapter 1; and Susan Braedley, 'Accidental Health Care: Masculinity and Neoliberalism at Work', in Meg Luxton and Susan Braedley (eds), *Neoliberalism and Everyday Life* (Montréal: McGill-Queen's University Press, 2010), pp. 136–62. For a more general analysis linking problems of resource allocation with questions of social communication and mediation, see Joseph Stiglitz, 'Inequality and Economic Growth', in Michael Jacobs and Mariana Mazzucato (eds), *Rethinking Capitalism: Economics and Policy for Sustainable and Inclusive Growth* (Chichester: Wiley, 2016), pp. 134–55.
41 On the question of the relations between law and the environment from a systems-theoretical perspective, see the essays collected in Andreas Philippopoulos-Mihalopoulos (ed.), *Law and Ecology: New Environmental Foundations* (London: Routledge, 2012), especially chapters 1, 2, and 5.
42 The present book pursues this objective and as such further elaborates attempts to sketch the path of research first outlined in Schecter, *Critique of Instrumental Reason* and *Critical Theory in the Twenty-First Century*.
43 Luc Boltanski and Eve Chiapello make this clear in *Le nouvel esprit du capitalisme* (Paris: Gallimard, 1999), available in English as *The New Spirit of Capitalism*, trans. Gregory Elliott (London: Verso, 2005). Also see Pierre Dardot and Christian Laval, *La Nouvelle raison du monde: Essai sur la société néolibérale* (Paris: Découverte, 2009), available in English as *The New Way of the World: On Neoliberal Society* (London: Verso, 2013). Dardot and Laval have updated their views in *Ce cauchemar qui n'en finit pas: Comment le néolibéralisme défait la démocratie* (Paris: La Découverte, 2016). A similarly critical assessment of neoliberalism is offered by Wendy Brown, in *Undoing the Demos*. For a general introduction and overview, see Harvey, *Brief History of Neoliberalism*. As the British example suggests, a comparison between the public housing policies of the Baldwin and Macmillan governments with those of Cameron and May highlights the differences between liberalism and neoliberalism on the very crucial issue of social welfare. See A. J. P. Taylor, *English History, 1914–1945* (Oxford: Clarendon Press, 1965), chapter 6.
44 John Gerard Ruggie, 'International Regimes, Transactions and Change: Embedded Liberalism in the Postwar Economic Order', in Stephen D. Krasner (ed.), *International Regimes* (Ithaca: Cornell University Press, 1983), pp. 195–232; and Hauke Brunkhorst, 'The Return of the Crisis', in Poul F. Kjaer, Gunther Teubner, and Alberto Febbrajo (eds), *The Financial Crisis in Constitutional Perspective: The Dark Side of Functional Differentiation* (Oxford: Hart, 2011), pp. 133–72, at p. 169.
45 Paul Mason, *PostCapitalism: A Guide to Our Future* (London: Allen Lane, 2015); and Streeck, *Buying Time*. Also see Streeck's 'How will capitalism end?', *New Left Review*, 87 (2014), 35–66.
46 It is in this context that Berthold Vogel discusses 'society's need of the state' (*Staatsbedürftigkeit*) in his book *Die Staatsbedürftigkeit der Gesellschaft* (Hamburg: Hamburger Ed., 2007).
47 Schmitt, *Legalität und Legitimität*, pp. 23–7, available in English as *Legality and Legitimacy*, pp. 20–6.
48 It can be added that Marx's vision of the Paris Commune as 'the political form at last discovered under which to work out the economic emancipation of labour'

does not differ significantly from that of Rousseau on this topic. See Marx, 'Civil War', p. 635. Whilst it is true Marx at times praises and at times criticises the Commune, it is clear that he has no coherent model of democratic legitimacy. The latter can be found with exemplary clarity in G. D. H. Cole, *Guild Socialism Re-Stated* (London: Leonard Parsons, 1920). The antiquated connotations of the word 'guild' do not detract from the originality and, with some modifications, feasibility of some of Cole's main proposals. For an analysis see Darrow Schecter, *Radical Theories: Paths beyond Marxism and Social Democracy* (Manchester: Manchester University Press, 1994), chapter 3.

49 Aristotle, *The Politics*, ed. Stephen Everson (Cambridge: Cambridge University Press, 1988), Book 3, pp. 61–2, and Montesquieu, *L'Esprit des lois*, Vol. I, Book 7, chapter 2, pp. 225–30, available in English as *The Spirit of the Laws*, pp. 96–101.

50 Bob Jessop alludes to some of these issues in *State Theory: Putting the Capitalist State in its Place* (Cambridge: Polity, 1990), but does so within the framework of regulation theory and political economy, thus neglecting the normative and socio-logical issues raised by constitutional and critical theory.

4

Dilemmas of contemporary statehood: on the sociological paradoxes of weak dialectical formalism and embedded neoliberalism

FD simultaneously refers, within the parameters defined by public law and centralised post-feudal states in Europe and elsewhere, to diverse instances of de-centralisation. The latter are commonly denoted by the separation of powers as well as the protected status of the private individual and the rights of a variety of non-state actors in civil society. Differentiation thus implies de-centralisation, but it does so in a somewhat paradoxical sense relating to the reality of a historically unique example of institutional form (the early modern state in Europe and North America, subsequently imposed or adopted elsewhere) which is capable, to significantly differing extents depending on the country in question, of reconciling countervailing tendencies. That is, differentiation and de-centralisation unfold within a framework that in principle remains centralised with regard to the key domains of taxation, military authority, public courts, and questions of justice. One is thus trying to explain a series of processes that unite, without fusing, and that separate, without permanently isolating. In short, one is trying to explain processes of mediation without relying on a central mediating foundation in the ways that weak and strong models of mediated unity tend to do. Hence it is noted at various junctures that centralisation does not mean hermetically sealed off, and that it is unlikely that states were ever territorially integral units that only now are being forced to grudgingly cede bits of their sovereignty to the institutions of international governance. This is not to say that there have been no changes in the relations between the national and transnational dimensions of law and statehood. Whilst 1945 and 1989 can be seen to represent moments of transition, it is as yet unclear, in the light of Brexit and a number of unfolding, unresolved issues, whether the financial crisis of 2007–2008 and its ongoing aftermath also represent a moment of transition in this regard.[1]

In this study, dialectics and critical theory are enlisted in an attempt to respond to the methodological and sociological challenges posed by the paradoxical realities of pluri-directional mediation observed in the dynamics between state building and FD. These challenges also offer various ways of investigating the extent to which modern states and their constitutions are still capable of synthesising manifestly divergent institutional dynamics, such as simultaneous inclusion and exclusion.[2] In Hegel's highly influential depiction, the organisations, corporations, and other associations active in civil society show signs of de-centralised self-steering capacities. But in his estimation, they are only able to do this thanks to the unifying juridical-political framework provided by the state. When Hegel asserts that civil society is a product of the modern world, he also makes clear that civil-societal self-steering is self-limiting self-steering that consciously refrains from making claims on the more fundamental prerogatives that must most definitely remain with the key institutions of statehood.[3] Leaving aside for the moment questions as to whether, and how successfully, states managed to do this in the past, one is entitled to ask what the future is likely to bring with regard to their ostensibly synthetic unifying capacity. It might in fact be countered that states are only called upon to unify and synthesise within the strong dialectical model that was definitively surpassed in 1989, and that successful modern states operate according to a weak dialectical model enabling them to provide flexible frameworks for societal self-steering. Both models presuppose mediated unity between citizens, law, government, and the state, however. Global history since 2007 entitles one to ask questions about the long-term viability of the weak dialectical, neoliberal variant of mediated unity.

Previous chapters point out that there are a number of latent and at times manifest tensions between political centralisation (the state, official public political will formation, and what is often casually assumed to be democracy), and social-systemic differentiation (society, specialised fields of knowledge functioning according to discrete operating principles, and the individual). It is also pointed out that consistent social-systemic differentiation implies that the formalised political system is evidently not simply synonymous with the state.[4] The relations obtaining between political centralisation and social-systemic differentiation therefore turn out to be anything but straightforward, and, as a consequence, it is very difficult to come up with convincing models that explain the mediations in play in any particular historical period. It has been seen that there are periods in which a determinate instance of central-isation and a specific instantiation of differentiation are clearly compatible, and conducive to good government and economic growth. When modern states are strong and stable, it would appear that there is in fact a mutually enforcing relation between centralisation and differentiation that can be characterised as constitutional in the broadest sense of the term which encompasses more than just constitutional law, constituent power, or even democracy.[5] When, on the contrary, modern states are weak and prone to authoritarian repression, it is often the case that the relation between the two is marked by conflict and highly antagonistic mediations. In such cases, the political system of the state is confronted with intensive demands for instances of social inclusion that the national political system in question is not adequately equipped to deal with.[6] It is typical of weak states, for example, that the state exercises insufficient control over the self-steering aspirations of military, religious, and economic elites and their respective environments. To the extent that these milieux become closed and self-referential, they at times manifest inchoate systemic properties whilst also exhibiting properties readily recognisable as distinct elements within an historical bloc.[7]

Whether the states of complex societies are strong or weak thus depends in large measure on a larger set of issues concerning modalities of public polit-ical centralisation and the extent to which those modalities can be success-fully synchronised with the operations of social systems. With this analysis, one is obviously quite some distance from Renaissance and early modern perspectives on constitutional breakdown that regard crisis to be the result of an excessive reliance on *fortuna* by the prince (Machiavelli) or the absence of civic virtue in democratic republics (Montesquieu). If it is possible that there is an ambiguous discrepancy, rather than a flagrant contradiction, between political centralisation and social-systemic differentiation, it is a discrepancy that finds a somewhat rough analogy in the incongruities between formal and substantive knowledge in a very qualified sense that will be explained pres-ently. At first glance, the plausibility of the analogy appears severely strained by the fact that there is no obvious correlation between political centralisa-tion and conceptually formalised knowledge of the kind that is often seen as actively coding the workings of individual social systems, such as ability or inability to pay, educational success or failure, legal versus non-legal, par-ties of government versus opposition parties, etc. It would seem to make far more sense to contrast political centralisation with anarchism or notions of indigenous communal rights, or formal democracy with direct democracy, or codified knowledge with the creativity of the intuitive imagination. Moreover, a purely descriptive account of the matter from a European or North American standpoint would probably highlight the overall compatibility, rather than discrepancy, between political centralisation and social-systemic differentiation, since that is what seems to be the case when one considers how modern nation states appear to function in practice. A very quick return to Kant, Hegel, Marx, Weber, and Simmel may be helpful in disentangling some of these issues. Their writings signal that conceptual formalisation complements political centralisation and social-systemic differentiation. Crucially, however, it only really does so within a specific historical-geographical context that cannot be taken to be universal. That is the context of modern Western rationalisation and the enduring legacies of Christian humanist culture, very broadly speaking, and the role within it played by the traditions of Roman law, common law, and their respective patterns of informal solidarity and legal positivism in the early modern and modern phases of state building. Within that tradition there is a clearly discernible correlation between political centralisation and the conceptually formalised codes of knowledge guiding social-systemic differentiation. Needless to say, it is also a tradition within which practices of military, socio-economic, and cultural imperialism have flourished and continue to assert their prerogatives.[8]

What is unclear, at this juncture, is the answer to the question as to whether political centralisation and social-systemic differentiation continue to be compatible and susceptible to moderately harmonious mediation within the framework of individual nation states. States are challenged by the ongoing evolution of what is increasingly a world society whose institutional and geographical contours are in a constant process of comprehensive redefinition. It is safe to say that once these contours are stabilised, world society will exhibit demands for political inclusion, broadly conceived, that differ significantly from the deeply ingrained patterns of inclusion that prevailed in what Luhmann refers to as 'old Europe'.[9] For a long time religion, family life, sport, work, education, newspapers and radio, trade unions and other professional associations, together with political parties, constituted the bedrock institutions of inclusion. How long will they be able to play this role going forward, or, in a related vein, will they continue to exist, but with markedly different functions than the ones they had in the recent past? The recent surge in calls for intensified border control in aid of national security and economic protectionism in service of the workers of whatever happens to be the domestic economy in question raises significant questions in this regard. These doubts are multiplied when, as has often been the case in the wake of Brexit, such calls are accompanied by demands for further de-regulation of trade and financial markets. At this point, the at times subtle discrepancies between political centralisation and social-systemic differentiation evolve in the direction of flagrant contradiction and acute conflict. The situation demands an investigation of the premises linking antagonistic conceptual thinking and a distinct tradition of state building, on the one hand, with the historical evolution of social systems and the persistence, or in some cases subtle modification, of the specific codes that continue to inform the workings of systemic operations within and across national boundaries, on the other. Globalisation is admittedly an important consideration when examining concept building, state building, and FD. But globalisation seems mainly to be looked at in relation to the state and categorised as a major cause for what is perceived to be the crisis of parties, politics, and democracy. The phenomena normally associated with globalisation have tended to command much more attention, due to their spectacular visibility, than other important features of what may be problematic about the version of FD that is currently in place. At this stage, it is no longer possible to ignore the potential impact of social media on mainstream political parties, just as it is not possible to ignore debates on the likely effects of artificial intelligence and computational thinking on the future of educational institutions, such as schools and universities. This is to say nothing about the possible effects of automatons and robots on the future of work. Investigating the extent to which social media, computational thinking, automation, and a range of related issues are linked with the most recent developments in the unfolding of FD is an immense subject that needs to be addressed in the sequel to the present study. It is clear, in terms of the main claims of this one, that FD has a history that has been overshadowed by the history of nations and states, and that FD is currently placing tremendous strains on what up until now have been the primary institutions of inclusion and integration. Moreover, there is a clearly discernible correlation between the intensification of differentiation processes and the widespread sense that communities and milieux are dissolving as the demands on people in late modern societies are multiplying and accelerating. In short, what was previously analysed as anomie or *Geworfenheit* may now in fact need to be re-examined with a new sociological focus.[10] The situation demands, moreover, that one does not fall prey to naturalistic fallacies or cybernetic fantasies about systemic self-steering that eliminate decision-making processes from consideration. For example, depending on the decisions structuring its internal constitution, an educational system can serve to provide citizens with different kinds of professional and intellectual training on an equal basis. But it also can be designed to entrench and exacerbate social inequality. Prisons and other correctional facilities can be constructed at determinate locations with the aim of taking advantage of anticipated high crime rates, amassing inmates, and thereby making profits, or they can be used to help rehabilitate people and give them the tools they will need upon leaving. Similar observations can be made about all social systems, including the crucially important economic, political, and legal systems. A new methodology is needed for an adequate understanding of the changes taking place in the dialectics of statehood/inclusion and of FD/specialised professionalisation. Part of what this entails is re-thinking the modalities of division, exclusion, non-identity, and difference; if these terms denote power and conflict, they also to some extent denote differentiation and autonomy. A contribution to meeting that challenge is attempted with the idea of socially constituted statehood looked at in the previous chapter, and the theory of societal constitutionalism examined in the next one.[11]

To the extent that law can now be analysed as a differentiated social system, one is confronted with an intricate political situation calling for a re-thinking of the sources of conflict and the various possible modes of conflict resolution within contemporary world society. The matter can be succinctly stated in the following terms: law is normally thought of as an integral part of a centralised state with a legally enforced monopoly on the legitimate use of force, and yet, at the same time, law is just one social system differentiated from all the other modern social systems, such as the economic, educational, political, and other systems. This is perhaps the most striking sociological corollary of the deconstruction of the mediated unity paradigm undertaken in chapter 1. The implications for prevailing notions of statehood, democracy, and citizenship have yet to be explored fully. Part of the complexity and confusion surrounding these issues relates to the argument about the partial politicisation of rights made in the previous chapter. One normally associates law with the legislature and the law-giving authority (in principle) of the demos, whilst also associating individual rights and justice with the courts and the judiciary. Although these processes pertain to distinct spheres of competence and knowledge, law and justice are both articulated in legal form, thus producing the appearance of mediated unity and a relatively high degree of centralisation. A closer look suggests that centralisation never means complete, vertically channelled, absolute centralisation. Similarly, differentiation never means categorically separated or hermetically sealed off. As emphasised at the start of chapter 1, literal interpretations can easily lead to misconceptions. The more fundamental historical issues concern the specific ways in which political power is centralised, the precise manner in which social systems are differentiated and coded, and the criteria according to which knowledge of codes and systems is established as knowledge, and demarcated from what are often taken to be extra-epistemological struggles over contestable interests and politicised values. Stated in these terms, one can see why it is important to consider existing and potentially alternative modalities of political centralisation in conjunction with existing and potentially alternative epistemological questions about systemic coding. It is clear that law, money, education, training, knowledge, politics, and power play some role in the workings of *each* social system. Yet it would be erroneous to deduce that individual social systems are states in miniature, or to believe that they function like regional states within the overarching nation state. Hegel shows that modern states are constituted with the express purpose of avoiding this scenario and the corruption and instability it brings in its wake. Luhmann and other systems theorists show that modern societies are constituted in ways that enable a specific social system, designated as the political system, to emerge and assume responsibility for the impersonal sharing and transfer of power, adjudicated on the basis of competitive elections. For Luhmann this means that the particular exercise of modern power deemed political is no longer subordinated to the whims and privileges of a family, class, or ethnic group. Whilst this can be considered rational and progressive according to fairly uncontroversial criteria, according to Luhmann and others it also means that officially recognised politics is pared down to the formal distinction between parties of government and parties of opposition.[12] More will be said below about the formalisation of politics and the simultaneous paring down of political knowledge to the instrumental knowledge of electoral strategy. The point for now is that within the parameters of world society, the distinction between incumbent and opposition parties guides the workings of political systems across states and national boundaries: systems do not start and cease to function in accordance with the arbitrary lines drawn by geographical borders. They can be thought of as polyvalent and dependent on their particular internal codes, which they use to organise and stabilise their operations, whilst also being dependent on their ability to read the information provided by the codes guiding the workings of neighbouring systems.[13] It is reasonable to believe that at some point in the near future, the institutions of normative integration around the world will have to deal with demands for political and other kinds of inclusion stemming from the global dynamics of systemic operations. These will be demands for inclusion into several systems at once, rather than demands for inclusion into a single nation or into a historically unique, territorially demarcated state. This could potentially transform rights claims from defensive demands for compensation into more affirmative claims relating to system-specific knowledge.[14]

Some systems theorists are adamant that social systems are closed and self-referential; other theorists maintain that systems can communicate with one another to varying degrees. A third model is suggested by the broad distinction between the lifeworld of communicative action and mutual understanding, and systemic imperatives directed by money and power.[15] Although there are notable differences between these approaches, all three mark significant departures from the models suggested by the simple private/public and state/society dichotomies. All three recognise the simplifications implied by the view that whilst modern states are democratic, modern societies are capitalist. All three, to different degrees, are willing to break with the assumption that thinking is an inherent and exclusive property of the *anthropos*. More pressing for the purposes of this chapter, however, is an illumination of the analogous tensions relating questions of political centralisation and social differentiation, on the one hand, with questions concerning different possible ways of positivising law, formalising knowledge, and coding systems, on the other. It would be far too schematic to imagine that whilst formal knowledge yields antagonistic inclusion (coercion), substantive knowledge might provide the bases of harmonious, successful integration (legitimacy). Yet when Adorno states that the critique of knowledge is social critique and vice versa, he intimates that the analogy is not completely speculative.[16]

As established in chapter 1, the political centralisation required for modern state building demands a series of constitutional separations and demarcations designating the mechanisms required for the sharing, controlling, and de-centralising of political power. Political centralisation could not be blindly centralist in view of the persistence of diverse religious worldviews, the emergence of autonomous scientific research bodies and learned societies, the proliferation of universities, the gradual separation of economic function and land ownership, as well as a great number of similar phenomena that can be seen as incipient stages in the unfolding of systemic differentiation processes. The stability and broadly speaking progressive patterns of rational normative integration achieved by post-feudal political centralisation happened within boundaries that are now by and large set by fixed geo-political realities.[17] This means that normative integration can no longer be repeated in tandem with territorial and administrative centralisation, as was the case during the early phases of post-feudal state building in Europe. States typically 'rewarded' individuals with rights of suffrage for their participation in wars and other violent means aimed at re-drawing territorial boundaries and seizing control of natural resources. Or individuals were integrated through dictatorial means, as happened in several European states during the interwar period of the twentieth century. Neither approach is viable for future practice. The normative and political tensions between administrative centralisation and social-systemic differentiation cannot be properly understood as questions of physical size or scale. Nor can they be grasped in terms of nation versus state or regional periphery versus main authority. Stated in these terms, the analogy between the discrepancy between political centralisation and social-systemic differentiation, on the one hand, and the discrepancy between formal and substantive knowledge, on the other, starts to seem less conjectural and speculative than it may have appeared at first glance. But in order to pursue this line of investigation fruitfully, it will be necessary to shift emphasis away from the juxtaposition of form and content/substance towards an analysis of the relation between form and function.

It is safe to say that questions of inclusion and exclusion will persist, and, at the same time, it would appear that there is no obvious way back to Keynesian economic management, steady expansion of the welfare state, or other means that were relatively successful in steering processes of integration in the recent past. The implication is that in order to confront the questions adequately which the dynamics of social-systemic expansion pose for normative integration, there will need to be a qualitative change in the relations between states and social systems, bearing in mind the non-identity of the state and the political system. The tensions pertaining to qualitative change in this regard are relevant to the dilemmas arising from a comparison between rival conceptualisations of the knowledge process. They are not, in other words, analogous to the tensions between the binary terms of foundational dialectics, such as those obtaining between subject and object or humanity and nature. Qualitative change will require new institutional forms that perform better than existing political systems currently do in response to demands for political inclusion. One can illustrate the point by examining the symmetries linking formal political inclusion (voting rights) with the imperative (strategy and 'common sense') to respect the systemic logic of parties of government versus parties of opposition as the only valid practical political knowledge appropriate for functionally differentiated societies. Clearly, however, this pared-down, instrumental knowledge is not the most appropriate or the only one available. Moreover, it is unlikely that pitting strategic politics against friend–enemy politics will illuminate anything fundamental about the political in functionally differentiated societies, just as, by extension, it is simplistic to juxtapose extra-normative social systems with democratically ratified political norms. The far more pertinent questions include the following: (a) under what conditions can the political system be re-coded in order to communicate better with other social systems, and (b) to what extent do social systems already communicate with each other, rather than with the state? Until one has at least approximate answers, one will not be in a position to assess accurately what neoliberalism signifies in socio-economic, legal, political, educational, and cultural terms.[18] One will be left inconclusively wondering whether neoliberalism is the result of a series of deliberate decisions to make sure that integration stops at party competition and electoral strategy, or whether formal political inclusion is always also post-political exclusion within the framework largely defined by modern Western rationalisation and Christian humanism.[19] It is therefore plausible to argue that the key epistemological tension is not that between formal versus substantive knowledge. It has more to do with the project to re-form conceptual and social constitutional processes of formalisation without confusing abstract, antagonistic, impersonal form with rigorous form. An exploration of theses issues could shift the boundaries that continue to define dominant methodological paradigms in a variety of fields, thus indicating new ways of thinking about qualitative reform. In other words, it may be possible to change the ways in which law, money, education, training, knowledge, politics, and power function in the workings of each social system, rather than demanding the abolition of law and money or passively accepting the way they currently function. Kant offers a pertinent point of departure for exploring these issues further.

Concepts, institutions, and historically contingent social-systemic codes

Kantian philosophy meditates on the non-identity of our knowledge of nature and events, which is dependent upon the subjective, human organisation that knowledge takes in consciousness and concepts, and the absolute, noumenal apprehension of nature and events that might in principle yield metaphysical knowledge of the 'things in themselves', if the latter could somehow be known without the mediating function of conceptual form. The concept of non-identity is relevant here because it denotes a relation that is not simply akin to a discrepancy, say, such as that between formal political inclusion and socio-economic inequality. Nor is it comparable to the different markers spaced along the various points of a continuum, such as those which in principle range from inequality to equality. Dialectical or mediated non-identity is not a means of achieving identity, unity, or order, as much as it is a way of thinking about the dynamics of institutional form and qualitative change without resorting to faith in historical progress or wishful thinking about the potential consequences of party political leadership changes. Given that his ideas on this topic have continuing political resonance well beyond academic debates about epistemology, there is much at stake when considering different possible responses to Kant and the questions he directly or indirectly raises in relation to what might be referred to as the impossibility of metaphysical essence and the reality of form. Academics and activists continue to think about how best to contend with the implicitly juridical claim that just as our knowledge is held in check by certain objective limits that lie outside of subjective control and manipulation, rationally exercised freedom presupposes objective institutional constraints. The latter can be seen to serve a dual purpose: whilst they safeguard against the subjugation of the individual citizen by the state, they integrate the citizen into a political community of rights-bearing equals. It is asserted, by extension, that humanity's capacity to institutionalise justice and legitimacy is also limited. In a post-feudal context, it is apparently limited by the codes and logic imposed by specific instances of political statehood and FD. The corollary claim is that these limits compel us to renounce any kind of re-coupling of justice and knowledge or of knowledge and legitimacy, since re-coupling of this kind would amount to reactionary de-differentiation, dogma, and obscurantism. Strictly speaking, FD dictates that whereas knowledge is attainable in fields of scientific research, law and politics operate according to an altogether different set of codes. But what would be the implications if one were somehow to posit political statehood and FD as incontestable constants, and then to deduce, from Kantian or approximately Kantian premises, that initially liberalism and now neoliberalism represent the natural and by and large only feasible responses to the challenge of governing legally and rationally within the said limits? One would be left with the virtually incontrovertible conclusion that neoliberal parties are the naturally governing parties of stable democratic states operating within societies that are functionally differentiated, to varying degrees, according to the patterns bequeathed by post-feudal statehood. Without commenting here on the prospects of the authoritarian neoliberalism of Trump and Marine Le Pen, one would also be forced to accept that some parties are condemned to perennial opposition. Once the issue is stated in these terms, one is entitled to ask if social democracy is in fact becoming a party of perennial opposition – and possible extinction – in the light of neoliberal hegemony.[20]

At any rate the 'Copernican Revolution' seems to pit formal knowledge and rationally distributed negative liberty against metaphysical mysticism and political adventurism. It also seems to invoke the legislative precedence of procedural consistency over the temptations of irresponsibly libertarian or potentially authoritarian experiment. In this context, two issues are particularly relevant to the central themes of this book and have already been touched upon at different stages. The first comes in the guise of an incipient politico-epistemological project to be discussed in greater detail in the next chapter. It is a project aimed at reforming existing constitutional frameworks currently guiding inter-systemic mediation, rather than projecting beyond any such framework into an informal, extra-systemic realm of unmediated democratic agency, or uncritically embracing ostensibly new manifestations of collective subjectivity that may seem to have no need of checks, balances, and related mechanisms for the dividing and sharing of power. Part of what that discussion in this and the next chapter entails is analysing existing patterns of inter-systemic mediation and investigating which particular instances are casually assumed to be inherently insusceptible, for allegedly scientific reasons, to modification and re-coding. It is often alleged in this regard that

attempts to enact qualitative reform are dangerous because they supposedly tamper with quasi-natural boundaries that are said to have evolved over
centuries, or that they flout universal anthropological realities of human and
social communication.[21] The categorisation of competent parties of government and suspicious parties of perennial opposition can be analysed as an
indirect consequence of enforcing these formal and informal rules. The second comes in the guise of a moment of doubt about the prospects for substantive knowledge and positive liberty. These are closely related issues that
can be taken up in terms of the following question: how might it be possible to provide a sociological methodological corrective to the widespread
tendency to assume that there is a natural fit between formal knowledge
and negative freedom? It may not be possible to do so in absolute terms as
the perfect reconciliation of concept/reality and humanity/nature that Hegel
may have had in mind. But it might at least be possible to adjust the existing boundaries between currently dominant institutional form and potentially
more elastic, responsive institutional form. Otherwise it will seem almost
certain that legitimacy and justice definitely exist, but cannot be known or
experienced beyond quantitatively measured electoral compromise and iterative procedure, or other than as the trace of absent legitimacy and justice in
this world. The attempt to displace existing boundaries shifts emphasis away
from the increasingly outmoded categories of left versus right, growth versus
stagnation, and so on, towards potentially far more fruitful debates about
the chances for systemic re-coding and inter-systemic re-coupling. Although
outdated in several respects, Hegel's critique of Kant and Marx's thoughts on
Hegel are still highly pertinent in this regard.

Hegel's theory of objective spirit is characterised by an unusual kind of
conservative utopianism that is seized upon by Marx and the Young Hegelians.
Marx takes Hegel to be saying that consciousness and society are in fact
evolving in a direction that is working towards overcoming formal conceptual
as well as socio-political dichotomies. He thinks Hegel thus provides a key
socio-historical corrective to Kant by noting that consciousness evolves historically, rather than naturally, haphazardly, or even purely logically, and that
concepts develop in conjunction with battles for religious and political freedom, as these unfold in conjunction with discernible patterns of state formation. In so doing, he reckons that Hegel reminds readers that our knowledge
of nature and events is inseparable from the dialectic between human subjectivity and institutional objectivity in the guise of individual rights, property
ownership, forms of state, and so on. The breakthrough thus achieved, which
acts as a caution against reification whilst also pointing towards Simmel's
sociology of social forms, is that institutional objectivity concerns manifold
relations between people and practices, rather than inventories of static

things, lifeless objects, or the numerical results of competitions of various kinds. Marx intuits that as a consequence of this pluralistic dynamism, felicitous changes in the life of institutions can change consciousness and thereby pave the way for radical conceptual innovation and a transition from formal to substantial knowledge. He believes that this transition could be the key to the transformation of subjectivity and the transcendence of negative liberty and weak dialectical modes of legitimacy. Mediation, in other words, is as much a question of institutional form as it is a question of conceptual form. Transcendence, in Hegelian-Marxist terms, means preserving the truth content of negative liberty and weak dialectics whilst simultaneously enhancing them. In other words, transcendence is not a simple instance of negation or abolition, as was largely the case with individual liberty in the former USSR. The key point for the present study is that analyses of mediated unity and mediated non-identity usually play a very minor role in most academic studies of the tensions between political centralisation, FD, social-systemic coding, and the division of powers; expert knowledge of these tensions is often assumed to be the exclusive domain of academic historians, political scientists, constitutional lawyers, and professional politicians. Whereas Hegel is wary of projects to accelerate the reconciliation of concepts and actual social life, Marx and his followers are confident that patterns of conflict are changing in ways that will lead to a reciprocal adjustment of subjective consciousness and the active capacity of a politically organised collective subject to revolutionise objective social reality. On his reading, socio-historical reality activates humanity's potential to emancipate itself from ignorance and oppression, that is, it is decidedly not reality that stands in the way of emancipation in a manner analogous to the way that original sin is sometimes thought to stand in the way of freedom and happiness. As he famously says in the eleventh of his *Theses on Feuerbach*, the dialectical nuances of form and content affecting knowledge and society are less important than the concrete project to change the world.[22]

First-generation critical theory may at times appear to be unduly pessimistic about the prospects for the kinds of revolutionary change imagined by Marx, his followers, and a great many other activists in search of a broadly speaking left-Hegelian solution to the problem of the Kantian dichotomies that does not culminate in coerced reconciliation.[23] This is partially explainable by the fact that critical theory was initially articulated in response to the debacle of Marxist theory in Soviet practice, and the failures of a number of avant-garde aesthetic projects, such as Dada and surrealism, for example, to move beyond liberal democracy by synthesising the spheres of aesthetic experience, political organisation, and pedagogical experimentation. Admittedly, the aesthetic avant-garde of this period rarely, if ever, took seriously the proposal that this synthesis could be accomplished through radical constitutional reform, thus avoiding coerced reconciliation. From a more contemporary perspective bearing in mind the broad analogies between the Kantian dichotomies and differentiation processes, it could be countered that this ostensible failure actually testifies to the qualified autonomy of art in modern society. If that is to a certain extent correct, it holds out the promise of an aesthetic social system steered by codes that elude the colonising tendencies of neighbouring systems, especially the one now largely steered by the sanctioning, antagonistic code of in/ability to pay. Anticipating some of the themes in the next chapter, it can be noted that depending on the constitutional modalities of their mediation, the apparently contrasting demands of systemic autonomy and inter-systemic communication might cease to be adjudicated as defensively poised environments.[24]

The crisis of democracy during the interwar decades of the twentieth century gives first-generation critical theory a palpably defensive quality; it is not difficult to detect a qualified appreciation of some of the Kantian dimensions of liberal democracy on the part of its most prominent exponents. In keeping with this, first-generation critical theorists sometimes appear to share a certain methodological stringency in matters of epistemology and social enquiry that one can find in J. S. Mill and other unusual liberals and unorthodox thinkers such as Kierkegaard, Nietzsche, Simmel, Schönberg, and a bit later, Theunissen.[25] At first glance one may be warranted in discerning common features linking the critical theory of this time with other approaches to the study of society that may seem politically suspect, or at any rate conservative. There is nonetheless a crucial difference between first- and even second-generation critical theory, on the one hand, and neoliberal apologies for austerity, privatisation, and extensive outsourcing today, on the other. Ostensibly, critical theory and neoliberalism are wary of strong dialectical modes of legitimacy, positive conceptions of liberty, and all instances of collective subjectivity that appear to foster oppressive inclusion rather than consensual integration. It would seem that both currents are united in opposing projects that harm individuals by putting an arguably arbitrary conception of the good before the right. One of the important differences, however, is that the conceptual arguments and material interests in support of embedded neoliberalism tend on the whole to a selective ignoring of dialectics. The exponents of austerity deny that there might ever be systemic re-coding and inter-systemic re-coupling in the senses used here. To this extent, neoliberalism perpetuates a dogmatic ideological tendency to naturalise and absolutise the markedly hierarchical structures of normative integration particular to early liberal democratic society (or what is often imagined to have been liberal democratic society during a highly circumscribed historical period) in various parts of Europe and North

America sometime before the putative onslaught of mass society and the supposed populist degeneration of politics. Those very unique conditions are typically elevated to the status of trans-historical realities about the failures of human nature, the limits of knowledge and human freedom, and the proper relations between citizens and authority. It has already been remarked that European states of that earlier epoch typically rewarded individuals with rights of suffrage for their participation in wars and other violent means aimed at re-drawing territorial boundaries and securing access to natural resources. States may have de-colonised since then, but the institutions of citizenship and statehood continue to be enmeshed in a variety of bio-political discourses and practices that have been intensified by neoliberal regimes to different degrees. Neoliberal governance does not really safeguard the right before the good. It tends instead to advance an arguably arbitrary conception of the right, presented as formal epistemological neutrality and procedural consistency, and to conflate the right and the good. In so doing, it steadfastly attempts to reject all rival conceptions of the right or the good. The methodological caveat offered at the start of chapter 2 remains relevant here: it is not being suggested that neoliberalism is a sorcerer with powers to manipulate knowledge and concentrate power in its hands. Ascertaining the degree to which one historically documented model of FD has eclipsed other possible models is much more important.[26]

The discussion in this chapter so far indicates that under the socio-historical conditions yielded by politically constituted statehood and the ongoing legacy of its imperialist past, the theoretical validity of such claims to neutral objectivity is weakened. These conditions raise questions about the ability to achieve consistently neutral form in conceptual and institutional terms, unless, that is, patterns of intra-systemic constitution and inter-systemic mediation are substantially reformed. The claims are weakened empirically by some of the clearly dysfunctional workings of typically neoliberal policies in higher education, labour markets, financial markets, environmental preservation, and health. More convincingly still, such arguments will be theoretically and empirically discredited if it can be shown that neoliberal governance helps create natural parties of government whilst also attempting dogmatically to prohibit social-systemic re-coding (see pp. 153–158). Dogma and inflexibility cannot be confused with methodological stringency, however much neoliberal doctrine may seem to enjoy the pedigree of Hayek and similarly oriented 'philosophical' economists. Whilst the method may be methodologically stringent according to certain economic criteria, it is sociologically deficient in a number of ways that indicate that FD and classical macroeconomics are by no means synonymous. Neoliberal doctrine often proceeds from the premise that any attempt to adjust the structure of inter-systemic mediations will be disastrous in practice, because it will inevitably fail to respect the logical and analytical postulates demonstrating the impossibility of fusing what should be and really are discrete instances of power, knowledge, specialised competence, and authority.[27] One can analyse this supposed undesirability of fusion with reference to the Kantian dichotomies, the reality of form, and the dynamics of conceptual and institutional innovation alluded to above. Key for the purposes of this study is awareness of the need to caution against conflating the reality of form with the unconditional dismissal of the possibility of new, dialectically supple institutional forms that respect the political-normative refusal of reconciliation under duress. The reality of form seems to favour a neoliberal approach to presiding over the functioning of FD because the alternative, at first glance, would seem to be dogmatic essence and authoritarian fusion of distinct entities. As indicated in chapter 1, in other words, liberal and neoliberal conceptions of knowledge, power, and the best ways of limiting power typically rely on dialectical arguments that are rarely stated in explicitly dialectical terms. Hence the most stringent counter-arguments will be able to highlight the ways in which hegemonic ideas could be developed in directions that are disclosed by certain kinds of hegemonic practice and dialectical possibility, yet simultaneously dismissed as utopian or authoritarian at the level of official discourse. The project to reform mediation processes is distinct from a project to fuse individuals and social systems or a forlorn attempt to reconstruct mediated unity. The effort to formulate a better and more complete theorisation of mediated non-identity is an important part of the struggle to achieve consistently neutral conceptual form. The preceding pages indicate that there is no way to do this without reference to critical theoretical and empirical sociology.

In more colloquial terms that seem like sound common sense, it is reasonable to believe that civil servants and other non-elected officials should not foist economic plans on the citizenry, governments should not tell journalists what they should write, spiritual leaders should not be allowed to transform debates about science and medicine into debates about religious truth, judges should not be intimidated by political parties, military leaders should not be in charge of political decisions, and so on. Hence it is frequently asserted that an extensive division of labour, separation of powers, and protection of individual rights is necessary to ensure that power is shared and that the authority to make legitimate decisions is distributed according to professional qualification. There is nothing ideological or inherently elitist about this claim. On the contrary: the critical theory elaborated in this book, which seeks to provide impetus for the emergence of the third generation, analyses arguments in favour of checks and balances and related constitutional provisions for holding power accountable to democratic control and ensuring, where applicable, that the exercise of power is subject to the control of citizens with the appropriate training. The book seeks to disentangle these arguments from those which, although they may also be expounded in the name of constitutional law, democratic politics, and preventative measures against authoritarian fusions, have become reliant on fixed ways of thinking about what are assumed to be the respective tasks of the economy, law, education, scientific research, politics, and so on in complex democratic societies in the twenty-first century. Stringent critical theory today therefore exhibits a wariness of premature reconciliation and coerced integration that is also salient in the writings of prominent liberal democratic thinkers and some of their Reformation precursors. But as the explanations offered in the current book illustrate, the fixation in question often encourages us to forget that definitions of appropriate competence and demarcations of systemic boundaries vary according to historical epoch and that social-systemic codes result in part from concrete decisions that can be overturned, adjusted, and recalibrated.

The critiques of instrumentally mediated unity, inconclusively post-feudal statehood, and highly selective FD offered here are not developed for the sake of polemical demands for something simplistic like 'reconciliation and solidarity now'. They are developed instead in order to show that prevailing notions of mediated unity, post-feudal nation-statehood, and post-feudal FD offer historically specific rather than timeless examples of how constitutional provisions might be enlisted to hold power accountable to democratic control and to ensure that the exercise of power is subject to the control of expert knowledge, guided by the appropriate systemic codes – especially when social evolution demands that the latter evolve in new directions. The critiques are also developed in order to show how constitutionally enforced austerity and other concrete examples of selective FD *are* authoritarian fusions in their own right. Many of these cases are in fact manifestations of the kinds of systemic de-differentiations against which constitutional law and democratic politics are in theory meant to safeguard in the name of the precedence of the right before the good.[28] Notions of rights and constitutions are normally associated with the so-called 'bourgeois revolutions' in Britain, the United States, and France in the seventeenth and the eighteenth century. There is a convincing critical-theoretical interpretation of the history and possible future development of FD, social systems and constitutional innovation that breaks with the premises and practice of the transhistorical model. That alternative cannot be outlined until the problems with this model are explored in detail. The rest of this chapter contributes to that exposition by developing a response to the claim that politicisation of the economy infringes upon FD whilst jeopardising the separation of powers and the neutrality of justice.

The autonomy of law and the independence of the judiciary: on the possibilities for planning in the late modern economy

Weber and Simmel provide complementary sociological translations of the Kantian dichotomies. Both thinkers are acutely sensitive to the paradoxes accompanying the logic of means and ends in a wide variety of distinct yet related social contexts in which nation states strive for stable modes of post-feudal integration. Whereas Hegel is able to declare confidently that the modern state is mind objectified, Weber has little doubt that it is a monopoly on the legitimate use of force within a given territory. In the light of this reality, he thinks one is best advised to understand the European state in terms of the largely apolitical means at its disposal, rather than in terms of the political ends it might in principle represent. Whilst Weber highlights the discrepancy between the ideal of substantive reason and the glaring realities of ubiquitous rationalisation, Simmel analyses the drifting apart of subjective and objective culture. Simmel intimates that the division of labour and other factors make it almost impossible to know the real value of the goods, services, and works of art that humans produce. Anticipating the analyses of Benjamin and the Frankfurt School, Simmel notes that drifting apart in this sense is not simply alienation or estrangement; it helps produce a wide variety of new social forms and unprecedented opportunities for individuals to step outside of traditionally assigned roles. This enables them to forge new values, exercise hitherto untested practices of autonomy in the city, and create audacious works of unconventional art. At the same time, however, the public institutional mediations between subjective and objective culture – especially those between law, politics, aesthetics, and the economy – visibly wane. Under these conditions, 'objective' increasingly tends to mean objectified, crudely quantified, and – anticipating Lukács, Heidegger, and others – misunderstood.[29] It is not difficult to see the parallels between Simmel's theory of social differentiation, Lukács's ideas on reification and false consciousness, and Heidegger's phenomenological account of present-to-hand modalities of subject/object relations. Yet it is also clear that when it comes to analysing the complexities and normative challenges facing late modern states and societies, Simmel is incomparably better positioned than much of first-generation critical theory, Western Marxism, and the exponents of fundamental ontology. His stress on the sociology of mutually interactive reciprocal exchange and social communication enables him to dispense with foundational dialectics in their weak and strong articulations, as well as with non-dialectical

appeals to authentic *Dasein* and national communities of fate.[30] Prefiguring
the systems-theoretical understanding of FD, Simmel points out that one
can study and understand the economic processes that produce objects
and services of value, but there is no longer any way to measure real value
effectively, beyond the quantitative measure of homogeneous monetary
units that effectively dissolve essential qualitative differences. It is almost
as if actual value becomes a thing in itself that is surely there, but, like the
thing-in-itself, cannot be known, save in formal terms.[31]

The main point is that Weber and Simmel can be seen as thinkers who highlight the affinities between instrumental reason and one historically contingent
and now dominant instantiation of statehood and FD. They show that, far from
being an inferior or degenerate form of substantive reason or the systemic
threat to the integrity of the lifeworld, instrumental reason corresponds neatly –
indeed, almost constitutionally – with the currently hegemonic modalities of
FD, prevailing institutional form, and existing systemic codes.[32] In *Politics as a
Vocation*, Weber draws attention to one of the notable paradoxes involved in
the differentiation of law, politics, economics, science, art, and education later
taken up by systems theorists. One consequence of the disparity between
apolitical means and political ends is that 'political' parties are called upon to
make use of means largely derived from the repertoire of economic competition, especially generic slogans and advertising, in order to defend the ostensibly universal ends of citizenship, such as freedom and equality. That is, at one
level politics and economics appear to be differentiated. Just as political power
in modern society has been detached from notions of divine right and religious
belief, one cannot directly buy political office, nor can one sell one's vote. At
another level, Weber points out, parties act like firms in a competitive market,
attempting to attract all potential political customers, and therefore adopting
populist strategies to expand their target audiences.[33] As a consequence, it can
be argued that just as instrumental reason prevails over potential rival models
for sociological rather than pathological or purely anthropological reasons, populist politics are partially explainable in terms of the structure of political communication demanded by distinct patterns of state formation and social-systemic
articulation that affect structures of collective bargaining and individual thinking.[34] The model of FD predominating in Western Europe and other parts of the
world can therefore be said to be formally differentiated in somewhat inconclusive and ambiguous ways that also create possibilities for the formal as well
as informal rapprochement of the differentiated systems in question. There are
a number of different ways of understanding these informal re-coupling processes. Theoretical and empirical evidence suggests that informal re-coupling
often coincides with projects to de-differentiate social systems as part of a
plan to bail out banks, enforce austerity, and implement financialisation as the

dominant mode of social communication and, by extension, of inter-systemic mediation. Interventionist steering persists precisely because social systems are not consistently autopoietic and self-steering – it is important not to confuse such strategic planning with contingency even if, at times, it looks like no one is in charge of what is going on, and the results are far from optimal. But steering usually assumes the guise of ostensibly apolitical managerial expertise, articulated in discourses of technocratic progress, and presented as rational responses to what are taken to be the realities of global competition. These realities are in turn defined by mainstream think tanks, rating agencies, and apparatuses of global governance in ways that legitimate specific decisions on how best to deploy scarce human, investment, and environmental resources.[35]

Why do these phenomena lead to the seemingly inescapable conclusion that stable, functionally differentiated societies with democratic states are characterised by the dominance of parties and coalitions of parties that manage to occupy the political centre from ideological positions slightly to the left or right of that figurative centre? Since it would be naïvely empiricist to suppose that centrist parties enjoy electoral success because the majority of voters hold moderate views, a different line of enquiry is required. There is a more incisive question, which is indirectly posed by Weber and Simmel and only tangentially taken up by Hegel and Marx. How and why have many modern societies been functionally differentiated in specific ways that make it virtually impossible to democratise the economy without oppressively centralising political power, reversing FD, and forfeiting the independence of the judiciary? An investigation into electoral behaviour that does not ask this second question will not be able to shed much light on the phenomenon of centrist voting, populism, or political alienation. When asking either of these two questions it is important to bear in mind that the formal constitutional separation of powers is only really conducive to political legitimacy and social stability when it is complemented by a series of informal institutional equilibria touching upon processes of political will formation and vital questions of education and occupational life chances. Informal re-coupling can and indeed now often tends to be used to implement financialisation and marketisation as the dominant modes of social communication and inter-systemic mediation. It will be seen in the next chapter that there is no objective reason why this must be the case, and that it is possible to rethink informal re-coupling and other means of re-orienting inter-systemic mediation in ways that could significantly alter the patterns of communication between key social systems. It may well be that Hegel was too schematic in his assessment of the dialectic of consciousness and institutional change, and too optimistic in his belief that the state responds adequately to the dysfunctional conflicts in civil society.

Simmel's analyses indicate that there is a plurality of dialectics and social forms that help shape the specific kinds of FD that are able to emerge in any particular context; in the process, potentially rival models of FD are variously affirmed as inevitable, casually ignored, or ruled out as unfeasible, undesirable, or unconstitutional. A certain degree of contingency and Machiavellian *virtù* does come into play in this regard. It is in any event extremely unlikely that a jarring imbalance of power in society can be compensated for and held in check by a stable balance of legislative, judicial, and executive powers at the level of the state. This question is all the more urgent today, when social democratic parties and trade unions everywhere are seemingly incapable of supplying the key components of the equilibrium sustaining the compromise often described as the post-war consensus. To the extent that these formerly key components become incapable of maintaining that equilibrium, the political centre will struggle to function as a stabilising foundation empowered to legitimise electoral results. It is likely that this in turn will severely strain relations between legislative, executive, and judicial branches of government.[36]

But perhaps a great deal that still needs to be explained is peremptorily bracketed out of the discussion if one accepts that each and every project to democratise the economy will end up centralising political power whilst also forfeiting the independence of the judiciary. For a start, it has already been established at the outset of this chapter that (1) political power *is* centralised in key respects, thus raising questions concerning the extent to which it is centralised in ways that make it virtually impossible to democratise the economy without overburdening it with what would appear to be extra-economic demands for equality and diverse kinds of social inclusion, and (2) law, money, education, training, knowledge, politics, and power play some role in the workings of *each* social system – why else would one speak of fiscal policy and labour market politics? The claim that systems must not be allowed to burden each other with their mutually illegible communications is thereby undermined. This is a somewhat complex matter; it is not being suggested that political centralisation has unfolded in this unwieldy manner as a result of fate, conspiracies, or arbitrary decisions on the part of an executive committee entrusted with the task of managing the affairs of the entire bourgeoisie, as Marx and Engels quip in 1848. Here a possibly difficult objection could be raised: it is scarcely possible to undo the historical processes that continue to make it difficult for the political system to read demands for economic democracy and equality as anything other than what systems theorists refer to as irritations or second-order observations carried out from the perspective of contingently circulated social information. But it is worth noting that whilst some extra-economic demands are permitted to steer the economy at crucial junctures, others are dismissed by the leading organisations of global governance as oppressively centralist or irresponsibly speculative. It has already been noted that commercial agreements between global non-state actors can have a tremendous influence on the financing of public deficits. The sanctity of privately negotiated decisions is constantly invoked by elites to forestall Keynesian and other approaches to questions of growth and the sharing of social burdens. There may be a decline in class politics and union militancy, but the question of how to finance public deficits looms larger than ever. Hence steering persists, as does selective systemic re-coupling. Just as it seems to make sense that political systems should not be overloaded with extra-political inputs, opposition to the decisive treaties invariably looks to be the lamentable protest of the weak and indebted countries against the strong and financially stable ones.[37]

It has also been established (3) that to the extent that social systems are differentiated but nonetheless continue to communicate with each other, social-systemic *differentiation* is always also a form of social-systemic *unity*, albeit not union, fusion, or organic bonding. This point explains the reference to paradox in the title of this chapter, and illuminates the notion that various social systems interact within each social system. A word of caution may be in order, in that the terminological emphasis on the simultaneity of differentiation and unity can easily deflect attention from the fact that the key semantic term in this context is *form*. In this case it is an instance of form that often encourages observers to think of unity as harmony, whilst also thinking of difference and differentiation as fractured unity and conflict. This is understandable, but neither historically accurate nor sociologically inevitable. As Weber and Simmel indicate, political power in liberal democratic states is centralised in specific institutions that coincide with the fact that parties working within those states are compelled to compete for power rather than to transform society. Indeed, any unmediated attempt at transformation in this sense will rightly be perceived as a regression of the law to command and a corresponding violation of individual rights. Changing fixed patterns of inter-systemic mediation therefore becomes a key issue. Since law, money, education, training, knowledge, politics, and power play some role in the workings of each social system, critical theorists do not demand the abolition of law and money. They ask instead how the form and function of law, money, educational training, and politics could be reformed. In the previous paragraph it is suggested that a political system constituted to produce government coalitions and opposition parties may work well when there are countervailing social alliances. The same system is likely to enter into crisis if it is widely perceived that professional politicians are becoming increasingly skilled in the business of gaining access to power whilst also losing contact with the needs of people and everyday life in educational, economic, and other systems. Phrased somewhat differently, there is nothing essentially democratic about a basic minimum income, properly funded social services, equal access to education, workers' councils in industry, or other attempts to democratise the economy through training, redistribution, or horizontally structured decision-making processes at work. It is conceivable that an authoritarian state might make this official policy, thus casting doubt on the quality of the training and the real power of the organs of industrial democracy. There is, however, something essentially anti-democratic about saying that all of these measures are by definition incompatible with the autonomy of the political and justice systems and therefore illegal, that is, virtually criminal. Here the currently hegemonic institutionalisation of the relation between law and democracy places them at manifest odds – but not for the reasons that Schmitt supposes. From a systems-theoretical perspective in search of a tentative alignment with critical theory, the terms 'democracy' and 'state' convey something about the quality of the unity – and simultaneous separation – of the legal, economic, educational, and political systems. Although such a perspective might share certain aspects of Schmitt's scepticism about the feasibility of pure procedure and the sanctity of legal norms, it dispenses with Schmitt's populist conception of democratic essence. It is in fact simplistic to demand the suspension of law in the name of the integrity of politics and democracy, just as it is misleading to say that constitutional limits on democracy and equality are the just price to pay for the autonomy of the judiciary. These reflections should thus invite observers to reflect on the precise nature of the autonomy of the judiciary in late modern states, before concluding that juridical autonomy would automatically be forfeited by a democratisation of the economy – no matter how one imagines this.

Notes

1 On the specific case of Brexit, see the chapters contained in William Outhwaite (ed.), *Brexit: Sociological Responses* (London: Anthem Press, 2017). Each of the contributions in that volume singles out distinct moments in the reorganisation of the relations between states, international governance, and transnational law. See in particular Chris Thornhill, 'A Tale of Two Constitutions: Whose Legitimacy, Whose Crisis?', in William Outhwaite (ed.), *Brexit: Sociological Responses* (London: Anthem Press, 2017), pp. 77–89, and Harry F. Dahms, 'Critical Theory, Brexit, and the Vicissitudes of Political Economy in the Twenty-First Century', in William Outhwaite (ed.), *Brexit: Sociological Responses* (London: Anthem Press, 2017), pp. 183–92. For a good analysis of the theoretical lessons to be drawn from the period linking the demise of the Bretton Woods agreements during the course of the 1970s to the ratification of the Maastricht Treaty in 1992, see Luca Frontini, *Moneta e impero* (Fermo: Zefiro SRL, 2016), pp. 66–7.
2 Niklas Luhmann, *Das Recht der Gesellschaft* (Frankfurt: Suhrkamp, 1993), p. 582, available in English as *Law as a Social System* (Oxford: Oxford University Press, 2004), pp. 487–8. According to a standard systems-theoretical view of these

dynamics, functionally differentiated societies do not actively exclude groups or individuals in the ways that segmented and stratified societies often do. The implication is that exclusion occurs on the basis of inadequate inclusion, and not, directly at any rate, as part of a strategy to target explicitly designated people or groups. To be more precise, it is unique to functionally differentiated societies that exclusion occurs as a result of social communication that is coded according to binary distinctions that fail adequately to integrate; exclusion results from faulty inclusion, rather than as a consequence of a consciously formulated plan to exclude. Stated in these terms, one can see why a purely systems-theoretical view of society tends to be somewhat conservative. Binary codes are explained as a response to complexity and contingency, rather than as deliberate racism or sexism. Although systems theory has a great deal to offer in terms of analysing FD, it lacks a critical edge when it comes to social conflict and questions of power. This point is developed with admirable clarity by Kolja Möller, 'Das Ganze der konstituierenden Macht', in Kolja Möller and Jasmin Siri (eds), *Systemtheorie und Gesellschaftskritik: Perspektiven der Kritischen Systemtheorie* (Bielefeld: Transcript, 2016), pp. 39–56, and by Sina Farzin, *Inklusion/ Exklusion: Entwicklungen und Probleme einer systemtheoretischen Unterscheidung* (Bielefeld: Transcript, 2006), pp. 100–102.

3 Hegel, *Grundlinien*, p. 339 (addition to paragraph 182), available in English as *Philosophy of Right*, pp. 220–1. It could be argued that his emphasis on self-limiting self-steering in civil society makes him an early exponent of societal constitutionalism.

4 Some theorists see parties and party systems as sub-systems of the political system. This understanding of that relation does not fully clarify the relation between the political system and the state, however. For an exploration of the theoretical and institutional issues involved, see Gunther Teubner, 'Polykorporatismus: Der Staat als Netzwerk öffentlicher und privater Kollektivakteure', in Hauke Brunkhorst and Peter Niesen (eds), *Das Recht der Republik. Festschrift für Ingeborg Maus* (Frankfurt: Suhrkamp, 1999), pp. 346–72; and Hans-Georg Moeller, *The Radical Luhmann* (New York: Columbia University Press, 2012), chapter 3.

5 Once could even include Gramsci's notion of common sense as one of the informal registers with an impact on constitutional arrangements in complex societies. See Mason, 'Corbyn's victory', and Dieter Grimm, *Die Zukunft der Verfassung II: Auswirkungen von Europäisierung und Globalisierung* (Frankfurt: Suhrkamp, 2012), pp. 36–64.

6 Chris Thornhill, *A Sociology of Transnational Constitutions: Social Foundations of the Post-National Legal Structure* (Cambridge: Cambridge University Press, 2016), chapter 5.

7 Bob Jessop is one of the first theorists fruitfully to combine the perspectives of Gramsci and Luhmann in the study of state building. See Jessop, *State Theory*, Parts III and IV. Jessop does a brilliant job of supplementing Gramsci and Luhmann with select elements of regulation school theory.

8 These issues have been taken up by a large number of distinguished scholars. Prominent amongst them are Berman, *Law and Revolution*; Brunkhorst, *Critical Theory of Legal Revolutions*; Andrew Linklater, *Violence and Civilization in the Western States-Systems* (Cambridge: Cambridge University Press, 2016); Peter H. Wilson, *The Holy Roman Empire: A Thousand Years of Europe's History* (London: Allen Lane, 2016); Emanuele Castrucci, *On the Idea of Potency: Juridical and Theological Roots of the Western Cultural Tradition* (Edinburgh: Edinburgh University Press, 2016); and Gil Anidjar, *Blood: A Critique of Christianity* (New York: Columbia University Press, 2014).

9 Luhmann, *Gesellschaft der Gesellschaft*, p. 893, available in English as *Theory of Society*, Vol. II, pp. 183–4.

10 David Berry and Anders Fagerjord examine the impact of computational thinking in David M. Berry and Anders Fagerjord, *Digital Humanities: Knowledge and Critique in a Digital Age* (Cambridge: Polity Press, 2017), chapters 3–4. On the relation between FD and the sense of accelerated temporal rhythms, see Hartmut Rosa, 'The speed of global flows and the pace of democratic politics', *New Political Science*, 27 (2005), 445–59. Readers of German with an interest in this subject should consult the chapters contained in Klaus Dörre, Stephan Lessenich, and Hartmut Rosa, *Soziologie – Kapitalismus – Kritik: Eine Debatte* (Frankfurt: Suhrkamp, 2009).

11 Class, race, gender, the Global South, age, and other categories will all retain their usefulness in this endeavour. The importance of age in the British parliamentary election of June 2017 suggests that this will continue to be the case for the foreseeable future. But critical theory can make a contribution to understanding how and why certain modalities of difference and exclusion assume the form of class, race, gender, and so on. On this topic see Anastasia Marinopoulou, *Critical Theory and Epistemology: The Politics of Modern Thought and Science*, Critical Theory and Contemporary Society (Manchester: Manchester University Press, 2017).

12 Luhmann, *Die Politik der Gesellschaft*, pp. 215–20, *Ausdifferenzierung des Rechts: Beiträge zur Rechtssoziologie und Rechtstheorie* (Frankfurt: Suhrkamp, 1981), pp. 149–52, and *Recht der Gesellschaft*, pp. 420–1, available in English as *Law as a Social System*, p. 367.

13 Gunther Teubner, 'Global Bukowina: Legal Pluralism in the World Society', in Gunther Teubner (ed.), *Global Law without a State* (Aldershot: Dartmouth, 1997), pp. 3–30, also available in Teubner, *Critical Theory and Legal Autopoiesis*.

14 By definition one cannot join a blood-based nation at will. Strangely, unless one happens to have been born there, it is almost as difficult to acquire citizenship in states that define themselves as republican and/or democratic. Given the right constitutional framework, inclusion on a social-systemic basis could potentially avoid many of the coercive dimensions of rival models of normative integration. See chapter 5 of the present book for a more detailed elaboration of this argument.

15 Whilst Luhmann insists on self-referential closure, Philippopoulos-Mihalopoulos and others intimate that systems communicate with one another – even if such communication takes the form of collisions. Habermas, by contrast, distinguishes between systemic and lifeworld dimensions of social reproduction and evolution. See Luhmann, *Soziale Systeme*, chapters 11–12; Andreas Philippopoulos-Mihalopoulos, 'Looking for the Space between Law and Ecology', in Andreas Philippopoulos-Mihalopoulos (ed.), *Law and Ecology: New Environmental Foundations* (London: Routledge, 2012), pp. 1–17; and Habermas, *Faktizität und Geltung*, available in English as *Between Facts and Norms*, chapter 1. Habermas updates his views on these issues in *Zur Verfassung Europas*, pp. 39–47, available in English as *Crisis of the European Union*, pp. 1–12.

16 Adorno, 'Zu Subjekt und Objekt', p. 158, available in English as 'Subject and Object', in Brian O'Connor (ed.), *The Adorno Reader* (Oxford: Blackwell, 2000), pp. 137–52, at p. 143.

17 The issue of stages and tempo acquires importance in this context. Where integration was very gradual, as in Great Britain, stability seems to have been achieved. Where integration was much more sudden and intensive, as in the case of the transition from the German *Obrigkeitsstaat* to the Weimar Republic, stability was always more fragile, as was shown in 1933. See Pincus, *1688: The First Modern Revolution*, and Detlev Peukert, *Die Weimarer Republik: Krisenjahre der klassischen Moderne*

(Frankfurt: Suhrkamp, 1987), available in English as *The Weimar Republic: The Crisis of Classical Modernity* (New York: Hill & Wang, 1st American edn, 1992).

18 These issues are discussed with clarity by Jamie Peck in *Constructions of Neoliberal Reason* (Oxford: Oxford University Press, 2010), and in the chapters in Jonathan Metzger, Philip Allmendinger, and Stijn Oosterlynck (eds), *Planning Against the Political: Democratic Deficits in European Territorial Governance* (London: Routledge, 2015).

19 Paul Cartledge offers some interesting thoughts on this matter in the epilogue to his *Democracy: A Life* (Oxford: Oxford University Press, 2016), pp. 305–13.

20 For an eloquent commentary on this issue, see Ashley Lavelle, *The Death of Social Democracy: Political Consequences in the 21st Century* (Aldershot: Ashgate, 2008), Part I, chapters 2–4; and Colin Crouch, *The Strange Non-Death of Neoliberalism* (Cambridge: Polity Press, 2011), chapters 3 and 5.

21 For a very incisive analysis of this tendency within recent social and political thought, see Michael Thompson, *The Domestication of Critical Theory* (London: Rowman & Littlefield, 2016), especially chapters 1 and 5.

22 Karl Marx, 'Theses on Feuerbach', in R. Tucker (ed.), *The Marx-Engels Reader* (New York: Norton, 2nd edn, 1978), pp. 143–5, at p. 145. Although Simmel and Adorno break with Hegel and Marx, they do not abandon a dialectical approach to questions of epistemology and social form. For an explicitly dialectical approach to questions of rights and constitutions, see Georges Gurvitch, 'Le Principe démocratique et la démocratie future', *Revue de Métaphysique et de Morale*, 36:3 (1929), 403–31. Simmel, Adorno, and Gurvitch reformulate the relation between non-identity and dialectics that first appears with Kant. The importance of this project for constitutional theory will be explored in greater detail in the next chapter. As has been stressed throughout, the key issue relates to understanding inter-systemic mediations, without which explanation of social communication becomes problematic.

23 The juxtaposition between Left Hegelianism and first-generation critical theory is probably best exemplified by the political and epistemological divergences between Adorno and Lukács. See Schecter, *Critique of Instrumental Reason*, chapters 2–3.

24 The first-generation critical theorists witnessed the crisis of democracy and the failure, by and large, of the Dada and surrealist movements to achieve their most important political objectives. The risk of repeating those failures was clear to Guy Debord and the Situationist International, as Debord himself realised well before Situationism actually unravelled at the end of the 1960s. See Guy Debord, 'Report on the Construction of Situations and on the International Situationist Tendency's Conditions of Organisation and Action', in Ken Knabb (ed.), *Situationist International Anthology* (Berkeley: Bureau of Public Secrets, revised and expanded edn, 2006), pp. 25–43; and Schecter, *The History of the Left*, chapter 5. It can certainly be said that the unification of aesthetic experience, political organisation, and pedagogical experimentation was a key component of the Bauhaus movement. As is well known, however, conservative and revolutionary tendencies competed within the diverse groups that composed it. See Eva Forgács, *The Bauhaus Idea and Bauhaus Politics* (Budapest: Central European University Press, 1995).

25 Theodor W. Adorno, *Zur Metakritik der Erkenntnistheorie: Studien über Husserl und die phänomenologischen Antinomien* (Stuttgart: Kohlhammer, 1956), translated into English somewhat oddly as *Against Epistemology: A Metacritique; Studies in Husserl and the Phenomenological Antinomies*, trans. Willis Domingo (Oxford: Blackwell, 1982). A number of these affinities can also be seen in the decades following World War II. See Adorno's 'Einleitung zum "Positivismusstreit in der deutschen

Soziologie" ', in *Soziologische Schriften I*, ed. Rolf Tiedemann (Frankfurt: Suhrkamp, 1979), pp. 280–353, and the chapters by him in Theodor W. Adorno, Hans Albert, Ralf Dahrendorf, Jürgen Habermas, Harald Pilot, and Karl R. Popper, *Der Positivismusstreit in der deutschen Soziologie* (Neuwied: Luchterhand, 1969).

26 The ideological character of such arguments is by no means lost on first-generation critical theory, as the analyses of Otto Kirchheimer and Franz Neumann show. For a very good overview of their research on the authoritarian turn of parliamentary democracy in the interwar period, see Scheuerman, *Between the Norm and the Exception*, chapters 6–8.

27 For a cogent analysis of neoliberal dogma see Wolfgang Streeck, *How will Capitalism End? Essays on a Failing System* (London: Verso, 2016), introduction and chapter 2, and Peck, *Constructions of Neoliberal Reason*, chapter 3.

28 On the lasting authoritarian consequences of inconclusive post-feudal statehood and selective FD, see Bruno Latour, *Nous n'avons jamais été modernes: Essai d'anthropologie symétrique* (Paris: La Découverte, 1991), available in English as *We Have Never Been Modern*, trans. Catherine Porter (Hemel Hempstead: Harvester Wheatsheaf, 1993), chapters 2–3 on revolutions and constitutions; Marcel Gauchet, *L'Avènement de la démocratie 1: La Révolution moderne* (Paris: Gallimard, 2007), introduction and chapter 4; and Alain Touraine, *La Fin des sociétés* (Paris: Seuil, 2013), Part III, chapter 3, and conclusion.

29 Georg Simmel, *Die Philosophie des Geldes*, Gesamtausgabe, 6 (Frankfurt: Suhrkamp, 4th edn, 1996 [1900]), p. 622, available in English as *The Philosophy of Money*, trans. Tom Bottomore and David Frisby, ed. David Frisby (London: Routledge, 3rd enlarged edn, 2004), p. 454 and *Soziologie: Untersuchungen über die Formen der Vergesellschaftung* (Frankfurt: Suhrkamp, 1992 [1908]), pp. 694–5, available in English as *Sociology: Inquiries into the Construction of Social Forms*, ed. and trans. Anthony J. Blasi, Anton K. Jacobs, and Mathew J. Kanjirathinkal, 2 vols (Leiden and Boston: Brill, 2009), Vol. II, pp. 548–9.

30 These issues are treated with subtlety and depth in two recent books by Austin Harrington and Elizabeth S. Goodstein. See Austin Harrington, *German Cosmopolitan Social Thought and the Idea of the West: Voices from Weimar* (Cambridge: Cambridge University Press, 2016), chapters 2 and 5; and Goodstein, *Georg Simmel and the Disciplinary Imaginary*, pp. 83–95 and chapter 8.

31 Georg Simmel, 'Exchange', in *On Individuality and Social Forms: Selected Writings*, ed. Donald N. Levine (Chicago: University of Chicago Press, 1971), pp. 43–69.

32 Georg Simmel, 'Die Arbeitsteilung als Ursache für das Auseinandertreten der subjektiven und der objektiven Kultur', in *Schriften zur Soziologie: Eine Auswahl*, ed. Heinz-Jürgen Dahme (Frankfurt: Suhrkamp, 1983), pp. 95–128.

33 Max Weber, 'Politics as a Vocation', in Hans Gerth and C. Wright Mills (eds), *From Max Weber: Essays in Sociology* (New York: Scribner & Son, 1946), pp. 77–128. Whilst the structuralist Marxist notion of 'determination in the last instance' offers an unconvincing explanation of informal social-systemic re-coupling, Gramsci's theory of the historical bloc can make valuable contributions to our understanding of extra-systemic political alliances. The more general point is that FD rarely means the hermetic separation of social systems. On the contrary, it usually implies a re-structuring of the mediations that place them into a communicative relation with one another.

34 Berry and Fagerjord, *Digital Humanities*, chapter 3.

35 Dieter Plehwe and Bernhard Walpen, 'Between Network and Complex Organization: The Making of Neoliberal Knowledge and Hegemony', in Bernhard Walpen and Gisela

Neunhöffer (eds), *Neoliberal Hegemony: A Global Critique* (London: Routledge, 2006), pp. 27–50.

36 The likelihood of such scenarios in France are analysed by Bruno Amable and Stefano Palombarini, *L'Illusion du bloc bourgeois: Alliances sociales et avenir du modèle français* (Paris: Raison d'agir, 2017). Amable's *Structural Crisis and Institutional Change in Modern Capitalism: French Capitalism in Transition* (Oxford: Oxford University Press, 2017) is available in English.

37 The Greek example springs most immediately to mind. See Paul Mason, 'Review of Yanis Varoufakis, *Adults in the Room: My Battle with Europe's Deep Establishment*', *Guardian* (6 May 2017), p. 6. Although Greece offers the paradigmatic example, similar dynamics structure the relations of the European Central Bank, European Commission, and Eurogroup with countries like Spain, Portugal, and Italy. For the Italian case see Frontini, *Moneta e impero*; and Vladimiro Giacché, *Costituzione italiana contro trattati europei: Il conflitto inevitabile* (Reggio Emilia: Imprimatur, 2015).

5

Re-thinking inclusion beyond unity and mediation beyond discretionary steering: on social systems and societal constitutions

Previous chapters have looked at the ways in which the evolutionary gains of political modernity and sociological modernity might be symbiotically maintained and further enhanced as the twenty-first century continues to unfold. Here the term 'evolutionary' is evidently not synonymous with peaceful, natural, predominantly consensual, or any other designation that suggests spontaneous progress towards harmoniously agreed norms of political legitimacy and social inclusion. It is neither new nor surprising that the achievements and progress towards the very possibility of consensual inclusion that have been made since the Industrial Revolution have been accompanied by a wide variety of struggles, including revolutions, violent conflicts, and bitterly negotiated, fragile collective compromises. Some of the most important of those collective compromises in Great Britain and elsewhere, such as the post-war social contract, are currently being re-negotiated and re-written in ways that are not always very clear to many of the participants. From a British perspective the Beveridge Report, Atlee government, NHS, and welfare state denote the political, educational, economic, health, and cultural dimensions of the concessions made and broad agreements reached across wide sectors of society. At the time, it looked like a kind of subtle revolution had been achieved and a unique paradigm of legitimacy had become a political reality as a result of the capacity of the state to successfully steer a series of processes aimed at democratic consultation and comprehensive reform.

The 1945 Labour government seemed to have found a viable path beyond the American and Soviet models by synthesising modest economic growth, social justice, transparent and plural political participation, expanded tertiary education, and universal access to health care. Analysing the period from a contemporary perspective, Felicity Lawrence remarks that 'the agreement at the heart of the post-war social contract, that work pays for a decent living, has been broken. Millions of people in the West work hard but do not earn enough to cover basic living costs or afford housing. The notion that the only alternative to market fundamentalism is a bureaucratic, inefficient state that leads in short order back to socialist totalitarianism has for too long stood in the way of change, paralysing even those politicians committed to change. So what would a modern "commons" charter look like?'[1] This chapter examines some of the issues involved in working towards a tentative response.

In more general terms, the relation between revolutionary conflict, war, law, rights, and the demand for innovative governance is a constant in modern constitutional history. One can regard the American, French, Russian, Chinese Cultural, and Velvet Revolutions as transitional moments when the relation between facts and norms is fundamentally reshaped into a new order with a qualitatively different institutional architecture. As Dieter Grimm remarks, every political community takes the form of a constitutional order.[2] Despite the ambiguities implied by the conceptual distinctions between political system and state, on the one hand, and the practical intersections and overlaps between national society and world society, on the other, it is now entirely possible to think of global humanity as a political community confronted with a common set of economic, juridical, educational, scientific, cultural, health, and ecological challenges. Hence, it is also possible to speak of a global constitution in empirical rather than utopian terms. The relations between legality and legitimacy, facts and norms, political system and state, and national society and world society are currently embroiled in processes of rapid transformation that, in turn, are responding to realignments and shifts in the mediations between diverse social systems on a world scale.[3]

Fundamental realignments of this kind can take shape in officially recognised and formalised agreements, such as the Weimar Constitution of 1918 or the Spanish Constitution of 1931. They can also materialise in much less visible ways, however, with unforeseen consequences and multiple risks. The collapse of the transnational order founded at Bretton Woods, or the more recent plans to set up a largely de-regulated transatlantic trade zone, for example, are cases where potentially major changes to the structures of governance are ratified with markedly varying degrees of active democratic involvement on the part of the citizens concerned. Inconclusive responses to the financial crisis of 2007–2008 indicate that whilst major changes are once again on the way, there are real questions concerning the degree of transparency and actual efficiency that will accompany them. There are also questions concerning the capacity of political parties to demand transparency when they are compelled, for the most part, to accept the separation of the ministry of the economy/treasury from the de facto power of an independent central bank in their respective countries, not to mention the power of the European Central Bank within the eurozone. One obvious risk is the regression towards a personalised and discretionary exercise of power that is likely to ensue if newly articulated and durable compromises cannot be established across a range of national, systemic, and environmental boundaries. To some degree, this is certainly a question of fairer income distribution, ensuring more widespread and diverse practices of recognition, legislating more equitable life chances, and enhancing lifeworld communication. But in line with the argument developed here, it may be more centrally a matter of finding an equilibrium between the normative capacity of states to limit the exercise of power and apply it evenly and predictably through positivised political centralisation, on the one hand, and the factual capacity of social systems for a constant re-articulation of the relation between knowledge and power in ways that are often highly dispersed and contingent, on the other. It has been emphasised throughout this study that there are urgent questions as to whether and for how long the nation state can sustain the balance between normatively regulated power, which is framed in generalised and formal terms, and social-systemic knowledge marked by high levels of specificity relevant to the system in question. It has been shown that whilst systems cannot be steered from a planning centre, they do not steer themselves according to the now fairly discredited model of self-regulating markets, either. If the nation state has become too inflexible, hierarchical, and territorially circumscribed to meet global challenges, another practice of statehood will be needed to mediate inter-systemic operations. At this juncture, it seems clear that the successor model will be called upon to co-ordinate social systems without fusing them in some kind of unwieldy authoritarian synthesis or instrumentally prising them apart and then re-suturing them later as part of short-term governance and electoral strategies. Such measures have been analysed in previous chapters as cases of reshuffled historical blocs and selective de-differentiation.

This stress on co-ordination reinforces the caveat that literal readings of terms such as centralisation and dispersal/de-centralisation can lead to misinterpretations. When applied to modern states, *centralisation* and the *division* of powers are mutually reinforcing rather than contradictory or incompatible. Similarly, social systems are dispersed and nonetheless in steady communication with one another through a wide range of mediations. This argument will not be delved into again in what follows below, since it has already been shown that dialectical de-coupling and re-coupling in this regard is one of the hallmarks of modern, functionally differentiated societies. Instead, chapter 5 examines some of the major challenges facing the project of reaching a constitutional equilibrium between key norms of political statehood and the facts of systemic pluralism. Meeting them will depend on the degree to which world-societal organisations and institutions can utilise existing constitutional experience and innovations as a resource to consult and learn from when attempting to solve problems and think about the best ways to reconcile knowledge, contingency, and justice in the near future. One could state the matter succinctly by saying that one of the central tasks of twenty-first-century citizenship is the pedagogical one of citizens helping social systems learn from states and the role played by constitutions in the history of weak and strong instances of statehood. This is not a completely utopian ideal if one bears in mind that collective learning is real and that it is distilled in the historically documented practice of constitutional evolution and practical struggles for constitutional change.[4] There are, of course, tremendous obstacles. For a start, it is not immediately apparent how to equip systems with a normative framework that is readily understood by the citizens involved in their various operations. This will have somehow to be accomplished, lest 'the dark side of functional differentiation' nullify the democratic potential embedded in horizontally structured, tendentially self-governing social systems.[5] The difficulties involved are indeed enormous when one considers the obvious limitations of the state for this purpose. To be more precise, it would seem that there are insurmountable problems for the particular form of political statehood that is conventionally conceived in its nationally defined and territorially delimited instantiations, and which frames questions of integration and legitimacy in terms of mediated unity or constituent power.[6]

It is easy to overlook the fact that there are more than casual affinities, both in historical and theoretical terms, between personalised authoritarian rule and more apparently democratic and republican notions of constituent power.[7] Moreover, at this juncture in the development of globalisation, it no longer seems feasible to separate normative lifeworlds from non-normative systems, or to hope that the state might somehow be able to maintain a precarious equilibrium between system and lifeworld. That thesis, as formulated by Habermas and others, hinges on the claim that a specifically democratic instance of equilibrium is reached because there are channels of communication between the lifeworld and legal and political institutions. This allows systemic steering imperatives to be balanced with freely agreed principles of conduct. The validity of that claim is called into question by the communicative properties of systems and manifest systemic disregard for the boundaries needed to maintain the integrity of the lifeworld against external encroachments. This line of argument might seem to point inevitably to a highly ephemeral, aesthetic vision of politics that offers little scope for meaningful intervention in mainstream debates on the conflicts besetting the economy, access to health care and education, environmental crisis, and the movements of refugees. One is then reduced to accepting ubiquitous instrumental reason and party political professionalisation as the ineluctable corollaries of FD, embracing some implausible fusion of theory and practice attributed to an arbitrarily chosen collective subject (that can be re-presented by a party), or aesthetic flight. Indeed, this always seems to be the major problem when attempting to wrest political solutions and alternatives from Adorno's incisive analyses of social processes.[8] Previous chapters attempt to demonstrate why a critical-theoretical approach to the history of state building and constitutional design, combined with a sociological approach to FD, can suggest paths of enquiry beyond empirical political science, a-historical analytical democratic theory, and aesthetic retreat.

Political statehood from the perspective of FD and constitutional history

States often rely on a constitution to spell out and give public expression to the fundamental compromises and alliances defining the institutional contours of a given order. The history of comparative state formation offers numerous examples where this event is distilled in a document with amendments and similar provisions enabling the state in question to alter the composition of that order in response to the need to adapt flexibly to changing circumstances. Such documents can only do so very approximately, given the diversity of communication, conflict, and compromise in complex societies. It is therefore relatively easy to see the desirability of a transition to a social form of statehood in which each of the primary social systems is publicly endowed with a specific constitution, coded in accordance with the discrete kinds of knowledge and likely disagreements that pertain to its particular operations. A move in this direction seems all the more important to the extent that the separation of normative lifeworlds from non-normative systems is no longer tenable and the task of maintaining a precarious equilibrium between system and lifeworld has become too complicated for the state.[9] The manifest gains, in terms of flexible steering and planning, would be especially tangible if the process is structured by transparency and open, informed deliberation. A system-specific constitution of this kind could be very effective in countering passive revolutions and decisionistic alterations in the structure of political compromise. Striking in this context are the implicit claims that (a) political agreements and compromises would cease to be considered extraneous or antithetical to epistemological ones, and that (b) constituent power would cease to be framed in terms of a mythically unmediated popular essence. The difficulties involved in organising such a transition are quite clearly staggering. One would be moving away from an order that in many respects is still fairly hierarchical (despite some purist systems-theoretical claims about functionally differentiated societies to the contrary). One would no longer be entrusting individual government ministries with the task of instituting an ad hoc dialogue between ministers and a network of elites and supposed experts standing in for and representing systemic functions. Instead, one would enjoy a far more horizontal order in which systemic functions and inter-systemic communication are guided by citizen councils acting in the political-pedagogical spirit invoked above, namely, with citizens taking active responsibility for enabling systems to learn from the role played by political constitutions in the history of weak and strong states. Equipping social systems in this way would almost certainly enhance their proven latent capacity to be self-governing, and, at the same time, enable citizens better to oppose selective de-differentiation and other instances of government manipulation of FD. In recent years, there have been numerous examples of such interventions intended to protect the privileges of the elites in charge of one system at the expense of the outmanoeuvred elites clinging on to control of others. Bailouts and other attempts to shore up the existing banking system (instead of re-coding the principles according to which it functions) are merely the most visible and obvious ones. This analysis confirms the thesis that hierarchy persists and is manifested in ways that extend well beyond differential incomes and so-called 'life chances'. It also confirms the related thesis that partisan factions continue to use interventionist steering in their power struggles against one another. The resulting policies often disturb systemic operations without correcting their destructive tendencies.[10]

Hence the analytical and normative arguments for societal constitutionalism seek to establish which of the preconditions for a transition to social statehood are demonstrably on hand; it is thus also incumbent on those who defend societal constitutionalism to ascertain which preconditions are not as yet available. These arguments are therefore distinct from those about (1) legitimation crises in late capitalism, (2) social democratic third ways, and, very obviously so, from (3) neoliberal and other positions embracing the ideas of Hayek and the practices of privatisation and rampant outsourcing. With regard to (1), it is no longer plausibly the case that the post-World War II state, through short-term corporatist compromise and limited strategic investment, becomes inextricably committed to more thorough and comprehensive egalitarian planning on an increasingly permanent basis. Prior to the onset of full-blown globalisation, it may have seemed analytically stringent to insist that by steadily increasing their active intervention in economic processes, late modern states would in effect be introducing the application of norma-tive and political criteria to what had previously been defined as a norm-free sphere of private exchange. Instead of opting for Soviet-style command econ-omies, in other words, theorists of legitimation crises in the 1970s thought that states everywhere would become so involved in matters of production and distribution that the relation between political control of the economy and democracy could be approached as a matter of equitable consultation of all citizens, universal rights, and rational macroeconomic forecasting. In principle, states gradually would be compelled to make the transition from stopgap Keynesianism and palliative welfare to a genuine and more consistent alterna-tive to the American and Soviet models of legitimacy. This was a very good argument at the time; it remains valid to the extent that states are so inex-tricably involved in the economic system that the distinction between public and private has become redundant to a significant extent.[11] But it has been seen that the contemporary state working within national contexts does not possess the resources needed to implement Keynesian policies under social democratic auspices. This lack is also part of the reason why social democratic parties anchored in the cultural traditions of national societies will struggle to spearhead credible third-way projects designed to bring citizens closer to decision-making processes that actually affect their daily lives. Demographic and other factors will also continue to play a notable role in the explanation of some of the pressing difficulties facing social democracy, which, since its inception, has been committed to forms of industrial production and redis-tributive justice that presuppose the validity of the mediated unity paradigm.

  Whilst the challenges facing social democracy seem especially acute today, we are probably witnessing the longer-term consequences of changes that really began to take effect as far back as 1945, when some of the cru-cially important steering capacities of nation states were transferred to trans-national agencies and organisations. It is only a matter of time before the consequences profoundly affect all political parties and states. In the immedi-ate aftermath of World War II, this must have seemed like the best way to alleviate states from the pressures for unrivalled as well as all-encompassing inclusion that contributed to fascist and authoritarian corporatist models of democratic unity in interwar twentieth-century Europe and thereafter. These openly dictatorial regimes can be seen as instances where weak dialectical modes of representation and legitimacy cede to strong ones even though, as is evident from precedent and the discussion in chapter 1, the term 'strong' in this context really means overstretched and overburdened, that is, factually

'weak'. The history of comparative state formation indicates that governments fall and states are often hollowed out when they attempt to be too
strong in the sense of directing the economy, education, scientific research,
and so on without the means to do so in a non-coercive way. Proponents
of societal constitutionalism suggest in different ways that it may now be
time for these operations to become self-governing in ways that enhance
rather than impede the self-governing aspirations of neighbouring operations.
Does this mean a return to the weak dialectical model normally associated
with liberal democracy, based on a firm distinction between public and private
spheres, and a clear but limited role for the state? This is not an option in
twenty-first-century world society. The metric obsessions and punitive realities of twenty-first-century neoliberalism offer clear evidence in support of the
view that the recognisably liberal stage of the era of liberal democratic hegemony has passed. One question that therefore arises is the following: is the end
of the neoliberal epoch now on the horizon? Despite the rhetoric of various
liberal, conservative, and Christian Democratic parties around the globe, the
state has become so enmeshed in economic, educational, and a wide range
of other systemic operations that there is no feasible return – if such a period
ever really existed – to an institutional configuration characterised by clear
and neat boundaries and distinctions. This means that the transition to a new
theory and practice of statehood has become urgent. What remains of local
and regional authority is characterised by complex networks of imbricated
competence and responsibility. What remains of national authority is shared
with and conditioned by international and transnational bodies. If the transfer
of steering capacities to transnational organisations and agencies has managed to relieve states from an array of acute inclusionary pressures, this has
not been accomplished without what has been analysed as an erosion in the
qualitative dimension of political statehood by Dieter Grimm and Udo di Fabio,
and aptly referred to as the irony of the state by Helmut Willke.[12]

The Greek case would stand out as a particularly virulent example of the
erosion of statehood if it were not for the fact that a similar set of criteria will
eventually be applied to most other states with histories of public debt and
nationally specific approaches to industrial relations. It is telling in this regard
that President Macron plans to reform the French Code du Travail and thereby
avert a scenario in which the Troika impose austerity on France. The catch is
that he and his team seem ready to take on that job by themselves, with major
implications for workers' rights.[13] If it is true that states and governments tend
towards negligence and corruption if they attempt to be too strong in the
sense used above, social constitutionalism and social statehood signal new
directions in thinking about alternatives. These are needed in order to push
the relevant debates beyond the impoverished choice between a state that

is hopelessly overburdened and inward-looking, relying on nationalist, protectionist, and other dubious notions of community, on the one hand, and a state that operates at the behest of international financial markets and private companies, in the name of remaining competitive according to very ill-defined standards of what this actually might mean apart from selling more cheaply and with visibly diminished quality, on the other. Typically, this happens when states are compelled formally to ratify informal agreements between key actors in civil society, the national government, and the relevant international bodies. This is, in Gramsci's analysis, the reality of mediated unity and political statehood under conditions of capitalist economic management: at a particular historical juncture a bloc of forces, interests, and values succeeds in bringing together crucial systemic functions on a temporary and precarious basis that stands in for what is meant to pass as democratic statehood. He analyses these changing formations as historical blocs that synthesise systemic operations in ways which, when virtuous in Machiavellian terms, momentarily establish a stable framework for the exercise of power by creating protean alliances and chains of command across the private/public and base/superstructure divides.[14]

If an historical bloc is stable, it can eventually become hegemonic as an integral state that at least approximates the ideal of mediated unity between the citizens, law, and public authority. This rarely happens in industrial and post-industrial societies marked by latent and overt conflict, however. In Gramsci's view, it is far more likely that a given society will stumble from one passive revolution to another – at least until the fundamental question of the economy and production in the widest sense is addressed with an eye to comprehensive and egalitarian inclusion. Whether the re-constitution of an historical bloc can be classified as a passive revolution or not depends on particularities of state formation and historical context. His theoretical sophistication on this issue is guided by the manifestly pre-modern characteristics of the Italian state and the highly uneven, erratic systemic differentiation of post-Risorgimento society. As he, Croce, Labriola, Gentile, and many others recognised at the time, the discrepancy between 'legal Italy' and 'real Italy' was flagrant. The discrepancy was equally obvious to observers such as Pareto and Mosca. But instead of thinking about the best approaches to integrating and including citizens on bases that would foster an institutional proximity to the workings of social systems, Pareto and Mosca anticipate Schumpeter's position on the relationship between citizens and states in modern democracies.[15] Pareto, Mosca, and Schumpeter can be seen as thinkers who regard populism to be the operating principle of the so-called 'normal' workings of parties and elections – it is certainly not an aberration or deviation in their view. Gramsci, by contrast, attempts to develop a model of legitimacy capable of reconciling the principles of self-governing systems and self-governing citizens. He never resolves the tension between that vision and his political commitment to a political vanguard. But he nonetheless highlights the importance of this issue whilst also developing a political sociology of the modern state that is neither naively idealist about the possibilities of harmonious mediation and foundational dialectics, nor anthropologically cynical about supposedly a-historical flaws in human nature. His work indicates that the project to re-think statehood will not be able to bypass a sociological analysis of FD or a consideration of inter-systemic communication as a key component of consensually normative, horizontally structured integration.[16]

Critical theory and the project to democratise inter-systemic mediation today

Many will rightly ask how systems might communicate with each other and co-ordinate their operations without the direction and generally cumbersome steering currently undertaken in large part by government ministries making use of high-level private contacts, personal connections, and institutions such as the *Grandes Ecoles* in France which are designed to reproduce technocratic and political elites.[17] It has been seen so far that this kind of steering normally occurs through ministerial or inter-ministerial interventions designed to re-couple discrete social processes and thereby retain a measure of supervisory control over the general direction of society in instances where this is broadly possible. The project to democratise inter-systemic mediation can be seen as a dual initiative aimed at enhancing citizen access to inter-systemic communication as a first step towards adjudicating inter-systemic conflicts and better co-ordinating their functions. At first glance, the project seems to encounter devastating obstacles, most notably the combined effect of antagonistic conceptual thought, flawed state formation (varying in degree depending on the case in question), and the colonial/imperialist background of most stable hegemonic states in the so-called developed world. It might be reasonably asked if enhanced access to systemic communication really needs to be preceded by comprehensive re-coding, so that the information received is no longer so thoroughly engulfed in power struggles and instrumental measurements of systemic performance. But would not such re-coding interfere with the dynamics of differentiation, and thereby forfeit the potential of de-centralised, horizontal organisation? It would seem, too, that the current model of FD is so enmeshed in a matrix of oppression and conflictual mediation that it will prove exceedingly difficult to extricate the horizontally structured, participatory dimension of de-centred differentiation and social-systemic communication from that ongoing legacy.[18] This impression is enforced by the fact that most systems theorists believe that inter-systemic communication inevitably stops at the point where systems sound out their respective environments. By way of a provisional response, it can be observed that the model of legitimacy suggested by informal links between ministers and select representatives of powerful interests in nominal charge of social systems is intrinsically oligarchic, hierarchical, and dramatically out of sync with the centrifugal evolutionary tendencies characteristic of late modern society. There is an evident need for rapid responses to rampant economic inequality and social exclusion, climate change, refugee movements, housing crises, and a wide variety of other policy matters; it is doubtful that the model of ministerial responsibility is suited to the challenges thereby posed.[19]

This point confirms the hypothesis that FD does not simply take over where political statehood left off. The radically democratic potential of FD continues to exist at manifest odds with the seemingly ineradicable residues of stratification that have plagued European societies since the early stages of political statehood in Europe. More recently, successive decades of deregulation and austerity have contributed to the perpetuation and exacerbation of entrenched inequality in Europe and around the world today.[20] Needless to say, the Glorious Revolution did not and probably could not have challenged some of these anachronisms. Others were largely left intact by the paradigmatic eighteenth-century revolutions in North America and France.[21] These specific patterns of political centralisation and social stratification may have been temporarily neutralised in Western Europe and North America during the thirty years following World War II. But the work of Piketty, Savage, and others indicates that the informal agreements can be turned into formal policy that protect political oligarchy and perpetuate socio-economic inequality; the closely related crises of political statehood, social democracy, and Keynesianism attest to the difficulties involved in trying to address these issues with what were, until the end of the 1970s, relatively efficient mechanisms of normative steering. Government ministers usually confer with a highly restricted group of domestic and international elites in industry, education, information technology, scientific research, and the like. The deals negotiated in this way cannot be confused with the democratic representation or civic participation required to enhance inter-systemic communication beyond reciprocal non-infringement. In many cases, they do not go beyond shoring up the compromises and alliances constitutive of a given historical bloc. At present, civic participation is largely confined to post hoc protests against measures that are already in the planning stage or have been taken. Participation is directed into the pre-formed channels dominated by professional parties compelled to behave like rival firms in a competitive market. From their standpoint, re-election to office and consolidation of power must be the guiding principles of political strategy and action. Operating within existing models of statehood and established patterns of FD, parties do not have the time, interest, or knowledge required to enable social systems to become self-governing or to empower citizens in a war of position against selective de-differentiation. It would thus seem that the chances for a transition to social statehood are fairly remote at the present juncture. Yet a very different set of conclusions is also tenable: it can be argued that the current model of ministerial responsibility and party political competition for power is simply ill-suited to the challenges facing global humanity, and as such, destined to be phased out. At that point, the need for a transition to a new model of statehood will necessitate changes in existing patterns of differentiation.

It is in any case misleading to speak about a decisive transition in this regard, as if some kind of absolutely 'clean break' had any real historical precedent – even revolutions sometimes seem to reinforce or accelerate rather than reverse pre-revolutionary trends in a given national society.[22] More central to the point are the numerous indications suggesting that however inchoately, social systems tend to exhibit constitutional properties alongside their manifestly horizontal structures of communication. Gunther Teubner's work provides some of the most convincing theoretical claims in this regard.[23] This observation complements the hypothesis that FD does not simply take over where political statehood left off, and supports the politically hopeful belief that horizontal structures of compromise and agreement have a better chance of flourishing in complex, internally divided social formations than they do in organic communities or even within supposedly unified nations.[24] In support of this assessment of the possibilities offered by complexity and differentiation, a number of legal theorists show that law is becoming increasingly reflexive and responsive to extra-legal information, and that at the same time politics is becoming increasingly transnational, that is to say global, and responsive to information from neighbouring social systems which, to an increasingly significant extent, also operate transnationally. These developments point towards two important and relatively recent transnational developments. First, the fact that law is becoming increasingly reflexive and responsive to extra-legal information means that legal systems do in fact communicate with other social systems in ways that point beyond Luhmann's rather a-historical notion that systems are self-referential and can only experience one another as 'irritations'; it is unlikely that legal systems are exceptional in having this communicative capacity.[25] Second, law and politics, to name just two examples, are evolving in specific ways that are likely to make it increasingly difficult for social democratic and all other parties to compete with each other for political power that is anchored in a territorially integral nation state. It is worth noting that the most articulate claims concerning the processes shaping the contemporary evolution of law and democratic politics stem from Luhmann's sociologically inflected legal theory, and, to a comparable extent, from certain strands of constitutional theory, rather than from Marxism, liberalism, bio-political theory, or deconstruction.[26] Luhmann signals that law and politics are steadily attaining functional qualities whilst shedding their exclusively national peculiarities. This point highlights the tensions between the practice of modern law as a differentiated social system and the normative ideal of democracy as a universally unifying political form from ancient Athens to the present, instituted in accordance with national political traditions. Indeed, as has been remarked in previous chapters, the lines between government, state, and political system are not always drawn with precision by Luhmann and other systems theorists, thus making democracy somewhat difficult to define.[27] Systems theory raises this problem without really addressing it squarely. Yet it can be convincingly argued that legal theory, Marxism, bio-political theory, deconstruction, and liberalism do not satisfactorily do so, either. Critical theory can now make a decisive contribution in this regard by drawing out some of the implications of the two points just mentioned. Admittedly, there are considerable obstacles to the project of enhancing citizen access to systemic communication and democratising inter-systemic mediation. Yet it has been shown that there are now equally formidable obstacles to preserving the institutional framework of the mediated unity paradigm. This conclusion appears all the more compelling if one considers that the reality of that paradigm is neither mediated unity nor Habermas's somewhat modified version thereof. Instead it is often patently incompetent steering misguided by personal contacts and private power. Technocratic and political elites have amply demonstrated their incapacity to respond quickly or efficiently to the normative challenges of FD and the organisational, informational, ecological, and epistemological challenges of systemic specificity. As a consequence, the emancipatory potential of FD is largely observable in its absence at the moment. It is what Regina Kreide in dialogue with Habermas refers to as a 'repressed democracy'.[28]

Within the framework of the mediated unity paradigm, law and politics are ostensibly united by democratic political form; here political form is tautologically predefined as intrinsically democratic, and characteristically applied in rather indiscriminate fashion, as in the idiomatic notion of a 'democratic society'. This kind of common parlance is very inaccurate and yet often reproduced, albeit with a bit more nuance, in a great deal of mainstream journalism and academic writing on the relations between law, democracy, and society. To this extent, it is also somewhat inaccurate to speak in terms of 'capitalist society'. The point about global law and transnational politics is highly relevant for a functionally differentiated world society where it becomes possible to open up a discussion about *which* particular social systems can be democratised and, crucially, *how* the term democratisation is to be interpreted in relation to processes that are not susceptible to the largely quantitative measures at the disposition of parties and governments, such as mathematical calculations related to coalition partners and provisions for the redistribution of wealth.[29] This issue raises a number of questions about the relevance of numerical measures of unity and difference, such as that between minority and majority, for operations that are more centrally concerned with knowledge, health, educational development, renewable energy sources, and considerations of integration and inclusion. The distinction between majority and minority will have to be reconceptualised in ways that build on the political experiences that made the separation of powers and judicial review vitally important constitutional steps in the evolution of democratic political statehood. Since power is not easy to quantify or measure numerically, it is all the more important that the exercise of power is divided, shared, and made transparent to the greatest possible extent. Although democratic politics has been fundamental in indicating how this dividing and sharing can be approached by states in relation to political systems, major questions remain as regards the comprehensive institutionalisation of checks and balances in other social systems. The matter was not particularly dramatic as long as states were relatively good at correcting market failure and educational exclusion, upholding decent standards of environmental protection, ensuring that the elderly could count on adequate care, and so on.

Much has already been written about the demise of the kinds of democracy characteristic of the medieval communes and Renaissance city-states. In the aftermath of that decline, during the early stages of modern state building, a new institutional reality slowly emerged in Europe before spreading to different parts of the globe thereafter. It was already recognised, if perhaps only implicitly, that a political system can only function well if it is sustained and flanked by parallel social systems functioning according to non-majoritarian codes. First and foremost amongst them was a legal system and a judiciary shielded, to the greatest possible extent, from the abuses of executive power. Later, around the middle of the nineteenth century with observers such as Mill and Tocqueville, the judiciary came to be regarded both as a safeguard against executive usurpation of legislative authority, and as a means for limiting the potential 'tyranny of the majority', as well. In the twentieth century, the public sphere and civil society have been discussed in similar terms as counterweights or balancing forces needed to fortify democracy and solidify the social and cultural dimensions of the mixed constitution of any given state.[30] Until recently, however, very few economists, political theorists, legal sociologists, or constitutional scholars would have described the processes involved in social-systemic terms or in terms related to the unfolding of FD.

It is too soon to interpret this increased attention to FD, social systems, and social constitutions as proof of enhanced societal reflexivity and citizen capacity to help guide systemic operations in ways informed by considerations of human flourishing and the need to protect the natural environment. Nationalism, populism, geo-politics, discourses of national sovereignty, and other allegiances rooted in territorial realities persist. Yet there are also clear signs that the predominance of the model of democratic governance based on the mixed constitution within the nation state is being challenged by global forces, some of which are at work in social systems with transnational constitutions. Theoretical research indicates that some of these systems are increasingly capable of communicating with each other without recourse to coupling via the legal system. More empirical research has to be done in order to get a clearer picture as to whether or not these systems and their constitutions are figuratively more legislative and judicial than executive in terms of internal structure. At first sight it would appear that the economic system of global society is organised according to the principles of the division of labour rather than the division of powers. In many cases, financial services proliferate with only a remote connection to the real economy. Under such conditions, it is not easy to see how decisions about production can be realigned with decisions about investment and taxation. It is problematic to simply advocate better communication between economic and educational systems in order to make a start in the right direction. When a government promises to scrap austerity because of a poor electoral result, or threatens to rate university courses in accordance with the likely salaries the degrees should be able to secure, it is not the clarity of the communication that is in question. It would be more direct and coherent to insist that it is time to re-code economic, political, and educational systems. Once the economic system is understood in terms of social form, and money is analysed as a medium of symbolic communication and as a code, one can decode the code, so to speak, and collectively opt for a differently coded economic constitution. Inequality is not simply the inevitable result of natural differences in talent and the just outcome of a fair fight for scarce resources. If one does assume this, it would seem that the only palliative is moderate redistribution and the establishment of the Financial Conduct Authority and other administrative agencies designed to monitor competition and anticipate deficits in consumer satisfaction. If, instead, one adopts a different code and accepts that economic power should and can be divided, shared, and made accountable to the greatest possible extent, and that an economic system will only be responsive to talent and genuinely fair when this is the case, one is no longer committed to the standard liberal democratic positions on property, competition for what are held to be scarce resources, and equality of opportunity. More to the point, there is no objective reason why diverse needs, satisfaction at work, respect for the natural environment, and other criteria cannot be granted constitutional status by the constituent authority of workers, consumers, and residents in deliberative dialogue. The history of democratic political evolution is marked by the capacity that citizens have acquired to amend the constitutions of their states. Can they now acquire the capacity to re-code some of the primary social systems? At first glance, the global dimension of transnational constitutions would seem to pose insuperable problems of scale. Yet everyone around the world has some direct experience and knowledge of educational, economic, political, legal, and other systems, and everyone around the world has a familiarity with different media of symbolic communication. It is true that there are as yet few convincing answers to the question of how best to represent systemic actors in abstraction from considerations of national and tribal territory. Yet globalisation and digitalisation indicate that it is increasingly important to distinguish between territory and space. The implications for the space of representation have not been fully explored.

Whilst it might be tempting, it would be imprecise to regard the diverse restrictions on suffrage, enclosure movements, rampant economic exploitation, persistent inequality, and other features of early liberal democratic national societies as simply the first stages in a movement towards twenty-first-century neoliberal patterns of global governance in which exclusion and inequality are merely perpetuated in new guises. The matter is far more complex than this vaguely conspiratorial and determinist view suggests.[31] It might also be tempting, but would be similarly incorrect, to dismiss the constitutional tenor of much liberal and republican thought as an apology for the formal political equality that obscures all kinds of real inequality and hierarchy in daily life. One could then easily conclude that liberal democratic and capitalist thinking and practice coalesce in constitutional orders, which is why radical contestation and authentic democratic transformation have to bypass constitutionalism and revert to the conquest of constituent power by a newly formed collective subject. The conclusion that we must thoroughly re-think prevailing conceptions of individual and collective autonomy is far more compelling.[32]

Speculative conjecture about the possible third coming (after the liberal democratic urban bourgeoisie and then the revolutionary socialist working class) of nationally sovereign constitutive power ignores the methodological point made above, namely, that post-feudal political systems can only function democratically if they are accompanied by a series of parallel social systems functioning according to a variety of incommensurable codes. The problem can now be addressed by focusing on democratising those codes in ways that are sensitive to systemic specificity, that is, by thinking about how best to democratise social systems without foisting markedly inappropriate codes on them for the purposes of hegemonic governance, or politicising those systems in accordance with strong dialectical criteria of inclusionary unity.[33] To do so is to presuppose mediated unity and corresponding forms of political authority that culminate in a spiralling pyramidal structure leading to the summit of the state. Apart from the fact that such a democratic imaginary is pre-Hegelian in many ways, it also fails to see that for obvious reasons there can be no global judiciary functioning in tandem with a global state. With a few possible exceptions, it is likely to prove very difficult to extend the process of territorial state building or to reproduce the dynamics of the emblematic eighteenth-century revolutions. In national territorial terms, the globe is already occupied by states and former colonies that have become variously weak and strong states. It is mistaken to conflate early modern Europe with the realities of a far more extensively differentiated world society in which land, nation, and state all play a significantly different role than they did prior to 1945. Enabling global social systems to develop their own functional equivalents of the judiciaries and legislatures of nation states offers a more promising path towards reforming democratic statehood. Whilst this may mean instituting constitutional provisions designed to respect the division of powers within certain systems, it also means challenging divisions in other systems that have insulated a number of such intra-systemic powers from critique, as in the case of central banks that demand independence from the political accountability brought to bear on national treasuries. This particular way of demarcating the jurisdiction of powers is extremely effective in producing the impression that whilst governments are wasteful and corrupt, banks are rational, efficient, and in any case too big to fail.[34]

The more general point is that depending on the system in question, distinct approaches to democratisation will be needed to reform the operation in question. To ignore these distinctions amounts to an attempt somehow to salvage the mediated unity paradigm, and, at the same time, to fall back on quantitative indices of inclusion in an historical period that demands qualitative reforms. Breaking with that model is not accomplished simply by declaring the need to embrace the post-foundational contingencies of late and post-modernity. Recognising that a political system can only function democratically if it is accompanied by parallel social systems functioning according to a wide variety of codes can only be the first step towards understanding that the constitutional division of powers at the level of states has evolved towards a proliferation of social-systemic operations that do not simply reproduce the public political division of powers on a smaller scale. It therefore becomes important to examine where the analogies between the separation of political powers, as applied to states, can be drawn in relation to social systems, and where, on the contrary, one can discern qualitative differences between political constitutions and social-systemic constitutions. Liberal political systems may normally help produce governments according to the principle of majority rule. However, political systems working within the liberal democratic nation state rely on the constitutional division of powers within that territory in order to function. Whilst the political systems supposedly function according to quantitative vote totals, the states, by contrast, function according to more complex, qualitative criteria. Some of these criteria, such as those informing the workings of independent legal systems and in (naïve) principle non-politicised economies, for example, are clearly at odds with a number of conceptions of democracy and justice. There is no way, moreover, that legal systems and economies ever really function in such pristinely neutral ways vis-à-vis entrenched patterns of power manifested in hierarchy, privilege, and discrimination. Critical systems theory does not defend this claim. It claims, instead, that (1) systemic operations are coupled, de-coupled, and re-coupled in ways that suggest that inter-systemic communication does in fact already take place and often does so in ways that are repressed and displaced by an inter-ministerial approach to managing social systems, and that (2) territorial nation states are increasingly unable to address entrenched patterns of hierarchy, privilege, and intersectional conflict which contribute to the repression in question. This is not simply due to neglect or vicious malevolence on the part of ruling elites – although austerity and other measures may often make it seem so. At this historical juncture, the inadequacy of political statehood in this regard can better be explained by the fact that (3) within the currently hegemonic model of FD, the differentiation of politics and economics is unfolding in ways that minimalise political control and accountability, and, in a related vein, that (4) it is highly implausible, within the constitutional terms of that model, to maintain that all social systems, especially the economic system, are on an equal footing.[35] This is not to say that political, religious, legal, educational, and other power is ultimately economic power. The crucial addendum to point (3) is that the expression 'political control' is intentionally vague, and begs the obvious question, 'political control of what?'. *Democratic* political statehood, at least in the terms projected by notions of constituent power and the rule of the people, implicitly promises citizens individual and collective control over all aspects of their lives. This is clearly not possible in a functionally differentiated late modern world society. It does not follow that heteronomy must be embraced as inevitable, in some kind of gleeful post-modernism. Instead, the question of democracy can now be reconceptualised in societal constitutional terms. It can be approached by showing that inter-systemic mediation may be able to take the place of what overarching, comprehensively unifying inclusionary political form promises but can only deliver in two ways. It can try to do so in a highly centralised authoritarian regime, or, as continues to be the case in most post-democracies, by ritualistically holding out but constantly failing to fulfil the promise of individual and collective control over familial, legal, political, economic, educational, scientific, technological, medical, and other processes. The crucial addendum to (4) is that the challenges and obstacles to putting the economic system on a genuinely equal footing with the other primary social systems can be interpreted in a wide variety of ways. Doubts will certainly arise in view of the fact that just as legal systems and economies never really function in pristinely neutral ways, it is hard to see how a situation of social-systemic parity might be possible in constitutional terms. There will be more to say about this below and in the conclusion to this book. The more general point for now is that the liberation of social form from a predefined conception of political unity marks the potential start towards addressing the diverse modalities of coerced integration in late modernity in a coherent, critical way.[36]

How and to what extent are social systems currently capable of developing societal constitutions?

In Western Europe during the first three decades following 1945, social democratic governments committed to Keynesian management of the money supply and an array of welfare policies were periodically able to align the wider criteria of justice referred to above with a broadly egalitarian vision of social inclusion based on solidarity and diverse instances of recognition. On this basis, it was possible to reach relatively durable compromises reconciling the numerical dimension of democracy with more substantive conceptions of justice, and to do so in ways that did not flagrantly violate the constitutional division of state powers. It is probably unwise to read vote totals literally, or to deduce that social democratic parties have simply become less popular. The analysis offered here suggests instead that the capacity for a certain measure of political control of the money supply that once functioned under largely social democratic auspices within the nation state has been undermined by a coupling of certain sub-systems of the global financial system with sub-systems of the global judicial system, thus conjuring up the somewhat apocalyptic possibility of a world run by large corporations with their own privately controlled courts (and armies and intelligence agencies). If this re-coupling thesis is at least partially correct, it is now possible to speak in terms of an international historical bloc that has relied on and continues to rely on the institutions of global governance to provide and hegemonically establish the foundations of a practice of statehood largely de-coupled from the results of national elections and demands for various kinds of rights. This does not mean that there is some kind of conspiracy between elites across states; it indicates that inter-systemic communication on a global scale has diminished the qualitative capacity states once had to read rights claims as demands for democratic inclusion and more than merely procedural justice. These claims are now more likely to be read not by states, as such, but by social systems which, since the ascent of neoliberalism, have been gradually re-coded to read them, in key instances and boundary situations between systems and systemic environments, as demands for enhanced competitive advantage. The foregoing analysis serves to reinforce the point that within the currently hegemonic model of FD, the differentiation of political and economic systems largely nullifies political control of the economy as well as the political signifi-cance of other social systems. The implications for diverse practices of repre-sentation are only slowly starting to emerge. To a steadily increasing degree the citizens of twenty-first-century world society may be compelled to com-municate their demands for social inclusion as demands for (partially politi-cised) rights of inclusion in distinct and nonetheless overlapping global social systems. This would mark a subtle but really rather revolutionary break with the practice of articulating those demands to governments via political parties firmly anchored in territorial states governed by distinctly national approaches to the dialectics of legality and legitimacy.[37]

It is difficult to overestimate the stakes involved or the challenges implied by the apparent demise, at this historical junction, of what Wolfgang Streeck refers to as democratic capitalism.[38] The first signs of this demise appeared with the abrupt return to fiscal orthodoxy by the Mitterrand government in the early 1980s, and the subsequent election of the Blair and Schröder governments in Britain and Germany towards the end of the 1990s. The predicament of the French Socialist Party since the departure of Lionel Jospin reinforces the point. The stakes are delineated by the juxtaposition between Keynesian economic management and an inclusive vision of social integration based on solidarity and recognition, on the one hand, and the scenario of a world run by large corporations with their own privately controlled courts, armies, and intelligence agencies, on the other. It is too early to tell if the crisis of democratic capital-ism is now definitive. If it turns out to be, the juxtaposition cedes to a situation that is closer to what some first-generation critical theorists occasionally allude to as the dystopian possibility of a totally administered world. Advocates of social constitutionalism, by contrast, do not shy away from the implications of the advent of what has been investigated here as the possibility of social statehood and an alternative scenario in which twenty-first-century world society citizens communicate their demands for social inclusion as demands for rights of inclusion in individual global social systems. In light of the demise of the social democratic capacity to 'tame capitalism', it is not completely speculative to believe that there may be a clash between the privatised corporate model of highly attenuated mediation and the societal constitutionalist one. A number of first-generation thinkers long for a pluri-centred dialectics that mediates social processes without managing or directing them, and hope that this is possible beyond the fields of modernist art and music. Within this potential framework in waiting, it is conceivable to have an economic system that functions on a genuinely equal footing with the other primary social systems. Alternatively, it is certainly possible to try to organise world society as a global race for tangible metrics of competitive success such as cost cutting in health, education, housing, science, production, and elsewhere, and it is true that organised competition does provide one way of institutionalising integration both within and across social systems. But these are largely instrumental governance strategies that conflate the struggle for enhanced competitive advantage with demands for democratic inclusion, and therefore imply a selective de-differentiation of educational, economic, and political systems. Leaving that issue aside for the moment, the central question at hand concerns the capacity of social systems to read demands for democratic inclusion in ways that carry forward and develop further the historical lessons of political modernity and state formation. Key in this regard is the indispensability of the separation of powers for the possibility of non-coerced integration, that is, for democratic inclusion. One can begin by investigating the extent to which something like this is already at work within specific social systems.

When the basic compromises and alliances constituting a given historical bloc show signs of disaggregation, it is not always immediately apparent that the order in question is entering a process of rapid re-composition and realignment. Where the bases of social stability are undermined as a result of relatively minor shocks, such as unexpected interim electoral results, sensationalised corruption scandals, or similarly transitory phenomena, it is likely that one is observing a case of faulty FD. Power is manifestly over-centralised when an autocrat such as Erdogan can manipulate the justice system and have academics, lawyers, and journalists dismissed or imprisoned, or when a musical group is deemed to be dangerous and subversive.[39] But what are we to make of more complex events, as when, say, financial crises become full-blown crises of state? At the heart of this study is a close examination of the concept of mediated unity, and a concomitant analysis of the extent to which specific political milestones, most notably the division of powers informing the conceptualisation of modern statehood, exist in a relation of tension with assumptions about sovereignty and constituent power borrowed from the mediated unity paradigm. Institutions have a practical history and an ongoing daily life that coexists with their intellectual history. It is often the case that distinct ideas are mixed together, as for example when the division of powers and popular sovereignty are lumped together and said to provide the foundations of democracy. Similarly, it is schematically asserted that whilst the division of powers and individual rights are the domain of liberalism, popular sovereignty ensures that democracy is legitimate in content rather than merely legal in form. Both approaches are inaccurate and neglect the considerable role played by states, constitutions, and FD. There can be no doubt about the conceptual boldness (Hegel and others) and institutional innovation (states as opposed to aggregates of private power and feudal hierarchies) associated with the mediated unity paradigm. In view of some of the contemporary realities of transnational 'democracy' and global governance, however, doubts do arise in relation to the feasibility both of the composition of the unity in question and the key mediating instances often taken to be constitutive of that unity. Whilst for Hegel and Gramsci, the latter are to be found in civil society, other observers may be more likely to point to political parties and their traditional electorates. Whilst the Socialist Party of Spain could always count on the support of the miners of Asturias, and the Communist Party of France knew it had safe seats in certain suburbs of Paris, Christian Democratic parties typically relied on a similar mechanism of translating the cultural values prevalent in easily identifiable social milieux into votes. It may have seemed that the complexities of mediation and inclusion were straightforwardly resolved by re-presenting the pillars of society in paradigmatic state institutions. Now that the mechanisms of this kind of corporatist governance appear to be in disarray in the wake of neoliberalism and globalisation, many members of those milieux feel excluded, neglected, and forgotten. Colin Crouch sums up the situation by saying that 'No political family can look forward to a comfortable future'.[40]

There may be an understandable temptation to look back with nostalgia upon what, however briefly in actual historical terms, may have been the epoch of integral statehood and national community in Europe and other parts of the world. Some advocates of this nostalgia may say that without these preconditions, democracy has to be inadequately representative and chronically populist. A closer look reveals that the era of political families was considerably more nepotistic and hierarchical at both national and international levels than most people may care to recall. Corporatist structures of bargaining typically favoured well-organised sectors of the work force employed in traditional trades at the expense of others. The application of human rights after 1945 has to be examined bearing in mind the acute dependence of African, Asian, and South American colonies and ex-colonies on aid and development from their respective mother countries. Observers wont to bemoan the passing of these arrangements often overlook the vertical chain of command that structured the world order throughout the early modern and subsequent phases of state building. It would of course be far too simplistic to say that authoritarian paternalism and corporatist structures of patrimony are the only realities underlying the supposed unity of citizens, law, representative governments, and democratic states. By contrast, one can claim that (1) the transition from aggregates of private power and feudal hierarchies to modern states was never fully conclusive, even if residual hierarchies tend to shed their expressly feudal character during the course of global history, and that (2) the transition from segmented societies to functionally differentiated societies can also be seen as incomplete and ongoing. The enduring legacy of these two points is discussed in previous chapters in terms of antagonistic concept building, the partially inclusive statehood of politicised rights, and erratic patterns of FD frequently characterised by the distortions of strategic de-differentiation. One can now tentatively outline the possible further trajectory of these transitions as they continue to evolve.

This chapter suggests that there are good reasons to believe that the evolutionary gains of political modernity and sociological modernity can be reconciled and mutually enforcing, and that a great deal turns on how effectively social systems are able to learn from the history of modern state building in one specific sense. Two questions arise in this regard. Can systems develop capacities akin to the reflexivity enlisted by states that have enabled them, albeit to widely varying degrees depending on the state and historical period in question, to establish even and consistent patterns of inclusion, whilst also purposely designing power in ways that limit the arbitrary exercise of power? Can citizens be educated to learn from the history of states and the sociology of systems, in order to enable systems better to co-ordinate social processes? To many this may seem menacingly like re-education. But given the relations currently prevailing between systems, it is specious to think that an educational system that is now to a large extent de-coupled from the political system can become anything other than a subservient sub-system of the global economic system. There is, in any case, an acute and obvious need for the constitutional re-ordering of the relations between educational, political, and economic systems across a wide variety of states around the world. It can be compared to the need for parliaments to exert control over executives during decisive transition periods in the evolution of statehood. It may otherwise prove impossible to restore some of the mediated proximity between (at that time elite) citizens and binding decision-making processes that may have characterised facets of liberal democratic statehood during the heyday of the public sphere.[41] One can make a start towards some tentative answers to these questions by analysing how states were able to develop constitutional provisions to safeguard the division of powers, and by an assessment of the evolutionary capacity of systems to do so in operations that are not, strictly speaking, limited to the exercise of political power, but instead pertain to scientific knowledge, economic growth, aesthetic experience, environmental health, or legal procedure. It might be objected that the currently hegemonic model of FD gradually emerged in tandem with the consolidation of merely formally democratic states, which in notable cases experienced authoritarian interludes and embarked on imperialist conquests that were not rectified until very recently or, because of enduring legacies of colonial dependence, have not yet been sufficiently rectified.[42] It could therefore be deduced that social systems generated on this basis have little chance of developing the requisite degree of reflexivity needed in order for them to re-code their operations in accordance with considerations of human wellbeing and environmental safety.

One very reasonable reply is that there is little point in asking whether systems can develop reflexive and self-steering capacities, since, as the example of law and transnational constitutions indicates, they are in the process of doing just this in manifest disregard of national borders. They will continue to perform these tasks in ways that are still inchoate and not easy to research due to the conspicuous absence of organised citizen input into inter-systemic mediation. Legal and other social systems across the world exhibit a marked propensity towards *autopoiesis* and active adaptation to their neighbouring social-systemic environments, thus raising the question as to how inter-systemic mediation might be organised in the coming decades. Luhmann remarks that in the process of systemic differentiation, individual systems tend to generate internal constitutions that enable them, in markedly different degrees and in qualitatively different ways, to achieve re-coupling with other social systems.[43] It is Luhmann who insists that social systems exist, that they communicate, and that, over time, they tend to generate internal constitutions. Admittedly he does not seem seriously to consider the possibility that there could be anything like organised citizen input into inter-systemic mediation. Yet it is that communication and those decisions that could map the path from self-referential social systems to societal constitutions.

Notes

1 Felicity Lawrence, 'A modern Commons Charter', *Guardian* (8 November 2017), p. 32. Ian Bullock notes that during the interwar years of the twentieth century, voices within the Independent Labour Party (ILP) articulated a coherent alternative to market dogma and state socialism. A key figure in those debates was G. D. H. Cole, the author of *Guild Socialism Re-Stated*, who in some ways can be regarded as a

precursor to societal constitutionalism. For Cole's theory of functional democracy and his influence on the ILP see Ian Bullock, *Under Siege: The Independent Labour Party in Interwar Britain* (Edmonton: Athabasca University Press, 2017), pp. 50–61. Bullock's conclusion stresses the living legacy of left libertarian organisational principles both within and outside of the international labour movement. Some of these have been taken up and renewed by certain strands of feminism, environmentalism, and champions of 'the commons'. Derek Wall shows how in *Elinor Ostrom's Rules for Radicals: Cooperative Alternatives Beyond Markets and States* (London: Pluto, 2017).

2 Grimm, *Die Zukunft der Verfassung II*, p. 11. Similarly, Chris Thornhill speaks of the inclusionary structure of modern society as, broadly speaking, a constitutional one, and, to an ever increasing extent, a transnational one. See his introduction to *Sociology of Transnational Constitutions*, pp. 1–30. Anticipating the discussion to follow, it should be clear at this stage that the very notion of 'a British perspective' (or any national perspective) on constitutions will have to cede to a far more nuanced notion of observation from social-systemic, rather than national perspectives.

3 Niklas Luhmann, 'Globalization or World Society: How to Conceive of Modern Society?', in Albert Scherr (ed.), *Systemtheorie und Differenzierungstheorie als Kritik: Perspektiven in Anschluss an Niklas Luhmann* (Basle: Beltz, 2015), pp. 38–55.

4 In this context, Luhmann refers to constitution building as an evolutionary resource. See his 'Verfassung als evolutionäre Errungenschaft', *Rechtshistorisches Journal*, 9 (1990), 176–220, at p. 176, and *Recht der Gesellschaft*, pp. 450–3, available in English as *Law as a Social System*, pp. 388–91.

5 Two main controversies are debated in the literature on this subject. The first concerns the degree to which individual systems develop normative structures autonomously as part of their evolution towards stability vis-à-vis other systems. The second turns on disagreements about whether or not social-systemic norms generated in this manner qualify as constitutional in any meaningful sense. David Sciulli argues yes on both counts. See his pioneering *Theory of Societal Constitutionalism*. For a much more sceptical view, see Grimm, *Die Zukunft der Verfassung II*.

6 Rawls and Habermas are two of the few thinkers to frame questions of justice and legitimacy outside of those paradigms. For a very good look at the issues involved, see the chapters included in James Gordon Finlayson and Fabian Freyenhagen (eds), *Habermas and Rawls: Disputing the Political* (New York: Routledge, 2011). Luhmann does so, too, and in ways that are much more in tune with the sociological dynamics of modern society.

7 Schmitt and the crisis of Weimar provide the emblematic examples in this regard. For an analysis, see Kennedy, *Constitutional Failure*, chapters 2 and 5. For a somewhat more favourable assessment of Schmitt, see Kalyvas, *Democracy and the Politics of the Extraordinary*, Part II.

8 Some of these issues are addressed by Andrew Bowie, *Adorno and the Ends of Philosophy* (Cambridge: Polity, 2013). Valerie Whittington's research shows that the matter is more complex, and the alternatives more varied, than is suggested in the text here. See her work on 'The Challenges of Deliberative Democracy' (D.Phil, University of Sussex, forthcoming).

9 It might be countered that the displacement of decision-making and steering functions to transnational bodies has already rescued late modern statehood from an excess of intensive inclusionary demands on the part of manifold local actors in diverse national societies. For a comprehensive overview of the debates on this thesis with specific reference to the present and future of the EU, see the chapters included in Outhwaite (ed.), *Brexit: Sociological Responses* and Kjaer *et al.* (eds), *Financial Crisis in Constitutional Perspective*.

10 Dani Rodrik remarks that to most observers, Yanis Varoufakis and Wolfgang Schäuble would seem to represent utterly irreconcilable positions on questions of public debt, austerity, and the function of the European Central Bank and IMF. Rodrik points out that despite this apparent chasm of opinion on EU matters, both share the premise that economic union should have been the basis of political union, and that without the latter, economic union would eventually be undermined. Of course, whilst Schäuble sees political union as a means to impose strong fiscal discipline on member states, Varoufakis sees it as a means to counter the power that creditors have over the Greek economy. Without explicitly referring to systems-theoretical methodology, Rodrik suggests that the relations between the fiscal, financial, and monetary sub-systems need to be re-coded so that a transnational banking union is possible without thereby having to accept a transnational fiscal union, so that fiscal policy can be guided by broader political concerns as well as regional and national realities. The short-term goal then becomes that of de-coupling private finance from public finance, so that the latter can be re-coupled to a mediated instance of citizen control. See Dani Rodrik, 'Does Europe really need fiscal and political union?', *Social Europe*, 8 January (2018).

11 Habermas's *Legitimation Crisis* offers the most persuasive and coherent statement of the arguments involved. Also see Claus Offe, 'Structural problems of the capitalist state', *German Political Studies*, 1 (1974 [1972]), 31–56. For a detailed analysis of this essay in the light of some of the broader themes in Offe's work, see Jens Borchert and Stephan Lessenich, *Claus Offe and the Critical Theory of the Capitalist State* (New York: Routledge, Taylor & Francis Group, 2016).

12 For an analysis of the erosion of statehood since 1945, see Thomas D. Zweifel, *International Organizations and Democracy: Accountability, Politics, and Power* (London: Lynne Rienner, 2006) and Grimm, *Die Zukunft der Verfassung II*, pp. 330–42. For a brilliant discussion of the contradictory imperatives facing states since the end of the Cold War, see Udo Di Fabio, *Der Verfassungsstaat in der Weltgesellschaft* (Tübingen: Mohr Siebeck, 2001), pp. 50–6 and pp. 129–30, and Helmut Willke, *Ironie des Staates: Grundlinien einer Staatstheorie polyzentrischer Gesellschaft* (Frankfurt: Suhrkamp, 1992), chapter 4. Willke skilfully addresses the question of what kind of expressly *political* authority is possible in highly complex, polycentric societies. The standard answers range from a highly pared-down Weberian definition to the intimate 'politics of friendship' espoused by Derrida and others. Notions of communicative action and recognition often occupy the middle ground between Weber and Derrida. Willke's comparative methodological strength in this regard stems from the fact that he develops his position with consistent reference to the important role played by FD in the constitution of modern society. For a similarly nuanced and sociological approach, see Peter Fuchs, *Die Erreichbarkeit der Gesellschaft: Zur Konstruktion und Imagination gesellschaftlicher Einheit* (Frankfurt: Suhrkamp, 1992), pp. 67–81; and the chapters contained in Renate Mayntz, Bernd Rosewitz, Uwe Schimank, and Rudolf Stichweh (eds), *Differenzierung und Verselbständigung: Zur Entwicklung gesellschaftlicher Teilsysteme* (Frankfurt: Campus, 1988). It is of great interest that Teubner's *Recht als autopoietisches System* (Frankfurt: Suhrkamp, 1989) and the studies by di Fabio, Willke, Mayntz et al., and Fuchs all appear just before and immediately after the end of the Cold War, i.e. in the period in which globalisation is set to reach a new level of intensity.

13 Alain Supiot, 'Et si l'on refondait le droit du travail...', *Le Monde Diplomatique* (October 2017), pp. 1 and 22–23.

14 Gramsci, *Quaderni del carcere*, Vol. II, Q.6, pp. 690–1 and Q.11, pp. 1505–6. Readers of English can consult the relevant passages on Gramsci's conception of

the historical bloc in *Prison Notebooks*. For supplementary exegetical analysis see Schecter, *The History of the Left*, chapter 2.

15 For a detailed analysis of all of these thinkers, see Bellamy, *Modern Italian Social Theory*.

16 For a more detailed discussion of Gramsci's views on these matters see Schecter, 'Gramsci's unorthodox Marxism' and 'Historical Bloc'.

17 Pierre Bourdieu, *La Noblesse d'Etat: Grandes Ecoles et esprit de corps* (Paris: Les Minuit, 1989), available in English as *The State Nobility: Elite Schools in the Field of Power* (Oxford: Polity, 1996), Parts IV–V.

18 These issues are covered in detail by Gurminder K. Bhambra, *Rethinking Modernity: Postcolonialism and the Sociological Imagination* (Basingstoke: Palgrave, 2007).

19 Pierre France and Antoine Vauchez, *Sphère publique, intérêts privés: Enquête sur un grand brouillage* (Paris: Presses de Sciences Po, 2017), chapter 3.

20 When the much-vaunted transition to parliamentary democracy took place in Spain, many of these longer-term problems were ignored, thus contributing to the severity of the situation in Catalonia today. Commenting on the matter shortly before things actually came to the impasse of October 2017, Inigo Errejon remarks that 'we are the children of the incompetent political elites of the regime of 1978' (p. 43). See Iñigo Errejón and Josep Ramoneda, 'Conversación', *La Maleta de Portbou*, 21, January–February (2017), 39–44. Knud Andresen and Stefan Müller confirm the importance of the 1970s as a pivotal transition period and unofficial abrogation of the constitutional compromises that prevailed in Europe after 1945. See their 'Contesting Deregulation: The 1970s as a Turning Point in Western History? Introductory Remarks', in Knud Andresen and Stefan Müller (eds), *Contesting Deregulation: Debates, Practices and Developments in the West since the 1970s* (New York: Berghahn Books, 2017), pp. 1–20.

21 On the case of the Glorious Revolution, see Pincus, *1688: The First Modern Revolution*, Part V. Although there was no feudal history to oppose in the North American case, Michelle Alexander shows that malevolent political control of electoral constituencies prevailed until the Voting Rights Act (1965). She also points out that the reforms supposedly guaranteed by that measure are by no means safe from further manipulation. See Michelle Alexander, *The New Jim Crow: Mass Incarceration in the Age of Colorblindness* (New York: New Press, 2010), chapters 3 and 5.

22 In relation to the French Revolution, for example, Tocqueville maintains that the Revolution continued the process of political centralisation that had been initiated by the absolute monarchy. See Tocqueville, *L'Ancien Régime et la Révolution*.

23 Teubner, *Critical Theory and Legal Autopoiesis*. The volume includes an excellent introduction and afterword by Andreas Philippopoulos-Mihalopoulos and Alberto Febbrajo. It might be objected that just because social systems develop constitutional features, this does not necessarily mean that they are capable of intersystemic co-ordination, thus returning us to the point where we were at the outset, relying on ministerial responsibility and informal agreements between elites circulating within and across social systems. This point is addressed below. For a further look at these crucial issues, see the chapters included in Paul Blokker and Chris Thornhill (eds), *Sociological Constitutionalism* (Cambridge: Cambridge University Press, 2017).

24 See Durkheim, *De la division du travail social*, available in English as *Division of Labor*, chapter 2 on mechanical solidarity. Durkheim observes that stratified societies and organic communities define their members' functions by relying on some notion

of natural similarity between person and function. This makes for a fairly rigid division of labour and somewhat stunted structures of communication that are poorly adapted to conditions of complexity and contingency. Alex Elliot addresses some of these questions in 'On the Concept of Solidarity' (D.Phil, University of Sussex, 2018). His comparison between Durkheim and Habermas is of particular relevance to an assessment of contemporary instances of inter-systemic communication.

25 Uwe Schimank, *Gesellschaft* (Bielefeld: Transcript, 2013), pp. 51–2. For an analysis of the various points of intersection between aesthetic and technological systemic rationalities, see Edward A. Shanken, 'Reprogramming Systems Aesthetics', in Edward A. Shanken (ed.), *Systems* (Cambridge, MA: MIT Press, 2015), pp. 123–9; and Francis Halsall, 'Systems of Art', in Edward A. Shanken (ed.), *Systems* (Cambridge, MA: MIT Press, 2015), pp. 130–6.

26 Moritz Renner goes so far as to say that a critique of the economic system today is only possible as a systems-theoretical critique, and that, perhaps even more surprisingly, Luhmann's *The Economy of Society* [*Die Wirtschaft der Gesellschaft* (Frankfurt: Suhrkamp, 1988)] should be understood as a classic example of a critique of capitalism appropriate for the global neoliberal period. See Moritz Renner, 'Die Wirtschaft der Weltgesellschaft: Möglichkeitsräume für eine systemtheoretische Kritik', in Marc Amstutz and Andreas Fischer-Lescano (eds), *Kritische Systemtheorie: Zur Evolution einer normativen Theorie* (Bielefeld: Transcript, 2013), pp. 219–36, at p. 219. His argument may strike many as an exaggeration of the critical potential of systems theory in general and of Luhmann's theoretical oeuvre in particular. Yet Renner highlights the very valid point that systems theory is an apposite point of departure for critical interdisciplinary social research that is not limited by normative commitments to an anthropology of communicative action or interpersonal recognition.

27 For a discussion of some of the ambiguities in Luhmann's writings on this subject, see Michael King and Chris Thornhill, *Niklas Luhmann's Theory of Politics and Law* (Basingstoke: Palgrave Macmillan, 2003), pp. 69–82 and pp. 99–109.

28 Regina Kreide, 'Die verdrängte Demokratie: Kommunikations- und Handlungsblockaden in einer globalisierten Welt', in Smail Rapic (ed.), *Habermas und der historische Materialismus* (Munich: Karl Alber, 2014), pp. 229–60.

29 This is by no means to say that wealth redistribution is therefore unimportant or outdated. But it does indicate that redistribution in various senses will be best furthered by constitutional reform that pays close attention to diverse patterns of FD. For a more anthropological approach, see Nancy Fraser and Axel Honneth, *Redistribution or Recognition? A Political-Philosophical Exchange* (London: Verso, 2003). Dogmatic systems theorists will probably say the term democratic should be applied exclusively to the political system precisely because the idea of a 'democratic society' is so vague.

30 Helmut Willke makes the valuable exegetical point that the development of systems-theoretical reflections on FD can be seen as the latter part of a line of thinking that issues from Adam Smith on specialisation, Durkheim on the division of labour, and Simmel on differentiation. He notes that this theoretical trajectory culminates in the concept of self-referential social systems, thus raising the pressing question of how best to co-ordinate their respective operations without diminishing their evolving capacity for self-government. See Helmut Willke, *Regieren: Politische Steuerung komplexer Gesellschaften* (Wiesbaden: Springer VS, 2013), p. 16. One may deduce, first, that the public sphere and a vibrant civil society are the necessary conditions of non-authoritarian democracy during the period of national society

and political statehood, and conclude, second, that inter-systemic communication and mediation are indispensable in this regard during the currently unfolding period of world society and social statehood. Despite the persistence of notable vestiges of national society and political statehood, it is difficult to deny that world society has become a factual reality. Social statehood, by contrast, must still be instituted. Showing that social systems are developing constitutional properties is the first in a series of steps needed in order to make the normative case for social statehood plausible.

31 For a far more nuanced view, see David Feldman, 'Migrants, immigrants and welfare from the old poor law to the welfare state', *Transactions of the Royal Historical Society*, 13 (2003), 79–104.

32 Skilful refutations of this line of argument can be found in Bellamy, *Political Constitutionalism*, Part II; and Gunther Teubner, 'Constitutional Drift: Spontaneous Co-evolution of Social Ideas and Legal Form', in Michael W. Dowdle and Michael A. Wilkinson (eds), *Constitutionalism Beyond Liberalism* (Cambridge: Cambridge University Press, 2017), pp. 79–95.

33 With specific reference to the global educational system, John Smyth forcefully makes the case that a variety of flexible and pluralist codes are being ruled out as not sufficiently competitive in favour of narrowly defined criteria of popularity and consumer satisfaction. See John Smyth, *The Toxic University: Zombie Leadership, Academic Rock Stars and Neoliberal Ideology* (London: Palgrave Macmillan, 2017).

34 Pettifor, *Production of Money*, chapter 6; Michael Hudson, *The Bubble and Beyond: Fictitious Capital, Debt Deflation and the Global Crisis* (New York: Inlet, 2012), introduction.

35 Werner Bonefeld, *Critical Theory and the Critique of Political Economy: On Subversion and Negative Reason*, Critical Theory and Contemporary Society (New York: Bloomsbury, 2014), chapter 2 (on political economy and social constitution), pp. 21–51; Rodrigo Cordero, Aldo Mascareño, and Daniel Chernilo, 'On the reflexivity of crises: lessons from critical theory and systems theory', *European Journal of Social Theory*, 20:4 (2017), 511–30; and Uwe Schimank, 'Die Prekarität funktionaler Differenzierung – und soziologische Gesellschaftskritik als "double talk"', in Albert Scherr (ed.), *Systemtheorie und Differenzierungstheorie als Kritik: Perspektiven in Anschluss an Niklas Luhmann* (Weinheim and Basle: Beltz-Juventa, 2015), pp. 80–103.

36 Simmel is the great pioneer in this line of sociological enquiry who anticipates the work of thinkers as diverse as Heidegger and Luhmann in a number of ways. For a fine analysis linking Simmel and first-generation critical theory, see Goodstein, *Georg Simmel and the Disciplinary Imaginary*, pp. 125 and pp. 296–306.

37 It is certainly possible to overstate the extent to which parties, governments, and states are currently challenged by social systems and inter-systemic communication. There is also a risk involved when analysing the modalities of the possibilities for transition in this regard. One can be mistakenly seen to be advocating privatisation simply because most attempts to circumvent existing channels of authority and representation tend to be strategies for avoiding tax and consolidating existing patterns of highly unequal wealth accumulation. This argument is made in different ways by Piketty, Streeck, Held, and Crouch. They show how it is possible to buttress existing practices of statehood, and thereby achieve the equality and justice prevalent in European societies during the three decades following 1945. Also see William Mitchell and Thomas Fazi, *Reclaiming the State: A Progressive Vision of Sovereignty for a Post-Neoliberal World* (London: Pluto, 2017).

38 See Streeck, *Buying Time*.
39 Many people may be inclined to regard the Erdogan and Putin regimes as similar in composition and hierarchical structure. For an opposing view that highlights the independence of the Constitutional Court in the Russian Federation, see Thornhill, *Sociology of Transnational Constitutions*, pp. 219–29.
40 Colin Crouch, 'Globalization, Nationalism, and the Changing Axes of Political Identity', in William Outhwaite (ed.), *Brexit: Sociological Responses* (London: Anthem Press, 2017), pp. 101–10, at p. 108.
41 Jacques Rancière has done some very valuable research into the history of libertarian socialism, and has found that there are historical precedents for this kind of re-ordering. See his *La Nuit des prolétaires: Archives du rêve ouvrier* (Paris: Fayard, 1981), chapters 7 and 11.
42 For example, the organisation responsible for uniting the French Colonies of Africa may have been renamed as the Financial Community of Africa, but the states that comprise it still need permission from Paris to print money and make financial decisions of any importance. See Dominic Johnson, 'Liberté? Na ja', *Fluter. Magazin der Bundeszentrale für politische Bildung*, 59 (2016), 33.
43 Although he does not explicitly state the matter in such romantic terms, it sometimes sounds almost as if systems long to achieve a relationship with other systems that moves beyond that of mere external irritations from their respective environments. See Niklas Luhmann, 'Die Unterscheidung von Staat und Gesellschaft', in *Soziologische Aufklärung 4: Beiträge zur funktionalen Differenzierung der Gesellschaft* (Wiesbaden: VS Verlag für Sozialwissenschaften, 4th edn, 2009 [1987]), pp. 69–76, at pp. 73–4.

Conclusion

Democratic state, capitalist society, or dysfunctional differentiation?

When the Institute for Social Research was founded in Frankfurt in 1923, its members began work on different facets of an interdisciplinary critique of what they, following Marx, designated as capitalist society. Like Marx, they were in no doubt that it is illusory to think that the state can function in a democratic way if society is not democratically organised as well. Thanks to generous funding through the private resources of Felix Weil, the Institute enjoyed a considerable degree of autonomy from the University of Frankfurt and from the trade unions and the political parties of the Weimar Left. The desideratum of political-epistemological distance from prevailing patterns of institutional mediation was as important to critical theory then as it is today. The distance in question can be likened to the spaces needed to supplement the divisions between the legislative, judicial, and executive branches of the state with additional public resources designed to promote the sharing and control of power. In terms of taking critical theory further, then, it is imperative to help create new configurations of democratic legitimacy that develop the affirmative possibilities intermittently disclosed by the otherwise largely prohibitive injunction to limit power and control authority. Critical theorists today continue to pose questions related to Marx's quip in the *German Ideology* that ruling class ideas are, in every epoch, the ruling ideas. One of those questions is the following: where are truer, less ideological ideas than the ruling ones to be sought, and how are more truthful ideas to be generated? This cannot be done through narrowly academic philosophy or conformist traditional theory. Nor can it be achieved through the general will of an improbable collective subject-object of history. Moving from the Weimar period towards a critical theory of contemporary society nurtured by a positive vision of potential change anchored in ongoing sociological processes, a related question concerns the quality and composition of the countervailing and mutually balancing powers in society. If the state can only function in a democratic way if society is democratically organised as well, it will be necessary to do more than supplement the divisions between the legislative, judicial, and executive branches of the state with a vibrant public sphere. The question as to how best to do so might be formulated as an investigative search for the evolutionary threshold beyond which the ruling ideas and pervasive domination Marx alludes to can be reformed into a continual battle of opposed ideas, contrasting values, and new institutions. Although this might seem like a chimerical threshold, it is implied by the very real historical examples of FD and mixed constitutions. One is of course no longer talking about the mixed constitution or contrasting visions of liberty respectively defended by the noble and popular elements of ancient and Renaissance republics. Nor is this about the supposedly neutral adjudication of the contractual claims and competing interests characteristic of what some Scottish Enlightenment thinkers refer to as commercial society. Moreover, the socio-economic, political, and educational compromises undergirding the mixed corporatist constitutions and welfare states of the post-1945 order in Europe and beyond have been overhauled by the unrelenting austerity measures and dogmatically quantitative metrics of growth imposed by neoliberalism.

There is no going back to the Renaissance republics, the commercial societies of early industrialisation, or the collective bargaining arrangements of corporatist Fordism. There is nonetheless a link between a factual analysis of mutually balancing social forces, FD, and mixed constitutions, on the one hand, and the evidence that ruling ideas and pervasive domination can be reformed into a continual battle of ideas and emergent institutions, on the other. It has been shown in previous chapters that contemporary societies are characterised by the difficulties and discoveries inherent in trying to co-ordinate the operations of discrete social systems functioning according to incommensurate codes, and that some of these difficulties could be remedied to a significant extent in the course of a gradual transition from political to social statehood. It has also been shown that FD produces and also depends on the development of social-systemic autonomy, and that historical modalities of differentiation in their turn have a major impact on what are considered to be viable and less viable models of statehood. Emphasis has been placed on continuity rather than rupture in this regard. Social systems have been in existence as long as there have been human societies. They have been managed, to greater and lesser extents, by a wide variety of power structures operative within diverse forms of statehood. Politically constituted modern states had to perform and continue to perform the numerous governmental tasks bound up with strategies to track and anticipate the likely future trajectories of various social systems. They have tended to do this without sufficient attention to the details of systemic coding or historical patterns of inter-systemic communication, thereby mismanaging the processes involved in many instances. What is more, these states are still desperately trying to channel systems on the basis of strategic decisions stemming from informal assemblies of ministerial elites, consultancy firms, lobbies, and what amount to different kinds of private clients. These are usually vantage points with little theoretical or social proximity to the specific systems in question, thus exacerbating the tendency to misdirect systems whilst coercively integrating citizens. Explicating the link between abuse of systems and coercive integration of citizens is therefore important in terms of the overall project pursued here. It might otherwise seem absurd to borrow from systems theory for the purposes of sketching a critical theory of society capable of indicating possible paths towards such proximity. Most systems theorists will agree that systems are coded. But they will also insist that there is no meaningful communication between social systems, since individual systems register other systems as environments rather than as complementary partners in the reproduction of society and its highly diverse media of symbolic communication. Orthodox proponents of the theory are likely to caution against any attempt to amalgamate systems in some form of social unity that could only be achieved though arbitrary de-differentiation and disrespect for the realities of FD. However, if systems theorists and critical theorists both object to arbitrarily de-differentiated aggregations of systems, they may come a step closer to agreeing that such aggregations can be analysed as states that attempt to manage the systems or, in less conventional terms, as historical blocs. Here one can see an unsuspected affinity between the emphasis on political-epistemological distance from prevailing patterns of institutional mediation in critical theory, on the one hand, and the stress on what systems theorists take to be the necessarily indirect and mediated quality of second-order observations of neighbouring systems, on the other. The disagreements will undoubtedly start again if systems theorists are asked to comment on the claim that the constant restructuring of states and historical blocs is part of an ongoing battle for hegemony that cannot be adequately explained through the descriptive study of social systems. Disagreement is then likely to deepen when intellectual historians and discourse analysts show that in genealogical terms, incommensurable systemic codes first came into existence as incommensurable value systems and as the result of conflictual symbolic communication. Once that genealogical process has been documented, however, the movement to re-code systems may start to look much more like the democratic struggle for a new culture and hegemony in which the theoretical and social proximity referred to above is widely accepted to be a primary condition of the possibility of collective self-government. It will certainly look a lot less like the random manipulation of supposedly inviolable systemic functions. Most systems theorists may not want to take these steps in the direction of critical theory and Gramscian political sociology. But by objecting to flagrant violations of FD, they have already broadly subscribed to the thesis that social-systemic amalgamation is authoritarian and tantamount to dysfunctional differentiation, and that dysfunctional differentiation can be analysed in terms of flawed mediation that massively contributes to coercive integration. It is important to point out that critical theory and Gramscian political sociology do not manage to arrive at these conclusions without any help at all from systems theory. They in fact need systems theory in order to develop a consistently sociological observational standpoint on the issue of how systems are currently coded and differentiated.

Despite the persistence of mixed constitutions and the continuity between competing models of statehood, the financial crisis of 2007–2008 and its ongoing aftermath have drawn public attention to what have become major deficits in democratic steering and the rational mediation of social-systemic operations. This may well be the consequence of intensified systemic differentiation and the lack of a viable model of territorially based statehood in an increasingly globalised world. This is a world in which knowledge, which cannot be consolidated within national borders, is fundamentally important for both social systems and active citizenship. During the course of the preceding chapters it has been asked whether the existing nation state can continue to steer on so many fronts, and whether the model of ministerial responsibility still offers a framework for flexible and responsive administration. In theoretical terms, it is tempting to see the time from the publication of the *Philosophy of Right* (1821) to *Between Facts and Norms* (1992) as the historical period in which the public sphere and the lifeworld are capable, in a number of nationally instituted civil societies around the world, of playing a central role in this endeavour to co-ordinate and informally plan within the territorial boundaries of the nation state. One could choose different texts or rely on historical events to frame the political transitions of this epoch. But one wonders about the extent to which the public sphere and civil society can still be relied on to perform that crucially important planning function today. Moreover, going forward, one has to ask what role social democratic parties will be likely to play in this regard, and whether politically constituted democratic states will be able to survive authoritarian populism without the parliamentary opposition provided by an electorally stable centre-left with roots in contemporary world society.[1]

It has also been asked whether and to what extent social systems exhibit reflexive and self-steering properties that are transforming the bases of statehood in ways pointing beyond the territorially defined sovereignty of the geographically demarcated nation state. Although cultural nationhood and territorial statehood will definitely persist in the immediate term, there are major uncertainties as regards their likely future forms. Marx is often unstinting in his praise of the emancipatory potential of capitalism vis-à-vis all previous modes of production. But he rarely acknowledges the great normative leap forward represented by the collapse of the ancien régime and its replacement, at varying speeds and to markedly different degrees depending on the national context, by the modern state. He largely dismisses the crucial mediating capacities that Hegel attributes to key institutions of civil society, insisting instead that capital and the managers of the industrial economic system have become the commanding power of the civil sphere and of society more generally. In his early writings, he contrasts the democracy of unfreedom characteristic of the feudal period with the political emancipation ushered in by the early modern revolutions in Britain, North America, and France. But he is quick to add that political emancipation will soon be made redundant by human emancipation. Just over a hundred years ago many observers regarded the Russian Revolution of 1917 and the German Revolution of 1918 as decisive steps on the way to human emancipation in the guise of a classless and stateless world society that had been glimpsed, however fleetingly, during the Paris Commune of 1871. A world society certainly exists and continues to evolve. But it is characterised by transnational constitutions and by global social systems rather than by classlessness or statelessness. These realities place the future of the nation state, what Marx refers to as political emancipation, and nationally enacted constituent power in some doubt.

What was described, without reference to FD, as capitalism by Marx, has thus far managed to outlive what Hegel designates, similarly without reference to FD, as the rational state. This does not vindicate Marx in any unqualified sense, however. There are manifest explanatory inadequacies inherent in heaping together defectively differentiated, non-identical social systems. This is typically done by casually using shorthand, such as 'democratic state' or 'capitalist society'. It is possible to individuate a plurality of social systems – conceptually represented as if unified – by each of these expressions. Defective differentiation and coercive mediation are thus closely related phenomena that are imprecisely explained with traditional theory or an insufficiently sociological approach to the critique of instrumental reason. Coercive mediation is coercive in the precise sense that non-identical social systems are assumed to have common properties that distract attention from the importance of recognising the singularity of the discretely coded processes at work in each specific system. It will not be possible to re-code or redirect these processes until their incommensurability is openly discussed and debated as a crucial issue for democratic decision-making by an informed citizenry. These explanatory inadequacies show that a critique of *capitalist*

economic systems is necessary, but insufficient for the articulation of a critical theory of society. The latter must focus on the dynamics operative in each
of the primary systems as well as the communication between them. There
are many conceivable ways of coding economic and other social systems.
Part of the problem with lumping distinct social systems together is that this
prevents social research from adequately addressing the fact that it is now
entirely possible to conceive of progressive innovation in one system accompanied by obvious regression in another. Moreover, whilst it is unlikely that
there will be another general revolution on the French or Russian model, it
is likely that there will be far less conspicuous revolutions in education, science, aesthetics, law, medicine, and economics. The legacies of distinctly
national traditions of state formation will continue to have enduring effects on
these processes. Without a transition from ruling ideas to a continual battle
of contrasting ideas stemming from the challenges inherent in co-ordinating
social systems, what is now casually called democracy could revert to some
of the markedly undemocratic practices associated with the ancien régime.
The looming prospect of neo-feudalism armoured with significantly enhanced
military and surveillance capacities underscores the urgency of maintaining a
certain degree of political-epistemological distance from prevailing patterns
of institutional mediation. The spaces between systems have to be provisionally maintained, at least conceptually, so that the question of the mediations
between them can be reformulated with a view to re-coding key systems and
re-constitutionalising statehood.

The Frankfurt School thinkers found themselves in a highly unusual socio-
historical and political situation that helped sustain what could be described
as an epistemological position of engaged detachment. In addition to the fact
that the Institute was set up to ensure a measure of autonomy from the
educational system and the conflicts stemming from the economic system
of the Weimar Republic, the founding members were situated within a highly
contradictory social structure which made their status both privileged and precarious. It was privileged due to the relatively elite personal profiles of the first
generation of critical theorists, and yet it was also precarious because of their
ethnic backgrounds, which forced them into exile in 1933. It can be conjectured that this condition of simultaneous inclusion and exclusion contributes
to the methodological rigour, originality, and depth of their writings. It can also
be conjectured that there is no social class, gender, ethnic category, or any
other group in contemporary society that is both integrated and excluded in
quite the same way that the Frankfurt School thinkers were during the interwar period of the previous century. But maybe the condition of simultaneous
inclusion/exclusion is simply part of what it now means to live in a modern,
dynamic, functionally differentiated society in which progressive innovation in

one system is accompanied by regression in another. Social systems divide and converge; questions of race, class, and gender – to name but the most prominent – are all related and yet also distinct. Some of the theoretical and empirical literature on intersectionality is very adept at illuminating some of the issues at stake. It reinforces the point that it is entirely possible for the same individual to be confronted with exclusionary practices in one social system whilst enjoying more inclusionary ones in another. Just as it is advisable to avoid grouping social systems together under general rubrics such as those denoted by the notions of capitalist society or the superstructure, it is also important to refrain from speaking about subjectivity or inter-subjectivity in very general, undifferentiated terms. Theory that does not do so tends to rely on anthropological assumptions about human nature that do not always stand up to sociological scrutiny.[2]

Until relatively recently, the very possibility of confronting ruling class ideas with more stringent ideas presupposed hierarchical structures of power and authority particular to segmented societies. In the era prior to pervasive FD, trenchant critique appeared to depend on the existence of an almost intrinsically critical and avant-garde perspective voiced from outside of the main institutional mediations between the hegemonic and subordinate cultures and classes in the public sphere and civil society, such as unions, parties, universities, the mainstream media, and the like. The first generation of Frankfurt School thinkers and select modernist movements incorporated this perspective for a brief time. To be radical no longer meant going to the root of the matter, as it did for Marx. For some critical theorists it now became more of a question of observation from beyond or outside the general norm, rather than trying to gain majority control of it. That historical period has in any case passed; its overt hierarchies and barriers have undergone considerable changes. The period of what one might call intrinsically democratic mediation, focused on inclusion via educational qualifications and incremental increases in equal access to labour markets, has also passed. The post-1945 structures of corporatist negotiation bringing the representatives of governments together with those of trade unions and the representatives of capital have been largely superseded by more frankly neoliberal arrangements and populist discourses. As neoliberalism and austerity in turn begin to exhibit symptoms of decline, the question concerning the quality and composition of countervailing and mutually balancing norms and powers in society must be posed anew, if, that is, the ideal and reality of democracy are to be reformed in step with sociological change. In this regard, there can be no doubt about the importance of the linguistic turn in social and political theory in the 1980s and the subsequent focus on recognition and performance at the centre of most attempts to reconceptualise mediation with the help of inter-subjective frameworks. Instead of adopting one of those approaches, however, the present book investigates the historically specific ways in which FD constitutes the background against which all discussions of mediation, communication, and integration in modern societies have to be articulated. It does so because of the overwhelming historical and sociological evidence in support of the claim that FD provides the factual dimension in the relation between facts and norms investigated by Habermas in his celebrated book of 1992.

To say that modern societies are functionally differentiated is not to say that the social systems and institutions that comprise them are hermetically separated. Previous chapters have taken care to use the terms function, differentiation, centralisation, de-centralisation, and mediation with this in mind. With a view to contemporary debates about democracy and the future of statehood, it seems uncontroversial to maintain that modern societies are not politically organised for democracy, that they are not economically organised for equality, that they are not legally organised for justice, and that they are not scientifically organised for truth and objectivity. They are not religiously, militarily, aesthetically, or educationally organised, either. The great advantage secured by this situation is that a society that is politically organised for democracy, like a society that is legally organised for justice, and so forth, would have to be organised in ways that would almost certainly impede the other social systems from functioning. They can only function properly if they are differentiated from one another. They cannot be differentiated from one another if they are all coded to pursue democracy, equality, justice, objectivity, beauty, or any other explicitly designated overarching goal, nor can they be differentiated from one another if they are completely detached and isolated in a condition of permanent separation. The implication is that the relation between differentiated social systems is characterised by mediation, communication, and a form of dialectics which, it has been shown here, is misdiagnosed when described as the inherently democratic dialectics of mediated unity (this does not mean that they must instead be coded in a quantitatively pared-down, binary fashion). It has also been shown that the dynamics of systemic coupling, de-coupling, and re-coupling offer a much more accurate description of the processes in question than the models that juxtapose (1) the state of nature and civil society; (2) public and private; (3) civil society and the state; or, much more recently and importantly, (4) lifeworld and system. Habermas's model is superior to all of the others because he acknowledges and grapples with the realities of FD. But as indicated, there are problems with uniting the great variety of modern social systems under the generic category of 'the system'. He often categorises the system as closed and non-democratic by definition, and contrasts closed systemic functions with the open rationality of the lifeworld, which is characterised as communicative and democratic by definition. Some of these problems are fundamental for an understanding of what democratic statehood might mean when considered without the foundation provided until now by some conception of mediated unity that may have irrevocably passed since 1992. The problems are touched upon in the concluding remarks below.

The systems-theoretical approach to these issues does not coerce systems together under overarching conceptual categories. A number of its proponents underline the formal, ostensibly neutral, and binary description of the codes currently steering the operations of most systems in world society. At first glance, then, and against the dogmas of politically or otherwise organised societies reliant on strong dialectical models of legitimacy and inclusion, functionally differentiated societies are distinguished by high levels of pluralism and contingency and are not, as a rule, susceptible to centralised management or command planning. In principle, political power is shared and held accountable, economies are regulated by supply and demand, educational attainment is measured by achievement and clear criteria of selection rather than personal acquaintances, and research in the sciences, social sciences, and humanities is always open to new facts and evidence. Each social system steers itself, to some degree, but it does so without completely reliable criteria of judgement as far as the operations of neighbouring systems are concerned. The exact geography of the term 'neighbouring' in this context is far from precise; boundaries are loosely assembled as a variegated field of systemic environments that are equally distant from one another. It is certainly not a case of a unitary lifeworld confronting 'the system'. Does this suggest that inter-systemic phenomena, such as capitalism and the state, which are clearly far broader than the economic and political systems, for example, do not exist? They manifestly do exist, thus raising difficult methodological and substantive issues for pristine versions of systems theory. Such a version of systems theory is rejected in this book. Indeed, the argument developed here calls for a disaggregation of concepts like capitalism and the state. Systems theory helps accomplish this task, but forfeits its considerable theoretical gains when insisting on the natural inevitability of reductively binary codes.

Terms like capitalist society and capitalist state enjoy a certain amount of plausibility because political power is not democratically shared or held accountable to a sufficient degree. Economies are patently not regulated by neutral laws of supply and demand, educational attainment continues to be largely shaped by social origins, and so on. But how is it possible to explain why trades are increasingly professionalised, how informal management is accomplished through algorithmic calculations, how artificial intelligence affects learning in children and others, how the relation between money and the goods and services money allegedly buys is changing, or how, for that matter, instrumental reason coexists with other possible rationalities? How does one distinguish between economic realities and the fears produced by them? The dogmatic systems-theoretical approach to FD is often naïve, a-historical, and ill-equipped to explain inter-systemic organisations and institutions. Yet explanatory concepts such as capitalist society or the capitalist state often tend to reduce all social pathologies to a single cause. Advocates of that vocabulary might reply that FD really means government bailouts of banks and other financial sectors deemed 'too big to fail'. On this reading, the libertarian potential of differentiation is nullified by socialising risks and privatising profits, thus displacing financial burdens from private businesses on to taxpayers. It could thus be argued that the reality of FD consists in distinctly capitalist types of technocratic steering. The problem with this model of causality is twofold. If, in the last analysis, law, education, economics, and health are essentially capitalist in capitalist society, then is it not also the case that science, religion, sport, aesthetics, love, and friendship also function in an essentially capitalist way? This critique is one-sided and somewhat conspiratorial. It also points to a problematic 'solution' by suggesting that in order to remedy the situation, humanity will need to organise politically for state socialism. It is not difficult to see that this kind of organisation could only be secured by a return to vertical structures of command in an oppressively inclusive people's democracy of the kind that collapsed in Europe in 1989–1991. The reality of this version of constituent power is likely to be socialist education, socialist science, socialist medicine, socialist philosophy, and so on.

Modern societies are neither functionally differentiated in neutral, spontaneous ways, nor are they centrally directed by a technocratic power elite. They are functionally differentiated in defective ways that make austerity, ubiquitous outsourcing, large-scale privatisations, and state-sponsored bailouts seem like common-sense responses to public spending deficits and crises in growth and investment. Moreover, they are functionally differentiated within a long history of state formation that can at times make conflicts about public deficits seem like national conflicts between Greece and Germany, or even a personal one between Varoufakis and Schäuble. It is difficult to know what the right responses are, given that command central planning manifestly is not one, and that states no longer seem to have the requisite planning resources at their disposal that might enable them to reintroduce Keynesian management or co-ordinate the efforts of capital and labour through corporatist compromise. The matter can be stated succinctly as follows: FD holds out the promise of a post-traditional, non-hierarchical world governed by consistently horizontal exchanges of knowledge and communication. At times, functionally differentiated societies thus exhibit some of the evolutionary learning capacity required to initiate a transition from a society constituted by political

emancipation to a society constituted by social emancipation of the kind anticipated by the young Marx and early first-generation critical theory. It may seem
odd that the evidence for the eventual viability of this transition has in recent
years been furnished by systems theory, which is often regarded as essentially conservative. Despite that reputation, which is well founded in some
respects, the theory accomplishes three important tasks: (1) it foregrounds
FD as the bedrock of sociological facticity and the indispensable condition for
an immanent critique of the relation between facts and norms; (2) it implicitly
challenges a number of anthropological premises informing much theorising
about communicative action, constitutional patriotism, cosmopolitan democracy, constituent power, recognition, and performance; and (3) it indicates
how inter-systemic communication could actually be deepened and broad-
ened to develop in the direction of inter-systemic mediation and new ways of
institutionalising de-centralised and flexible forms of planning and steering.

Point 3 merits two substantial qualifications. First, it is certainly not true
of all systems theory; Luhmann and orthodox systems theorists would insist
that codes are binary and that inter-systemic mediation is always severely
limited by the fact that systems ultimately experience neighbouring systems
as environments.[3] Second, the collapse of corporatism and the demise of
Keynesianism would seem to demand the reconstruction of the politically
constituted state as the only feasible response to the shrinking of statehood
pursued with such ruthless vehemence by the powerful proponents of global
neoliberal governance. Although this demand makes eminent sense, it is not
clear how this work of reconstruction is to proceed.[4] What is clear, however,
is that economists and other academics, elected politicians, entrepreneurs,
journalists, and trade unionists have been talking over the course of several
decades about how to restructure work, reduce unemployment, improve the
conditions of immigrant workers, and raise standards of consumer and environmental protection. The fact that relatively little in the way of tangible results
has been achieved does not unequivocally confirm the axiom that social systems are operationally closed and self-referential.[5] On the contrary, it confirms
that inter-systemic communication exists, however embryonically at present,
and that social systems continue to be embedded within entrenched patterns
of FD that could be significantly rectified through social-systemic re-coupling
and re-coding by a global citizenry educated in the intricacies of the relevant
processes. Three objections immediately spring to mind. Would not the proposed re-coupling of the educational system to the economic system violate
systemic integrity? Would it not, moreover, amount to the return to a politically organised society in new guises? Is the model of agency underlying the
proposal in any way feasible? It is possible to begin sketching a provisional
response by returning very briefly to Adorno, Habermas's distinction between

the system and lifeworld, and the systems-theoretical distinction between system and systemic environment.

Adorno probably would have been somewhat sceptical about Habermas's claim that post-traditional societies can and do draw on accumulated knowledge to learn from the collective successes (national constitutions, state formation, and transnational constitutional foundations) and setbacks (fascism and other instances of state failure, Brexit and other instances of nationalist regression) of the past. Although extremely loath to embrace any notion of historical progress, Adorno would broadly adhere to the postulate that modern societies are internally fragmented and divided, and he would also agree that any attempt to unify them is likely to result in coerced integration rather than genuinely legitimate authority. As signalled in the introduction to this book, however, Adorno would add that division and fragmentation are not simply synonymous with alienation and heteronomy; the antagonistic structure of these formations opens up an invaluable space for critical thinking and action. That distance enables citizens to subject the socio-historical mediations between humanity and nature, as these are institutionalised in society, to an immanent critique. The implication is that people need not passively accept 'the way things are', or rail against existing socio-economic conditions in highly subjective terms, or in the shrill tones of moral outrage. Nor need they entrust the political organisation of society to any kind of restricted steering elite. Adorno sees that internal distance and fragmentation are primarily related to communications that affect and are affected by the labour process, but are not reducible to it. Habermas effectively incorporates this insight into the distinction between work and interaction that recurs in his early writings.[6]

A series of reflections on critical theory, defective FD, and possible future forms of statehood can begin by linking the reality of mediation with an analysis of the specific modalities of differentiation that contrive to make outsourcing, austerity, and privatisation seem like the right or even the only solution to questions of collective decision-making, allocation of housing and health care, and provision of education, to say nothing of climate change and the movements of migrants and refugees. It has been remarked that a number of national and transnational judiciaries have had considerable success in reading the demands of citizens as bearers of rights. National territory does not provide adequate guidance for states dealing with displaced persons or environmental problems. These are matters that now exceed the current planning capacities of governments and the geographical boundaries of nations. Privatising public services whilst retaining public financial responsibility for the miscalculations of powerful (and often inept) private interests patently does not lead to the most efficient or just allocation of resources in health, education, and housing. There is no centrally planned political solution to these issues, nor is it likely that the market will sort them out. If regulated and fair competition is needed in certain social systems, it is not a blanket remedy that will enhance the responsiveness of all of them. Access and integration need to be carefully considered in conjunction with systemic specificity. It is important to ask why, for example, banks are empowered to create the cash in circulation and to direct where it goes by deciding, in many cases in restricted boardrooms, who can access credit and who cannot. This gives them the power to determine the level and composition of investment, to steer consumer demand, and to shape production decisions. The problem is not banks or bankers – the economy of society depends on a banking sub-system empowered to stimulate investment and plan in the immediate and long terms. It is the party political and financial discretionary power to decide, in closed circles, if a bank is going to be geared towards productive lending and investment, or if it will be geared towards speculation and protecting the interests of shareholders shielded, in many cases, from awareness of the working conditions and management practices in the companies concerned. Hence questions of systemic codes have to be considered with reference to the specific incentives that are written into the inchoate constitution of a given social system. Evidence from the United States, for example, suggests that the incentive to make collectively binding decisions and settle disputes through litigation is widespread. Even if people there are not any more litigious than people elsewhere, they are strongly incentivised to be so due to institutional pressures that have little to do with supposed flaws in human nature or the greed of American lawyers.[7]

At the moment it is far easier to envisage states such as Spain and Britain being forced to cede sovereignty to Catalonia and Scotland than it is, for example, to envisage hospitals, insurance providers, and pharmacies sharing their resources to care for patients, or to imagine banks working together with enterprises and communities so that financial services can be re-coupled to production, investment, and the real economy. There is no objective or scientific economic, political, or legal reason why these realignments cannot be pursued and at least partially achieved. That goal may seem somewhat vague and distant right now. It has been suggested here that much depends on the codes and constitutions within social systems and on utilising the chances to make creative interventions in the mediations between them. At times, social systems exhibit reflexive, self-limiting, and constitutional properties; at other times, they exhibit a barely containable tendency to colonise, expand, and marginalise their respective environments. One thinks in the first instance of the economic system of modern society, which has been very adept at ignoring the best of efforts of communist central planning, and, after a relatively brief period, of demonstrating the limits of Keynesian demand management, as well. Both of these attempts at political regulation of economic processes experienced initial successes that were followed by stalemate and eventual defeat. Neoliberalism seems to be following a similar trajectory, as it becomes obvious once again that markets will not reliably regulate themselves, and that competition within a given system, such as health or education, can be ruinous, depending on how this competition is structured. The economic regulation of economic processes therefore makes very good sense if the self-limiting and power-sharing constitutional properties of that system can be nurtured in ways that do not make it dependent on the failures of neigh-bouring systems. Somewhat paradoxically, there is no way for the economic system to achieve this degree of autonomy without communication from the legal, political, and educational systems of world society. If this happens, it would be, in Gunther Teubner's words, 'a constitutional moment'. Hence it is not a question of returning to a politically organised society. This is the crux, and additional evidence in support of the claim that re-coupling the educational system to the economic system need not violate systemic integrity. Everything depends on how the process of re-coupling is imagined and enacted.[8]

Adorno would not have bemoaned the collapse of the people's democracies which, like any attempt to organise society politically, had to forfeit the independence of the media and judiciary. Since a functionally differentiated society is more attuned to sociological modernity than a politically, legally, economically, or similarly organised society, much rides on the qualitative dimensions of FD. Modern societies are not ensembles without organisation, however, as states, constitutions, and social systems attest. Although Habermas never endorses the idea of a politically organised society, he nonetheless knows that it is crucial for a legal state and any constitutional democracy that there be a discernible channel of communication between citizens in the lifeworld, legal institutions, educational institutions, and state-level political authority. Somewhat akin to Hegel in the *Philosophy of Right*, Habermas posits a mediated unity between citizens, law, the public sphere/civil society, and the state. Determining the precise composition of mediation in mediated unity is therefore important for understanding his endeavour to stake out a clear position on freedom and democracy. Habermas suggests that the challenge is to envisage a constitutional architecture that goes well beyond mutual non-infringement, but stops well short of the establishment of a politically organised people's democracy. But it may be the case that the future of statehood and systems now depends less on undifferentiated notions of agency or inter-subjectivity than it depends on equipping inter-systemic spaces with representative institutions. It is too easy to dismiss this point as speculative and abstract. Conceptions of the public sphere, civil society, and public/private have always included an extra-territorial dimension that defies conventional ideas about spatial distance and literal geographical location. Hegel and many others have little doubt that the distinction between possession and property is the law, that the distinction between private and public depends on the state, and that a valid contract presupposes a valid state. None of those very accurate statements indicate where, exactly, law and the state can be located in physical terms, however.[9]

Habermas's reading of Durkheim is instructive in this regard. He thinks Durkheim believes that law was once embedded in traditional institutions such as the church, and that as political authority gradually became secularised, legal institutions and juridical reasoning were de-coupled from religion and tradition. In the course of this process, law develops into a medium of communication with its own norms. He understands Durkheim to be saying, broadly, that after passing through various stages of cultural proximity to religious institutions, law evolves in the direction of state juridical law. But for Habermas, it does so without ever ceasing to be firmly rooted in the lifeworld of communicative action and inter-subjective reason. Although his own thinking on these topics takes a number of different turns and shifts in emphasis, he consistently maintains that social integration and system integration are propelled by different rationalities and distinct institutional realities. In his account, democratic law is somehow distinct from other social systems and exceptional in that it manages to acquire systemic properties whilst retaining its bases in inter-subjective communication. He thus warns that systems-theoretical models of explanation ignore this point, and as a consequence, offer no remedies when systemic imperatives undermine communicative reason.[10] Systems theorists agree that law becomes differentiated from religion and develops into a medium of communication with its own norms. The problems for traditional theories of democratic legitimacy start when one considers the possibility that as FD unfolds, the law gradually loses its bases in inter-subjective communication. Indeed, things would have been a bit too neat had law somehow been able to develop systemic properties whilst also remaining rooted in the lifeworld. Systems theorists add that law is not an unusual social system in this respect. To insist on the privileged relation between law and political authority is somewhat akin to reverting to the anthropological premises of a quasi-religious worldview. The fact that a religious legal-anthropological idiom is converted into a democratic legal-anthropological idiom does not really alter that a great deal. Just as law develops its own norms and media of communication, it can be seen that the economy, which begins with the simplest forms of production and then barter, develops the medium of money. Politics develops the medium of power. As seen in chapter 1, one of the astounding chapters in the history of early modern statehood recounts the ways in which the political system of society attempts to develop norms for applying power in an unrivalled, rather than in an all-encompassing way. Education develops examinations and the criteria pertinent to the selection process. Science makes fact and evidence the basis of objective validity, and so on. Citizens who might otherwise vociferously disagree on basic orientations might well nevertheless agree that imprisoning people without a trial should be illegal, that the arbitrary exercise of power is violent, that buying one's way into a degree programme is pedagogically unsound and corrupt, that conflating lay opinion and scientific fact is foolish. So one cannot maintain that incommensurable systemic codes first came into existence as incommensurable value systems exclusively in relation to the law, as opposed to other social systems, and thereby hope to salvage the chain of command leading from interpersonal legal obligations to political authority in the name of democracy. The problem with the framework of analysis suggested by the lifeworld/system dichotomy is not only that it unites a great variety of modern social systems under the generic category of 'the system'. It also adamantly holds on to the postulate that there is a conduit between citizens and the non-administrative dimension of government, emblematically illustrated by the roots of law in the lifeworld, which mediates between citizens and the state.[11] Whilst Luhmann argues that constitutions can act as instances of coupling between the legal and political systems, less dogmatic systems theorists argue that social systems can be seen to develop their own constitutions. The distinctions between mediating, re-coupling, and incipient auto-constitutionalism are not pedantic precisely because they each attribute very different degrees of self-steering capacity and, by extension, of capacity for self-government to society. It has been argued here that if social systems have always existed, they have not always been functionally differentiated, and, they have certainly not always been functionally differentiated in the ways they are now. It has been argued, further, that if statehood has always been about managing social systems to a considerable extent, social statehood does not depart from political statehood so much as it socialises the communication between social systems. In this context socialised does not mean socialist as opposed to liberal. Nor does it mean public rather than private ownership. It is a description of the possibility, inscribed within the contours of political statehood, for systems constantly to educate citizens, and for citizens, in turn, to have a far more active role in re-coding the systemic constitutions that are educating them. In this sense socialised social-systemic communication can be seen as offering a completely different model of democratic legitimacy than the one reflected in the personal squabbles between Schäuble and whoever happens to be his opponent in the headlines.[12]

Habermas is a critical and, in some of his writings, a radical thinker who defends republican democracy, communicative action, constitutional as opposed to nationalist patriotism, as well as consensual norms of inclusion. His theory of civic-legal-political communication is based on the model of a vertically directed flow and presupposes a modified version of Hegelian mediated unity, albeit recently updated with cosmopolitan and transnational emphases. Thus, whilst the theory is rational, there are questions about the extent to which it is actual. It certainly appears to be more flexible and humanist than systems theory. By refusing to posit a democratic conduit that links civic education to the institutions of legal reform and political authority, Luhmann seems to discount the very possibility that citizens could be the collective authors of the laws that govern them. The critical and quietly utopian moment in the modified systems-theoretical account adopted in this book is its consistently horizontal approach to understanding the relation between social systems in a functionally differentiated society. This method also lacks rational actuality precisely because world society is decidedly not, at present, consistent or transparent in its institutionalisation of FD. This assessment is borne out by the analyses in previous chapters of historical blocs, bailouts, the TTIP and similar economic treaties, discretionary steering of social systems by parties and states, makeshift de-regulation followed by frantic re-regulation, and recourse to selective de-differentiation. From that perspective, it is evident that the still prevalent model of ministerial responsibility – exacerbated by the first-past-the-post electoral system and similarly flawed constitutional mechanisms in Great Britain, to name just one geographical location – is hopelessly bureaucratic, cumbersome, and even residually feudal. Given the social complexities of contemporary world society, it is impossible for government ministers of health, education, transport, housing, sport, and the economy to be accountable and responsible for the unique and particular logics that guide the operations and communication organised by each of those systems. It has been seen that the economy, in principle, is just one of those systems, and that FD is and remains the defining feature of sociological modernity. Endowed with the appropriate constitutions and inter-systemic mediations, FD might provide decisive impetus for the transition from political statehood to social statehood.

Notes

1 Colin Crouch, David Held, Wolfgang Streeck, Jacques Rancière, and Wendy Brown, amongst many others, are all grappling with this question. For an analysis of the most important questions involved, see David Gonsalves, 'Democracy and Political Control of the Economy' (D.Phil, University of Sussex, forthcoming).

2 Marcel Stoetzler, 'From interacting systems to a system of divisions', *European Journal of Social Theory*, 20:4 (2017), 455–72 and 'Intersectional individuality: Georg Simmel's concept of "the intersection of social circles" and the emancipation of

women', *Sociological Inquiry*, 86:2 (2016), 216–40. As is well known and widely acknowledged, the term intersectionality was first developed by Kimberlé Crenshaw. See her 'Mapping the margins: intersectionality, identity politics, and violence against women of color', *Stanford Law Review*, 43:6 (1991), 1241–99. For a more general overview, see Michele Tracy Berger and Kathleen Guidroz, *The Intersectional Approach: Transforming the Academy Through Race, Class, and Gender* (Chapel Hill: University of North Carolina Press, 2009).

3 The systems theory discussed in this book is broadly oriented by Luhmann, but draws more directly on some of his more innovative readers, such as Andreas Fischer-Lescano, Kolja Möller, Andreas Philippopoulos-Mihalopoulos, Uwe Schimank, Gunther Teubner, Chris Thornhill, and Helmut Willke. Fischer-Lescano, Möller, Teubner, Thornhill, and Willke fruitfully combine some of the insights of systems theory and constitutional theory in ways that have had a major impact on this study.

4 For two contrasting approaches see Mitchell and Fazi, *Reclaiming the State*; and John Micklethwait and Adrian Wooldridge, *The Fourth Revolution: The Global Race to Reinvent the State* (London: Penguin, 2014).

5 Willke, *Regieren*, pp. 36–7.

6 Jürgen Habermas, *Knowledge and Human Interests* (Boston: Beacon Press, 1971), originally published in German as *Erkenntnis und Interesse* (Frankfurt: Suhrkamp, 1968), chapters 3 and 7.

7 Rudenstine, *Age of Deference*, chapters 11–12.

8 Gunther Teubner, 'A Constitutional Moment? The Logics of Hitting Bottom', in Poul F. Kjaer, Gunther Teubner, and Alberto Febbrajo (eds), *The Financial Crisis in Constitutional Perspective: The Dark Side of Functional Differentiation* (Oxford: Hart, 2011), pp. 3–42, also available in Teubner, *Critical Theory and Legal Autopoiesis*.

9 See Philippopoulos-Mihalopoulos, 'Looking for the Space between Law and Ecology'.

10 Habermas, *The Theory of Communicative Action*, Vol. II, pp. 77–92.

11 Habermas, *Faktizität und Geltung*, in English available as *Between Facts and Norms*, chapters 7–8.

12 Luhmann, *Die Politik der Gesellschaft*, pp. 105–6; Möller, *Formwandel der Verfassung*, pp. 201–9. The most comprehensive statement outlining the reasons why a modern, functionally differentiated society can be self-governing is articulated by G. D. H. Cole in *Guild Socialism Re-Stated*. The present book attempts to update some of Cole's ideas in ways that are relevant for twenty-first-century world society.

References

Abromeit, John, *Max Horkheimer and the Foundations of the Frankfurt School* (Cambridge: Cambridge University Press, 2011).

Adorno, Theodor W., *Aesthetic Theory*, ed. Gretel Adorno and Rolf Tiedemann (London: Athlone, 1997).

——, *Against Epistemology: A Metacritique; Studies in Husserl and the Phenomenological Antinomies*, trans. Willis Domingo (Oxford: Blackwell, 1982).

——, *Ästhetische Theorie*, ed. Gretel Adorno and Rolf Tiedemann, Gesammelte Schriften, 7 (Frankfurt: Suhrkamp, 1970).

——, *Drei Studien zu Hegel: Aspekte. Erfahrungsgehalt. Skoteinos oder Wie zu lesen sei* (Frankfurt: Suhrkamp, 1963).

——, 'Einleitung zum "Positivismusstreit in der deutschen Soziologie" ', in *Soziologische Schriften I*, ed. Rolf Tiedemann (Frankfurt: Suhrkamp, 1979), pp. 280–353.

——, 'Gesellschaft', in *Soziologische Schriften I* (Frankfurt: Suhrkamp, 1979 [1965]), pp. 9–19.

——, *Hegel: Three Studies* (Cambridge, MA: MIT Press, 1993).

——, *Lectures on Negative Dialectics: Fragments of a Lecture Course 1965/1966* (Cambridge: Polity, 2008).

——, *Minima Moralia: Reflections from Damaged Life* (London: Verso, 1978).

——, *Minima moralia: Reflexionen aus dem beschädigten Leben* (Berlin and Frankfurt: Suhrkamp, 1951).

——, *Nachgelassene Schriften: Vorlesung über Negative Dialektik – Fragmente zur Vorlesung 1965/66*, ed. Rolf Tiedemann (Frankfurt: Suhrkamp, 2003).

——, *Negative Dialectics*, trans. E. B. Ashton (London: Routledge, 1973).

——, *Negative Dialektik* (Frankfurt am Main: Suhrkamp, 1975 [1966]).

——, 'On Subject and Object', trans. Henry W. Pickford, in *Critical Models: Interventions and Catchwords* (New York: Columbia University Press, 1998), pp. 245–58.

——, 'Subject and Object', trans. E. B. Ashton, in Andrew Arato and Eike Gebhardt (eds), *The Essential Frankfurt School Reader* (New York: Continuum, new edn, 1982), pp. 497–511.

——, 'Subject and Object', in Brian O'Connor (ed.), *The Adorno Reader* (Oxford: Blackwell, 2000), pp. 137–52.

——, 'Zu Subjekt und Objekt', in *Stichworte: Kritische Modelle 2* (Frankfurt: Suhrkamp, 1969), pp. 151–68.

——, *Zur Metakritik der Erkenntnistheorie: Studien über Husserl und die phänomenologischen Antinomien* (Stuttgart: Kohlhammer, 1956).

Adorno, Theodor W., Hans Albert, Ralf Dahrendorf, Jürgen Habermas, Harald Pilot, and Karl R. Popper, *Der Positivismusstreit in der deutschen Soziologie* (Neuwied: Luchterhand, 1969).

Alexander, Michelle, *The New Jim Crow: Mass Incarceration in the Age of Colorblindness* (New York: New Press, 2010).

Algan, Yann, and Thomas Cazenave, *L'Etat en mode start-up: Le Nouvel Age de l'action publique, préface d'Emmanuel Macron* (Paris: Eyrolles, 2016).

Ali, Tariq, *The Extreme Centre: A Warning* (London: Verso, 2015).

Amable, Bruno, *Structural Crisis and Institutional Change in Modern Capitalism: French Capitalism in Transition* (Oxford: Oxford University Press, 2017).

Amable, Bruno, and Stefano Palombarini, *L'Illusion du bloc bourgeois: Alliances sociales et avenir du modèle français* (Paris: Raison d'agir, 2017).

Anderson, Perry, *In the Tracks of Historical Materialism* (London: Verso, 1983).

Andresen, Knud, and Stefan Müller, 'Contesting Deregulation: The 1970s as a Turning Point in Western History? Introductory Remarks', in Knud Andresen and Stefan Müller (eds), *Contesting Deregulation: Debates, Practices and Developments in the West since the 1970s* (New York: Berghahn Books, 2017), pp. 1–20.

Anidjar, Gil, *Blood: A Critique of Christianity* (New York: Columbia University Press, 2014).

Arendt, Hannah, *The Human Condition* (Chicago: University of Chicago Press, 1958).

Aristotle, *The Politics*, ed. Stephen Everson (Cambridge: Cambridge University Press, 1988).

Avineri, Shlomo, *Hegel's Theory of the Modern State* (Cambridge: Cambridge University Press, 1972).

Badiou, Alain, 'The communist hypothesis', *New Left Review*, 49: January–February (2008), 29–42.

Baecker, Dirk, *Form und Formen der Kommunikation* (Frankfurt: Suhrkamp, 2007).

Banet-Weiser, Sarah, and Manuel Castells, 'Economy is Culture', in Manuel Castells (ed.), *Another Economy is Possible: Culture and Economy in a Time of Crisis* (Cambridge: Polity, 2017), pp. 4–33.

Barnett, Hilaire, *Constitutional & Administrative Law* (London: Cavendish, 5th edn, 2004).

Bellamy, Richard, *Liberalism and Modern Society: An Historical Argument* (Cambridge: Polity, 1992).

——, *Modern Italian Social Theory: Ideology and Politics from Pareto to the Present* (Stanford: Stanford University Press, 1987).

——, *Political Constitutionalism: A Republican Defence of the Constitutionality of Democracy* (Cambridge: Cambridge University Press, 2007).

Bendix, Reinhard, *Max Weber: An Intellectual Portrait* (London: Heinemann, 1960).

Benhabib, Seyla (ed.), *Democracy and Difference: Contesting the Boundaries of the Political* (Princeton: Princeton University Press, 1996).

Berger, Michele Tracy, and Kathleen Guidroz, *The Intersectional Approach: Transforming the Academy Through Race, Class, and Gender* (Chapel Hill: University of North Carolina Press, 2009).

Berlin, Isaiah, 'Two Concepts of Liberty', in *The Proper Study of Mankind: An Anthology of Essays*, ed. Henry Hardy and Roger Hausheer (London: Pimlico, 1998), pp. 191–242.

Berman, Harold J., *Law and Revolution: The Formation of the Western Legal Tradition* (Cambridge, MA: Harvard University Press, 1983).

Berman, Sheri, *The Primacy of Politics: Social Democracy and the Making of Europe's Twentieth Century* (Cambridge: Cambridge University Press, 2006).

Bernstein, Richard J., *Beyond Objectivism and Relativism: Science, Hermeneutics, and Praxis* (Philadelphia: University of Pennsylvania Press, 1983).

Berry, David M., *Critical Theory and the Digital*, Critical Theory and Contemporary Society (New York: Bloomsbury, 2014).

Berry, David M., and Anders Fagerjord, *Digital Humanities: Knowledge and Critique in a Digital Age* (Cambridge: Polity Press, 2017).

Bhambra, Gurminder K., *Rethinking Modernity: Postcolonialism and the Sociological Imagination* (Basingstoke: Palgrave, 2007).

Bieling, Hans-Jürgen, 'Die Konstitutionalisierung der Weltwirtschaft als Prozess hegemonialer Verstaatlichung', in Sonja Buckel and Andreas Fischer-Lescano (eds), *Hegemonie gepanzert mit Zwang: Zivilgesellschaft und Politik im Staatsverständnis Antonio Gramscis* (Baden-Baden: Nomos, 2007), pp. 143–60.

Bingham, Tom, *The Rule of Law* (London: Allen Lane, 2010).

Blokker, Paul, and Chris Thornhill (eds), *Sociological Constitutionalism* (Cambridge: Cambridge University Press, 2017).

Blühdorn, Ingolfur, *Simulative Demokratie: Neue Politik nach der postdemokratischen Wende* (Berlin: Suhrkamp, 2013).

Bobbio, Norberto, 'Gramsci and the Conception of Civil Society', in John Keane (ed.), *Civil Society and the State: New European Perspectives* (London and New York: Verso, 1988), pp. 73–99.

Boltanski, Luc, and Eve Chiapello, *The New Spirit of Capitalism*, trans. Gregory Elliott (London: Verso, 2005).

——, *Le nouvel esprit du capitalisme* (Paris: Gallimard, 1999).

Bonefeld, Werner, *Critical Theory and the Critique of Political Economy: On Subversion and Negative Reason*, Critical Theory and Contemporary Society (New York: Bloomsbury, 2014).

Borchert, Jens, and Stephan Lessenich, *Claus Offe and the Critical Theory of the Capitalist State* (New York: Routledge, Taylor & Francis Group, 2016).

Bourdieu, Pierre, *La Noblesse d'Etat: Grandes Ecoles et esprit de corps* (Paris: Minuit, 1989).

——, *The State Nobility: Elite Schools in the Field of Power* (Oxford: Polity, 1996).

Bowcott, Owen, 'Half of victims would think twice on going through courts again', *Guardian* (11 September 2015), p. 17.

Bowie, Andrew, *Adorno and the Ends of Philosophy* (Cambridge: Polity, 2013).

Boyer, Robert, and Jean-Pierre Durand, *L'Après-fordisme* (Paris: Syros, 1993).

Braedley, Susan, 'Accidental Health Care: Masculinity and Neoliberalism at Work', in Meg Luxton and Susan Braedley (eds), *Neoliberalism and Everyday Life* (Montréal: McGill-Queen's University Press, 2010), pp. 136–62.

Breckman, Warren, *Marx, the Young Hegelians and the Origins of Radical Social Theory: Dethroning the Self* (Cambridge: Cambridge University Press, 1999).

Broeders, Dennis, 'The new digital borders of Europe', *International Sociology*, 22:1 (2007), 71–92.

Brown, Wendy, *Edgework: Critical Essays on Knowledge and Politics* (Princeton: Princeton University Press, 2005).

——, *States of Injury: Power and Freedom in Late Modernity* (Princeton: Princeton University Press, 1995).

——, *Undoing the Demos: Neoliberalism's Stealth Revolution* (Cambridge, MA: MIT Press, 2015).

Brunkhorst, Hauke, *Critical Theory of Legal Revolutions: Evolutionary Perspectives*, Critical Theory and Contemporary Society (New York: Bloomsbury, 2014).

——, 'The Return of the Crisis', in Poul F. Kjaer, Gunther Teubner, and Alberto Febbrajo (eds), *The Financial Crisis in Constitutional Perspective: The Dark Side of Functional Differentiation* (Oxford: Hart, 2011), pp. 133–72.

——, 'Some Conceptual and Structural Problems of Global Cosmopolitanism', in Anastasia Marinopoulou (ed.), *Cosmopolitan Modernity* (Oxford: Peter Lang, 2015), pp. 19–71.

Bullock, Ian, *Under Siege: The Independent Labour Party in Interwar Britain* (Edmonton: Athabasca University Press, 2017).

Cabo Martin, Carlos de, *Pensamiento crítico, constitucionalismo crítico* (Madrid: Trotta, 2014).

Cartledge, Paul, *Democracy: A Life* (Oxford: Oxford University Press, 2016).

Castoriadis, Cornelius, *The Imaginary Institution of Society* (Cambridge: Polity, 1987).

——, *L'Institution imaginaire de la société* (Paris: Seuil, 1975).

Castrucci, Emanuele, *On the Idea of Potency: Juridical and Theological Roots of the Western Cultural Tradition* (Edinburgh: Edinburgh University Press, 2016).

Clam, Jean, 'What is Modern Power?', in Chris Thornhill and Michael King (eds), *Luhmann on Law and Politics: Critical Appraisals and Applications* (Oxford: Hart, 2006), pp. 142–62.

Coicaud, Jean-Marc, *Legitimacy and Politics: A Contribution to the Study of Political Right and Political Responsibility*, trans. and ed. David Ames Curtis (Cambridge: Cambridge University Press, 2002).

Cole, G. D. H., *Guild Socialism Re-Stated* (London: Leonard Parsons, 1920).

Colón-Ríos, Joel I., *Weak Constitutionalism: Democratic Legitimacy and the Question of Constituent Power* (London: Routledge, 2012).

Cordero, Rodrigo, Aldo Mascareño, and Daniel Chernilo, 'On the reflexivity of crises: lessons from critical theory and systems theory', *European Journal of Social Theory*, 20:4 (2017), 511–30.

Cornell, Drucilla, *The Philosophy of the Limit* (London: Routledge, 1992).

Crenshaw, Kimberle, 'Mapping the margins: intersectionality, identity politics, and violence against women of color', *Stanford Law Review*, 43:6 (1991), 1241–99.

Cristi, Renato, 'Carl Schmitt on Sovereignty and Constituent Power', in David Dyzenhaus (ed.), *Law as Politics: Carl Schmitt's Critique of Liberalism* (Durham, NC: Duke University Press, 1998), pp. 179–93.

Crouch, Colin, 'Globalization, Nationalism, and the Changing Axes of Political Identity', in William Outhwaite (ed.), *Brexit: Sociological Responses* (London: Anthem Press, 2017), pp. 101–10.

——, *Post-Democracy* (Cambridge: Polity, 2004).

——, *The Strange Non-Death of Neoliberalism* (Cambridge: Polity Press, 2011).

D'Souza, Rohan, *Drowned and Dammed: Colonial Capitalism and Flood Control in Eastern India* (Oxford: Oxford University Press, 2006).

Dahms, Harry F., 'Critical Theory, Brexit, and the Vicissitudes of Political Economy in the Twenty-First Century', in William Outhwaite (ed.), *Brexit: Sociological Responses* (London: Anthem Press, 2017), pp. 183–92.

Dangerfield, George, *The Strange Death of Liberal England* (London: Constable, 1936).

Dardot, Pierre, and Christian Laval, *Ce cauchemar qui n'en finit pas: Comment le néolibéralisme défait la démocratie* (Paris: La Découverte, 2016).

——, *The New Way of the World: On Neoliberal Society* (London: Verso, 2013).

——, *La Nouvelle Raison du monde: Essai sur la société néolibérale* (Paris: Découverte, 2009).

Davies, William, *The Limits of Neoliberalism: Authority, Sovereignty and the Logic of Competition*, Theory, Culture & Society (London: SAGE, 2014).

Dean, Jodi, *Democracy and Other Neoliberal Fantasies: Communicative Capitalism and Left Politics* (Durham, NC: Duke University Press, 2009).

Debord, Guy, 'Report on the Construction of Situations and on the International Situationist Tendency's Conditions of Organisation and Action', in Ken Knabb (ed.),

Situationist International Anthology (Berkeley: Bureau of Public Secrets, revised and expanded edn, 2006), pp. 25–43.

Deitelhoff, Nicole, and Jens Steffek, *Was bleibt vom Staat? Demokratie, Recht und Verfassung im globalen Zeitalter*, Staatlichkeit im Wandel (Frankfurt: Campus-Verlag, 2009).

Derrida, Jacques, *Politics of Friendship* (London: Verso, 1997).

——, *Politiques de l'amitié, suivi de L'Oreille de Heidegger* (Paris: Galilée, 1994).

——, 'Violence et métaphysique', in *L'Ecriture et la différence* (Paris: Seuil, 1967), pp. 117–228.

——, *Writing and Difference*, trans. Alan Bass (London: Routledge, 1997).

Di Fabio, Udo, *Der Verfassungsstaat in der Weltgesellschaft* (Tübingen: Mohr Siebeck, 2001).

Dicey, A. V., *Introduction to the Study of the Law of the Constitution* (London: Macmillan, 8th edn, 1931 [1885]).

Dickinson, H. T., *Liberty and Property: Political Ideology in Eighteenth-Century Britain* (London: Methuen, 1977).

Dörre, Klaus, Stephan Lessenich, and Hartmut Rosa, *Soziologie – Kapitalismus – Kritik: Eine Debatte* (Frankfurt: Suhrkamp, 2009).

Dugan, Emily, 'Cruel court charge denies compensation to rape victim', *Independent* (28 October 2015), p. 1.

Dukes, Ruth, *The Labour Constitution: The Enduring Idea of Labour Law* (Oxford: Oxford University Press, 2014).

Durkheim, Emile, *De la division du travail social* (Paris: Presses universitaires du France, 4th edn, 1996 [1893]).

——, *The Division of Labor in Society* (New York: Free Press, 1933).

Dyzenhaus, David, *Legality and Legitimacy: Carl Schmitt, Hans Kelsen, and Hermann Heller in Weimar* (Oxford: Oxford University Press, 1997).

Elliot, Alex, 'On the Concept of Solidarity' (D.Phil, University of Sussex, 2018).

Elliot, Larry, 'As Kim and Lagarde talk, a fresh crisis brews', *Guardian* (10 October 2016), p. 22.

Errejón, Iñigo, and Josep Ramoneda, 'Conversación', *La Maleta de Portbou*, 21, January–February (2017), 39–44.

Esmark, Anders, 'Systems and Sovereignty: A Systems Theoretical Look at the Transformation of Sovereignty', in Mathias Albert and Lena Hilkermeier (eds), *Observing International Relations: Niklas Luhmann and World Politics* (London: Routledge, 2004), pp. 121–41.

Farzin, Sina, *Inklusion/Exklusion: Entwicklungen und Probleme einer systemtheoretischen Unterscheidung* (Bielefeld: Transcript, 2006).

Febbrajo, Alberto, and Francesco Gambino (eds), *Il diritto frammentato* (Milan: Giuffrè, 2013).

Febbrajo, Alberto, and Gorm Harste (eds), *Law and Intersystemic Communication: Understanding 'Structural Coupling'* (Farnham: Ashgate, 2013).

Feldman, David, 'Migrants, immigrants and welfare from the old poor law to the welfare state', *Transactions of the Royal Historical Society*, 13 (2003), 79–104.

Feldner, Heiko, and Fabio Vighi, *Critical Theory and the Crisis of Contemporary Capitalism*, Critical Theory and Contemporary Society (New York: Bloomsbury, 2015).

Finlayson, James Gordon, and Fabian Freyenhagen (eds), *Habermas and Rawls: Disputing the Political* (New York: Routledge, 2011).

Fischer-Lescano, Andreas, and Gunther Teubner, *Regime-Kollisionen: Zur Fragmentierung des globalen Rechts* (Frankfurt: Suhrkamp, 2006).

Forgács, Eva, *The Bauhaus Idea and Bauhaus Politics* (Budapest: Central European University Press, 1995).
Foucault, Michel, *Archaeology of Knowledge*, trans. A. M. Sheridan Smith (London: Routledge, 2002).
——, *The Birth of Biopolitics: Lectures at the College de France, 1978–1979*, trans. Graham Burchell (Basingstoke: Palgrave Macmillan, 2008).
——, *L'Archéologie du savoir* (Paris: Gallimard, 1969).
——, *Naissance de la biopolitique: Cours au Collège de France, 1978–1979*, ed. Michel Senellart, sous la dir. de François Ewald et Alessandro Fontana (Paris: Gallimard Seuil, 2004).
France, Pierre, and Antoine Vauchez, *Sphère publique, intérêts privés: Enquête sur un grand brouillage* (Paris: Presses de Sciences Po, 2017).
Fraser, Nancy, and Axel Honneth, *Redistribution or Recognition? A Political-Philosophical Exchange* (London: Verso, 2003).
Fraser, Nancy, and Rachel Jaeggi, *Capitalism: A Conversation in Critical Theory* (Cambridge: Polity, 2018).
Fromm, Erich, *Beyond the Chains of Illusion: My Encounter with Marx and Freud* (New York: Simon & Schuster, 1962).
Frontini, Luca, *Moneta e impero* (Fermo: Zefiro SRL, 2016).
Fuchs, Christian, *Digital Demagogue: Authoritarian Capitalism in the Age of Trump and Twitter* (London: Pluto, 2018).
Fuchs, Peter, *Die Erreichbarkeit der Gesellschaft: Zur Konstruktion und Imagination gesellschaftlicher Einheit* (Frankfurt: Suhrkamp, 1992).
Garton Ash, Timothy, 'Europe is being torn apart – but the torture will be slow', *Guardian* (9 March 2015).
Gauchet, Marcel, *L'Avènement de la démocratie 1: La Révolution moderne* (Paris: Gallimard, 2007).
Gentile, Giovanni, *Genesis and Structure of Society*, trans. H. S. Harris (Urbana: University of Illinois Press, 1960).
Gentleman, Amelia, '"We feel like we are dying slowly": the horror of the Calais refugee camp', *Guardian* (4 November 2015), G2, pp. 6–11.
Giacché, Vladimiro, *Costituzione italiana contro trattati europei: Il conflitto inevitabile* (Reggio Emilia: Imprimatur, 2015).
Gill, Stephen, 'Constitutionalizing inequality and the clash of globalizations', *International Studies Review*, 4:2 (2002), 47–65.
Giroux, Henry A., *Neoliberalism's War on Higher Education* (Chicago: Haymarket Books, 2014).
Gonsalves, David, 'Democracy and Political Control of the Economy' (D.Phil, University of Sussex, forthcoming).
Goodstein, Elizabeth S., *Georg Simmel and the Disciplinary Imaginary* (Stanford: Stanford University Press, 2017).
Görg, Christoph, *Gesellschaftliche Naturverhältnisse* (Münster: Westfälisches Dampfboot, 1999).
Gorz, André, *Farewell to the Working Class: An Essay on Post-Industrial Socialism*, trans. Michael Sonenscher (London: Pluto, 1987).
Graeber, David, *The Democracy Project: A History, a Crisis, a Movement* (London: Penguin Books, 2014).
Gramsci, Antonio, *Prison Notebooks*, trans. and ed. Joseph A. Buttigieg (New York: Columbia University Press, 1991).
——, *Quaderni del carcere*, ed. Valentino Gerratana, 4 vols, Vol. II, Edizione critica dell'Istituto Gramsci (Torino: G. Einaudi, 1975).

Griffith, J. A. G., *The Politics of the Judiciary* (Glasgow: Fontana/Collins, 1977).

Grimm, Dieter, *Die Zukunft der Verfassung II: Auswirkungen von Europäisierung und Globalisierung* (Frankfurt: Suhrkamp, 2012).

Gurvitch, Georges, 'Le Principe démocratique et la démocratie future', *Revue de Métaphysique et de Morale*, 36:3 (1929), 403–31.

Habermas, Jürgen, *Between Facts and Norms: Contributions to a Discourse Theory of Law and Democracy*, trans. William Rehg (Oxford: Polity, 1997).

——, *The Crisis of the European Union: A Response*, trans. Ciaran Cronin (Cambridge: Polity, 2012).

——, *Erkenntnis und Interesse* (Frankfurt: Suhrkamp, 1968).

——, *Faktizität und Geltung* (Frankfurt: Suhrkamp, 1992).

——, 'Hat die Demokratie noch eine epistemische Dimension? Empirische Forschung und normative Theorie', in *Philosophische Texte*, Vol. IV (Frankfurt: Suhrkamp, 2009), pp. 87–149.

——, *Knowledge and Human Interests* (Boston: Beacon Press, 1971).

——, *Legitimation Crisis* (Boston: Beacon Press, 1975).

——, *Legitimationsprobleme im Spätkapitalismus* (Frankfurt: Suhrkamp, 1973).

——, *The Philosophical Discourse of Modernity*, trans. Frederik Lawrence (Cambridge: Polity, 1987).

——, *Der philosophische Diskurs der Moderne: Zwölf Vorlesungen* (Frankfurt: Suhrkamp, 3rd edn, 1985).

——, *The Postnational Constellation: Political Essays*, trans. and ed. Max Pensky (Cambridge: MIT Press, 2001).

——, *Die postnationale Konstellation: Politische Essays* (Frankfurt: Suhrkamp, 1998).

——, *The Structural Transformation of the Public Sphere: An Inquiry into a Category of Bourgeois Society*, trans. Thomas Burger with the assistance of Frederick Lawrence (Cambridge: Polity, 1992).

——, *Strukturwandel der Öffentlichkeit: Untersuchungen zu einer Kategorie der bürgerlichen Gesellschaft* (Frankfurt: Suhrkamp, 2nd edn, 1991 [1962]).

——, *Theorie des kommunikativen Handelns*, 2 vols (Frankfurt: Suhrkamp, 1981).

——, *The Theory of Communicative Action*, 2 vols (Cambridge: Polity, 1984).

——, *Zur Verfassung Europas: Ein Essay*, Edition Suhrkamp: Sonderdruck (Berlin: Suhrkamp, 5th edn, 2014).

Halimi, Serge, 'Grand Marché transatlantique: les puissants redessint le monde', *Le Monde Diplomatique* (June 2014), p. 11.

Halimi, Serge, and Pierre Rimbert, 'Information sous contrôle', *Le Monde Diplomatique* (July 2016), pp. 12–13.

Halperin, Sandra, 'Modernity and the embedding of economic expansion', *European Journal of Social Theory*, 19:2 (2016), 172–90.

Halsall, Francis, 'Systems of Art', in Edward A. Shanken (ed.), *Systems* (Cambridge, MA: MIT Press, 2015), pp. 130–6.

Hampshire, James, *The Politics of Immigration: Contradictions of the Liberal State* (Cambridge: Polity, 2013).

Hardt, Michael, and Antonio Negri, *Empire* (Cambridge, MA: Harvard University Press, 2000).

Harrington, Austin, *German Cosmopolitan Social Thought and the Idea of the West: Voices from Weimar* (Cambridge: Cambridge University Press, 2016).

Harvey, David, *A Brief History of Neoliberalism* (Oxford: Oxford University Press, 2005).

Hegel, Georg Wilhelm Friedrich, *Elements of the Philosophy of Right*, trans. H. B. Nisbet (Cambridge: Cambridge University Press, 1991).

——, *Grundlinien der Philosophie des Rechts oder Naturrecht und Staatswissenschaft im Grundrisse*, ed. Eva Moldenhauer, Werke, 7 (Frankfurt: Suhrkamp, 1986).

——, *Phänomenologie des Geistes* (Stuttgart: Reclam, 1987).

——, *Phenomenology of Spirit* (Oxford: Clarendon Press, 1979).

——, *Vorlesungen über die Philosophie der Geschichte*, ed. Eva Moldenhauer, Werke, 12 (Frankfurt: Suhrkamp, 1986).

Heidegger, Martin, *Being and Time*, trans. Joan Stambaugh, revised and with an introduction by Dennis J. Schmidt (Albany: State University of New York Press, 2010).

——, *Sein und Zeit* (Tübingen: Niemeyer, 17th edn, 1993 [1927]).

Held, David, *Global Covenant: The Social Democratic Alternative to the Washington Consensus* (Oxford: Polity, 2004).

Hitzel-Cassagnes, Tanya, 'Paradoxien im Organisationsbereich: Global Governance', in Marc Amstutz and Andreas Fischer-Lescano (eds), *Kritische Systemtheorie: Zur Evolution einer normativen Theorie* (Bielefeld: Transcript, 2013), pp. 149–72.

Hobhouse, Leonard T., *Liberalism* (London and New York: Oxford University Press, 1964).

Honneth, Axel, *Kampf um Anerkennung: Zur moralischen Grammatik sozialer Konflikte* (Frankfurt: Suhrkamp, 1994).

——, *The Struggle for Recognition: The Moral Grammar of Social Conflicts* (Oxford: Polity, 2005).

Horkheimer, Max, 'Traditional and Critical Theory', in *Critical Theory: Selected Essays* (New York: Continuum, 1982), pp. 188–252.

——, 'Traditionelle und kritische Theorie', in *Traditionelle und kritische Theorie: vier Aufsätze* (Frankfurt: Fischer Taschenbuch Verlag, 1968), pp. 12–64.

Horkheimer, Max, and Theodor W. Adorno, *Dialectic of Enlightenment*, trans. John Cumming (New York: Herder and Herder, 1972).

——, *Dialektik der Aufklärung: Philosophische Fragmente* (Frankfurt: Fischer Taschenbuch Verlag, 1995 [1944]).

Hudson, Michael, *The Bubble and Beyond: Fictitious Capital, Debt Deflation and the Global Crisis* (New York: Inlet, 2012).

Hume, David, 'That Politics May Someday Be Reduced to a Science', in C. W. Hendel (ed.), *David Hume's Political Essays* (New York: The Liberal Arts Press, 1953), pp. 12–23.

Iglesias Turrión, Pablo, *Disputar la democracia: Política para tiempos de crisis* (Madrid: Akal, 2014).

James, David, *Hegel's Philosophy of Right: Subjectivity and Ethical Life* (London: Continuum, 2007).

Jameson, Fredric, *Late Marxism: Adorno, or, The Persistence of the Dialectic* (London: Verso, 1990).

Jenkins, Simon, 'The supreme court is doing MPs' dirty work for them on article 50', *Guardian* (8 December 2016), p. 39.

Jennar, Raoul Marc, 'Cinquante états négotient en secret la libéralisation des services', *Le Monde Diplomatique* (September 2014), pp. 12–13.

Jessop, Bob, *State Theory: Putting the Capitalist State in its Place* (Cambridge: Polity, 1990).

Joerges, Christian, 'A New Alliance of De-Legalisation and Legal Formalism? Reflections on the Response to the Social Deficit of the European Integration Project', in Hauke Brunkhorst (ed.), *Demokratie in der Weltgesellschaft*, Soziale Welt: Sonderband, 18 (Baden-Baden: Nomos, 2009), pp. 437–50.

Johnson, Dominic, 'Liberté? Na ja', *Fluter. Magazin der Bundeszentrale für politische Bildung*, 59 (2016), 33.

Jones, Paul K., *Critical Theory and Demagogic Populism*, Critical Theory and Contemporary Society (Manchester: Manchester University Press, forthcoming).

Kalyvas, Andreas, *Democracy and the Politics of the Extraordinary: Max Weber, Carl Schmitt, and Hannah Arendt* (Cambridge: Cambridge University Press, 2008).

Kant, Immanuel, 'An Answer to the Question: What is Enlightenment?', trans. H. B. Nisbet, in *Kant's Political Writings*, ed. Hans Reiss (Cambridge: Cambridge University Press, 1970), pp. 54–60.

——, 'Appendix to "Perpetual Peace" ', in *Kant's Political Writings*, ed. Hans Reiss (Cambridge: Cambridge University Press, 1970), pp. 116–30.

——, 'On the Common Saying: "This May be True in Theory, but it Does not Apply in Practice" ', in *Kant's Political Writings*, ed. Hans Reiss (Cambridge: Cambridge University Press, 1970).

Keating, Michael, and David McCrone (eds), *The Crisis of Social Democracy in Europe* (Edinburgh: Edinburgh University Press, 2013).

Kellner, Douglas, *Critical Theory, Marxism, and Modernity* (Baltimore: Johns Hopkins University Press, 1989).

Kennedy, Ellen, *Constitutional Failure: Carl Schmitt in Weimar* (Chapel Hill: Duke University Press, 2004).

Kerwer, Dieter, 'Governance in a World Society: The Perspective of Systems Theory', in Matthias Albert and Lena Hilkermeier (eds), *Observing International Relations: Niklas Luhmann and World Politics* (London: Routledge & Kegan, 2004), pp. 197–203.

Keucheyan, Razmig, *Hémisphère gauche: Une cartographie des nouvelles pensées critiques* (Paris: La Découverte, 2010).

——, *The Left Hemisphere: Mapping Critical Theory Today*, trans. Gregory Elliott (London: Verso, 2013).

——, 'Périssables démocraties', *Le Monde Diplomatique* (April 2015), p. 3.

King, Michael, and Chris Thornhill, *Niklas Luhmann's Theory of Politics and Law* (Basingstoke: Palgrave Macmillan, 2003).

Kirkpatrick, Graeme, *Computer Games and the Social Imaginary* (Cambridge: Polity, 2013).

Kitschelt, Herbert, *The Transformation of European Social Democracy* (Cambridge: Cambridge University Press, 1994).

Kjaer, Poul F., *Constitutionalism in the Global Realm: A Sociological Approach* (London: Routledge, 2014).

——, 'Law and Order within and beyond National Configurations', in Poul F. Kjaer, Gunther Teubner, and Alberto Febbrajo (eds), *The Financial Crisis in Constitutional Perspective: The Dark Side of Functional Differentiation* (Oxford: Hart, 2011), pp. 395–430.

Kjaer, Poul F., Gunther Teubner, and Alberto Febbrajo (eds), *The Financial Crisis in Constitutional Perspective: The Dark Side of Functional Differentiation* (Oxford: Hart, 2011).

Klare, Michael T., *The Race for What's Left: The Global Scramble for the World's Last Resources* (New York: Metropolitan Books, 2012).

Köhnke, Klaus Christian, *Der junge Simmel in Theoriebeziehungen und sozialen Bewegungen* (Frankfurt: Suhrkamp, revised edn, 1996).

Koskenniemi, Martti, 'Hegemonic Regimes', in Margaret Young (ed.), *Regime Interaction in International Law: Facing Fragmentation* (Cambridge: Cambridge University Press, 2012), pp. 305–24.

——, 'Legal Fragmentation(s): An Essay on Fluidity and Form', in Gralf-Peter Calliess, Andreas Fischer-Lescano, Dan Wielsch, and Peer Zumbansen (eds), *Soziologische Jurisprudenz: Festschrift für Gunther Teubner zum 65. Geburtstag* (Berlin: De Gruyter, 2009), pp. 795–810.

Koutsourakis, Angelos, *Politics as Form in Lars von Trier: A Post-Brechtian Reading* (New York: Bloomsbury, 2013).

Kreide, Regina, 'Die verdrängte Demokratie: Kommunikations- und Handlungsblockaden in einer globalisierten Welt', in Smail Rapic (ed.), *Habermas und der historische Materialismus* (Munich: Karl Alber, 2014), pp. 229–60.

Laclau, Ernesto, *On Populist Reason* (London: Verso, 2005).

Lagasnerie, Geoffroy de, *L'Art de la révolte: Snowden, Assange, Manning* (Paris: Fayard, 2015).

——, *La Dernière Leçon de Michel Foucault: Sur le néolibéralisme, la théorie et la politique* ([Paris]: Fayard, 2012).

Lansley, Stewart, and Joanna Mack, *Breadline Britain: The Rise of Mass Poverty* (London: Oneworld, 2015).

Latour, Bruno, *Nous n'avons jamais été modernes: Essai d'anthropologie symétrique* (Paris: La Découverte, 1991).

——, *We Have Never Been Modern*, trans. Catherine Porter (Hemel Hempstead: Harvester Wheatsheaf, 1993).

Lavelle, Ashley, *The Death of Social Democracy: Political Consequences in the 21st Century* (Aldershot: Ashgate, 2008).

Lawrence, Felicity, 'A modern Commons Charter', *Guardian* (8 November 2017), p. 32.

Lazzarato, Maurizio, *Governing by Debt*, trans. Joshua David Jordan (Cambridge, MA: MIT Press, 2015).

Le Sueur, Andrew, Maurice Sunkin, and Jo Eric Khushal Murkens, *Public Law: Text, Cases, and Materials* (Oxford: Oxford University Press, 2010).

Lefort, Claude, 'Les Droits de l'homme ne sont pas une politique', *Le Débat*, 16 (2000), 36–55.

Lieckweg, Tania, *Das Recht der Weltgesellschaft: Systemtheoretische Perspektiven auf die Globalisierung des Rechts am Beispiel der Lex Mercatoria* (Stuttgart: Lucius & Lucius, 2003).

Linden, Markus, and Winfried Thaa (eds), *Krise und Reform politischer Repräsentation* (Baden-Baden: Nomos, 2011).

Linklater, Andrew, *Violence and Civilization in the Western States-Systems* (Cambridge: Cambridge University Press, 2016).

Locke, John, *Two Treatises of Government* (London: Dent, 1978).

Lordon, Frédéric, *La Malfaçon: Monnaie européenne et souveraineté démocratique* (Paris: Les Liens qui libèrent, 2014).

Loughlin, Martin, *Sword and Scales: An Examination of the Relationship between Law and Politics* (Oxford: Hart, 2000).

Luhmann, Niklas, *Ausdifferenzierung des Rechts: Beiträge zur Rechtssoziologie und Rechtstheorie* (Frankfurt: Suhrkamp, 1981).

——, *Das Erziehungssystem der Gesellschaft*, ed. Dieter Lenzen (Frankfurt: Suhrkamp, 2002).

——, *Die Gesellschaft der Gesellschaft*, 2 vols (Frankfurt: Suhrkamp, 1997).

——, 'Globalization or World Society: How to Conceive of Modern Society?', in Albert Scherr (ed.), *Systemtheorie und Differenzierungstheorie als Kritik: Perspektiven in Anschluss an Niklas Luhmann* (Basle: Beltz, 2015), pp. 38–55.

——, *Law as a Social System* (Oxford: Oxford University Press, 2004).

——, *Die Politik der Gesellschaft* (Frankfurt: Suhrkamp, 2000).

——, *Das Recht der Gesellschaft* (Frankfurt: Suhrkamp, 1993).

——, *Social Systems* (Stanford: Stanford University Press, 1995).

——, *Soziale Systeme* (Frankfurt: Suhrkamp, 1987 [1984]).

——, *Soziologische Aufklärung 4: Beiträge zur funktionalen Differenzierung der Gesellschaft* (Wiesbaden: VS Verlag für Sozialwissenschaften, 4th edn, 2009 [1987]).

——, *Theory of Society*, 2 vols (Stanford: Stanford University Press, 2012–2013).

——, 'Die Unterscheidung von Staat und Gesellschaft', in *Soziologische Aufklärung 4: Beiträge zur funktionalen Differenzierung der Gesellschaft* (Wiesbaden: VS Verlag für Sozialwissenschaften, 4th edn, 2009 [1987]), pp. 69–76.

——, 'Verfassung als evolutionäre Errungenschaft', *Rechtshistorisches Journal*, 9 (1990), 176–220.

——, *Die Wirtschaft der Gesellschaft* (Frankfurt: Suhrkamp, 1988).

——, 'Der Wohlfahrtsstaat zwischen Evolution und Rationalität', in *Soziologische Aufklärung 4: Beiträge zur funktionalen Differenzierung der Gesellschaft* (Wiesbaden: VS Verlag für Sozialwissenschaften, 2009 [1983]), pp. 108–20.

Luhmann, Niklas, and Karl-Eberhard Schorr, *Reflexionsprobleme im Erziehungssystem* (Stuttgart: Klett-Cotta, 1979).

Luyendijk, Joris, *Swimming with Sharks: My Journey into the World of Bankers* (London: Guardian Books, 2015).

Lyotard, Jean-François, *La Condition postmoderne: Rapport sur le savoir* (Paris: Minuit, 1979).

——, *The Postmodern Condition: A Report on Knowledge*, trans. Geoff Bennington and Brian Massumi (Manchester: Manchester University Press, 1984).

MacCormick, Neil, 'Sovereignty and After', in Hent Kalmo and Quentin Skinner (eds), *Sovereignty in Fragments: The Past, Present and Future of a Contested Concept* (Cambridge: Cambridge University Press, 2010), pp. 151–68.

Madsen, Mikael Rask, and Chris Thornhill (eds), *Law and the Formation of Modern Europe: Perspectives from the Historical Sociology of Law* (Cambridge: Cambridge University Press, 2014).

Mairet, Gérard, *Le Principe de souveraineté: Histoires et fondements du pouvoir moderne* (Paris: Gallimard, 1997).

Marasco, Robyn, *The Highway of Despair: Critical Theory After Hegel* (New York: Columbia University Press, 2015).

Marcuse, Herbert, *One-Dimensional Man: Studies in the Ideology of Advanced Industrial Society* (London: Routledge, 2nd edn, 2002 [1964]).

——, 'Philosophy and Critical Theory', trans. Jeremy J. Shapiro, in *Negations: Essays in Critical Theory* (London: Allen Lane The Penguin Press, 1968), pp. 134–58.

Marinopoulou, Anastasia, *Critical Theory and Epistemology: The Politics of Modern Thought and Science*, Critical Theory and Contemporary Society (Manchester: Manchester University Press, 2017).

Marsh, David, *Europe's Deadlock: How the Euro Crisis Could Be Solved – and Why It Won't Happen* (New Haven: Yale University Press, 2016).

Marshall, Peter H., *Demanding the Impossible: A History of Anarchism* (London: HarperCollins, 1992).

Marx, Karl, 'The Civil War in France', in Robert Tucker (ed.), *The Marx Engels Reader* (New York: Norton, 1978), pp. 618–52.

——, 'Contribution to the Critique of Hegel's *Philosophy of Right*', in Robert C. Tucker (ed.), *The Marx-Engels Reader* (New York: Norton, 2nd edn, 1978), pp. 16–25.

——, 'Contribution to the Critique of Hegel's *Philosophy of Right*: Introduction', in Robert C. Tucker (ed.), *The Marx-Engels Reader* (New York: Norton, 2nd edn, 1978), pp. 53–65.

——, 'Theses on Feuerbach', in R. Tucker (ed.), *The Marx-Engels Reader* (New York: Norton, 2nd edn, 1978), pp. 143–5.

Mason, Paul, 'Corbyn's victory was not supposed to happen: but to disrupt logic is the first step in defeating Britain's ruling elite', *Guardian* (13 June 2017), G2, pp. 10–11.

——, *PostCapitalism: A Guide to Our Future* (London: Allen Lane, 2015).

——, 'Review of Yanis Varoufakis, *Adults in the Room: My Battle with Europe's Deep Establishment*', *Guardian* (6 May 2017), p. 6.

Maturana, Humberto R., and Francisco J. Varela, *Autopoiesis and Cognition: The Realization of the Living* (Dordrecht: Reidel, 1980).

Maus, Ingeborg, *Rechtstheorie und politische Theorie im Industriekapitalismus* (Munich: Fink, 1986).

Mayntz, Renate, Bernd Rosewitz, Uwe Schimank, and Rudolf Stichweh (eds), *Differenzierung und Verselbständigung: Zur Entwicklung gesellschaftlicher Teilsysteme* (Frankfurt: Campus, 1988).

McKinnon, Catriona, and Iain Hampsher-Monk (eds), *The Demands of Citizenship* (London: Continuum, 2000).

McLellan, David, *The Young Hegelians and Karl Marx* (London: Macmillan, 1969).

McNally, Mark (ed.), *Antonio Gramsci*, Explorations in Contemporary Political Thought (Ashgate: Palgrave Macmillan, 2015).

Meek, James, *Private Island: Why Britain Now Belongs to Someone Else* (London: Verso, 2014).

Menke, Christoph, *Kritik der Rechte* (Berlin: Suhrkamp, 2015).

Meret, Susi, and Birte Siim, 'Multiculturalism, Right-Wing Populism and the Crisis of Social Democracy', in Michael Keating and David McCrone (eds), *The Crisis of Social Democracy in Europe* (Edinburgh: Edinburgh University Press, 2013), pp. 125–39.

Merkel, Wolfgang, and Marcus Spittler, 'Disaffection or Changes in European Democracies?', in Ludolfo Paramio (ed.), *Desafección política y gobernabilidad: el reto político* (Madrid: Marcial Pons, 2015), pp. 61–105.

Metzger, Jonathan, Philip Allmendinger, and Stijn Oosterlynck (eds), *Planning Against the Political: Democratic Deficits in European Territorial Governance* (London: Routledge, 2015).

Michelsen, Danny, and Franz Walter (eds), *Unpolitische Demokratie: Zur Krise der Repräsentation* (Berlin: Suhrkamp, 2013).

Micklethwait, John, and Adrian Wooldridge, *The Fourth Revolution: The Global Race to Reinvent the State* (London: Penguin, 2014).

Mill, John Stuart, *On Liberty*, ed. Gertrude Himmelfarb (London: Penguin, 1982 [1859]).

Milne, Seumas, *The Revenge of History: The Battle for the Twenty-First Century* (London: Verso, 2012).

Mitchell, William, and Thomas Fazi, *Reclaiming the State: A Progressive Vision of Sovereignty for a Post-Neoliberal World* (London: Pluto, 2017).

Moeller, Hans-Georg, *The Radical Luhmann* (New York: Columbia University Press, 2012).

Möller, Kolja, *Formwandel der Verfassung: Die postdemokratische Verfasstheit des Transnationalen* (Bielefeld: Transcript, 2015).

——, 'Das Ganze der konstituierenden Macht', in Kolja Möller and Jasmin Siri (eds), *Systemtheorie und Gesellschaftskritik: Perspektiven der Kritischen Systemtheorie* (Bielefeld: Transcript, 2016), pp. 39–56.

——, 'Struggles for Law: Global Social Rights as an Alternative to Financial Market Capitalism', in Poul F. Kjaer, Gunther Teubner, and Alberto Febbrajo (eds), *The Financial Crisis in Constitutional Perspective: The Dark Side of Functional Differentiation* (Oxford: Hart, 2011), pp. 326–32.

Monbiot, George, *How Did We Get into This Mess? Politics, Equality, Nature* (London: Verso, 2016).

——, 'TTIP may be dead, but a worse trade deal is coming', *Guardian* (7 September 2017), p. 29.

Montesquieu, Charles de Secondat, *L'Esprit des lois* (Paris: Gallimard, 1992 [1748]).

——, *The Spirit of the Laws* (Cambridge: Cambridge University Press, 1989).

Moschonas, Gerassimos, *In the Name of Social Democracy: The Great Transformation, 1945 to the Present*, trans. Gregory Elliott (London: Verso, revised and updated edn, 2002).

——, 'Reforming Europe, Renewing Social Democracy? The PES, the Debt Crisis, and the Euro-Parties', in David J. Bailey, Jean-Michel de Waele, Fabien Escalona, and Mathieu Vieira (eds), *European Social Democracy during the Global Economic Crisis: Renovation or Resignation?* (Manchester: Manchester University Press, 2014), pp. 252–69.

Mouffe, Chantal, *The Challenge of Carl Schmitt* (London: Verso, 1999).

Müller, Jan-Werner, *Constitutional Patriotism* (Princeton: Princeton University Press, 2007).

Nakhimovsky, Isaac, *The Closed Commercial State: Perpetual Peace and Commercial Society from Rousseau to Fichte* (Princeton: Princeton University Press, 2011).

Negt, Oskar, and Alexander Kluge, *Public Sphere and Experience: Toward an Analysis of the Bourgeois and Proletarian Public Sphere*, trans. Peter Labanyi, Jamie Owen Daniel, and Assenka Oksiloff (London: Verso, 2016).

Neumann, Franz L., 'The Change in the Function of Law in Modern Society', in William E. Scheuerman (ed.), *The Rule of Law under Siege: Selected Essays of Franz L. Neumann and Otto Kirchheimer* (Berkeley: University of California Press, 1996 [1937]), pp. 101–41.

Nuzzo, Angelika, 'Dialectic as Logic of Transformative Processes', in Katerina Deligiorgi (ed.), *Hegel: New Directions* (Chesham: Acumen, 2006), pp. 85–103.

Offe, Claus, 'Erneute Lektüre: Die Strukturprobleme nach 33 Jahren', in *Strukturprobleme des kapitalistischen Staates: Aufsätze zur politischen Soziologie*, ed. Jens Borchert and Stephan Lessenich (Frankfurt: Campus-Verlag, revised new edn, 2006), pp. 181–96.

——, 'Structural problems of the capitalist state', *German Political Studies*, 1 (1974 [1972]), 31–56.

Offerle, Michel, 'Les Partis meurent longtemps', *Le Monde* (31 May 2017), p. 20.

Outhwaite, William (ed.), *Brexit: Sociological Responses* (London: Anthem Press, 2017).

Paterson, John, 'The Precautionary Principle: Practical Reason, Regulatory Decision-Making and Judicial Review in the Context of Functional Differentiation', in Andreas Philippopoulos-Mihalopoulos (ed.), *Law and Ecology: New Environmental Foundations* (Abingdon: Routledge, 2011), pp. 83–104.

Peck, Jamie, *Constructions of Neoliberal Reason* (Oxford: Oxford University Press, 2010).

Pettifor, Ann, *The Production of Money: How to Break the Power of Bankers* (London: Verso, 2017).

Peukert, Detlev, *The Weimar Republic: The Crisis of Classical Modernity* (New York: Hill & Wang, 1st American edn, 1992).

——, *Die Weimarer Republik: Krisenjahre der klassischen Moderne* (Frankfurt: Suhrkamp, 1987).

Philippopoulos-Mihalopoulos, Andreas (ed.), *Law and Ecology: New Environmental Foundations* (London: Routledge, 2012).

——, 'Looking for the Space between Law and Ecology', in Andreas Philippopoulos-Mihalopoulos (ed.), *Law and Ecology: New Environmental Foundations* (London: Routledge, 2012), pp. 1–17.

——, *Niklas Luhmann: Law, Justice, Society* (London: Routledge, 2010).

Pierson, Christopher, *Hard Choices: Social Democracy in the Twenty-First Century* (Cambridge: Polity Press, 2001).

Piketty, Thomas, *Le Capital au XXIᵉ siècle* (Paris: Seuil, 2013).

—— *Capital in the Twenty-First Century*, trans. Arthur Goldhammer (Cambridge, MA: The Belknap Press of Harvard University Press, 2014).

——, 'Global treaties have to be about more than trade', *Guardian* (17 November 2016), p. 39.

Pincus, Steven C. A., *1688: The First Modern Revolution* (New Haven: Yale University Press, 2009).

Pippin, Robert B., *After the Beautiful: Hegel and the Philosophy of Pictorial Modernism* (Chicago: University of Chicago Press, 2014).

Plehwe, Dieter, and Bernhard Walpen, 'Between Network and Complex Organization: The Making of Neoliberal Knowledge and Hegemony', in Bernhard Walpen and Gisela Neunhöffer (eds), *Neoliberal Hegemony: A Global Critique* (London: Routledge, 2006), pp. 27–50.

Poggi, Gianfranco, *The Development of the Modern State: A Sociological Introduction* (Stanford: Stanford University Press, 1978).

Preuß, Ulrich K., 'Disconnecting Constitutions from Statehood: Is Global Constitutionalism a Promising Concept?', in Martin Loughlin and Petra Dobner (eds), *The Twilight of Constitutionalism?* (Oxford: Oxford University Press, 2010), pp. 23–46.

Rancière, Jacques, *La Nuit des prolétaires: Archives du rêve ouvrier* (Paris: Fayard, 1981).

Rapic, Smail (ed.), *Habermas und der historische Materialismus* (Munich: Karl Alber, 2014).

Rawls, John, 'Justice as fairness: political not metaphysical', *Philosophy & Public Affairs*, 14:3 (1985), 223–51.

——, *The Law of Peoples, with 'The idea of public reason revisited'* (Cambridge, MA: Harvard University Press, 1999).

——, *Political Liberalism* (New York: Columbia University Press, 1993).

——, *A Theory of Justice* (Cambridge, MA: Harvard University Press, 1971).

Raz, Joseph, *The Authority of Law: Essays on Law and Morality* (Oxford: Clarendon Press, 1979).

——, *The Morality of Freedom* (Oxford: Clarendon, 1986).

Renner, Moritz, 'Die Wirtschaft der Weltgesellschaft: Möglichkeitsräume für eine systemtheoretische Kritik', in Marc Amstutz and Andreas Fischer-Lescano (eds), *Kritische Systemtheorie: Zur Evolution einer normativen Theorie* (Bielefeld: Transcript, 2013), pp. 219–36.

Requejo, Ferran, and Camil Ungureanu, *Democracy, Law and Religious Pluralism in Europe: Secularism and Post-Secularism* (London: Routledge, 2015).

Rivlin, Geoffrey, *Understanding the Law* (Oxford: Oxford University Press, 3rd edn, 2004).

Rodrik, Dani, 'Does Europe really need fiscal and political union?', *Social Europe*, 8 January (2018).

Rosa, Hartmut, 'The speed of global flows and the pace of democratic politics', *New Political Science*, 27 (2005), 445–59.

Rosanvallon, Pierre, *Democratic Legitimacy: Impartiality, Reflexivity, Proximity*, trans. Arthur Goldhammer (Princeton: Princeton University Press, 2011).

——, *La Légitimité démocratique: Impartialité, réflexivité, proximité* (Paris: Seuil, 2008).

Rose, Gillian, *The Melancholy Science: An Introduction to the Thoughts of Theodor W. Adorno* (London: Macmillan, 1978).

Ross, Kristin, *Communal Luxury: The Political Imaginary of the Paris Commune* (London: Verso, 2015).

—— *The Emergence of Social Space: Rimbaud and the Paris Commune* (London: Verso, 2008).

Rudenstine, David, *The Age of Deference: The Supreme Court, National Security, and the Constitutional Order* (New York: Oxford University Press, 2016).

Ruggie, John Gerard, 'International Regimes, Transactions and Change: Embedded Liberalism in the Postwar Economic Order', in Stephen D. Krasner (ed.), *International Regimes* (Ithaca: Cornell University Press, 1983), pp. 195–232.

Sahverdi, Umut, 'Transformations in the Turkish Educational System in Relation to the Islamic Turn in Turkish Statehood' (D.Phil, University of Sussex, forthcoming).

Salvadori, Massimo L., *Democrazie senza democrazia* (Bari: Laterza, 2009).

Samuels, Robert, *Psychoanalyzing the Left and Right after Donald Trump* (New York: Palgrave Macmillan, 2016).

Sassen, Saskia, *A Sociology of Globalization* (New York: W. W. Norton, 2007).

Schäfer, Armin, 'Liberalization, Inequality and Democracy's Discontent', in Armin Schäfer and Wolfgang Streeck (eds), *Politics in the Age of Austerity* (Cambridge: Polity, 2013), pp. 169–95.

Schäfer, Michael, *Die 'Rationalität' des Nationalsozialismus: Zur Kritik philosophischer Faschismustheorien am Beispiel der Kritischen Theorie* (Weinheim: Beltz Athenäum, 1994).

Schecter, Darrow, *Beyond Hegemony: Towards a New Philosophy of Political Legitimacy* (Manchester: Manchester University Press, 2005).

——, *Critical Theory in the Twenty-First Century* (New York: Bloomsbury, 2013).

——, *The Critique of Instrumental Reason from Weber to Habermas* (London: Continuum, 2010).

——, 'Gramsci's unorthodox Marxism: political ambiguity and sociological relevance', *Modern Italy*, 15 (2010), 145–59.

——, 'The Historical Bloc: Toward a Typology of Weak States and Contemporary Legitimation Crises', in Mark McNally (ed.), *Antonio Gramsci* (Basingstoke: Palgrave Macmillan, 2015), pp. 179–94.

——, *The History of the Left from Marx to the Present: Theoretical Perspectives* (London: Continuum, 2007).

——, 'Liberalism and the limits of legal legitimacy: Kant and Habermas', *King's College Law Journal*, 16 (2005), 99–119.

——, *Radical Theories: Paths beyond Marxism and Social Democracy* (Manchester: Manchester University Press, 1994).

Schermer, Henry, and David Jary, *Form and Dialectic in Georg Simmel's Sociology: A New Interpretation* (Basingstoke: Palgrave Macmillan, 2013).

Scheuerman, William E., *Between the Norm and the Exception: The Frankfurt School and the Rule of Law* (Cambridge, MA: MIT Press, 1994).

Schimank, Uwe, *Gesellschaft* (Bielefeld: Transcript, 2013).

——, 'Die Prekarität funktionaler Differenzierung – und soziologische Gesellschaftskritik als "double talk"', in Albert Scherr (ed.), *Systemtheorie und Differenzierungstheorie als Kritik: Perspektiven in Anschluss an Niklas Luhmann* (Weinheim and Basle: Beltz-Juventa, 2015), pp. 80–103.

Schmitt, Carl, *Der Begriff des Politischen* (Berlin: Duncker & Humblot, 3rd edn, 1996).

——, *The Concept of the Political* (Chicago: University of Chicago Press, 1996).

——, *Constitutional Theory* (Durham, NC: Duke University Press, 2008).

——, *Legalität und Legitimität* (Berlin: Duncker & Humblot, 5th edn, 1993).

——, *Legality and Legitimacy*, trans. and ed. Jeffrey Seitzer and with an introduction by John P. McCormick (Durham, NC and London: Duke University Press, 2004).

Schui, Florian, *Austerity: The Great Failure* (New Haven: Yale University Press, 2014).

Sciulli, David, *Theory of Societal Constitutionalism: Foundations of a Non-Marxist Critical Theory* (Cambridge: Cambridge University Press, 1992).

Scott, James C., *Seeing Like a State: How Certain Schemes to Improve the Human Condition have Failed* (New Haven: Yale University Press, 1998).

Scott, John, 'Modes of Power and Reconceptualization of Elites', in Michael Savage and Karel Williams (eds), *Remembering Elites* (Oxford: Wiley-Blackwell, 2008), pp. 27–43.

Seymour, Richard, *Corbyn: The Strange Rebirth of Radical Politics* (London: Verso, 2016).

Shanken, Edward A., 'Reprogramming Systems Aesthetics', in Edward A. Shanken (ed.), *Systems* (Cambridge, MA: MIT Press, 2015), pp. 123–9.

Sherwood, Harriet, Anu Anand, Maeve Shearlaw, and Jonathan Franklin, 'UN women: 20 years on from summit in Beijing, equality remains a distant dream', *Guardian* (11 September 2015), p. 29.

Sieyès, Emmanuel Joseph, *Qu'est-ce que le tiers état?* (Geneva: Droz, 1970).

——, *Political Writings: Including the Debate Between Sieyès and Tom Paine in 1791*, ed. Michael Sonenscher (Indianapolis: Hackett, 2003).

Simmel, Georg, 'Die Arbeitsteilung als Ursache für das Auseinandertreten der subjektiven und der objektiven Kultur', in *Schriften zur Soziologie: Eine Auswahl*, ed. Heinz-Jürgen Dahme (Frankfurt: Suhrkamp, 1983), pp. 95–128.

——, 'Exchange', in *On Individuality and Social Forms: Selected Writings*, ed. Donald N. Levine (Chicago: University of Chicago Press, 1971), pp. 43–69.

——, 'How Is Society Possible?', in *On Individuality and Social Forms: Selected Writings*, ed. Donald N. Levine (Chicago: University of Chicago Press, 1971), pp. 6–22.

——, *Die Philosophie des Geldes*, Gesamtausgabe, 6 (Frankfurt: Suhrkamp, 4th edn, 1996 [1900]).

——, *The Philosophy of Money*, trans. Tom Bottomore and David Frisby, ed. David Frisby (London: Routledge, 3rd enlarged edn, 2004).

——, *Sociology: Inquiries into the Construction of Social Forms*, trans. and ed. Anthony J. Blasi, Anton K. Jacobs, and Mathew J. Kanjirathinkal, 2 vols (Leiden and Boston: Brill, 2009).

——, *Soziologie: Untersuchungen über die Formen der Vergesellschaftung* (Frankfurt: Suhrkamp, 1992 [1908]).

——, 'Wie ist Gesellschaft möglich?', in *Soziologie: Untersuchungen über die Formen der Vergesellschaftung*, Gesamtausgabe, 11, ed. Otthein Rammstedt (Frankfurt: Suhrkamp, 1992 [1908]), pp. 42–62.

Skinner, Quentin, 'The Sovereign State: A Genealogy', in Hent Kalmo and Quentin Skinner (eds), *Sovereignty in Fragments: The Past, Present and Future of a Contested Concept* (Cambridge: Cambridge University Press, 2010), pp. 26–46.

Smith, Helena, 'Everything that Tsipras was promised was a fairytale', *Guardian* (10 May 2016), p. 21.

Smyth, John, *The Toxic University: Zombie Leadership, Academic Rock Stars and Neoliberal Ideology* (London: Palgrave Macmillan, 2017).

Snowden, Edward, 'Governments can reduce our dignity to that of tagged animals', *Guardian* (3 May 2016), G2, pp. 6–9.

Srnicek, Nick, and Alex Williams, *Inventing the Future: Postcapitalism and a World Without Work* (London: Verso Books, 2015).

Statham, Paul, and Hans-Jörg Trenz, *The Politicization of Europe: Contesting the Constitution in the Mass Media* (Abingdon: Routledge, 2013).

Stavrakakis, Yannis, *The Lacanian Left: Psychoanalysis, Theory, Politics* (Albany: State University of New York Press, 2007).

Stichweh, Rudolf, *Die Weltgesellschaft: Soziologische Analysen* (Frankfurt: Suhrkamp, 2000).

Stiegler, Bernard, *La Télécratie contre la démocratie: Lettre ouverte aux représentants politiques* (Paris: Flammarion, 2006).

Stiglitz, Joseph, 'Inequality and Economic Growth', in Michael Jacobs and Mariana Mazzucato (eds), *Rethinking Capitalism: Economics and Policy for Sustainable and Inclusive Growth* (Chichester: Wiley, 2016), pp. 134–55.

Stiglitz, Joseph E. and Bruce C. Greenwald, *Creating a Learning Society: A New Paradigm for Development and Social Progress*, Kenneth J Arrow Lecture Series at Columbia University, 1 (New York: Columbia University Press, 2014).

Stoetzler, Marcel, 'From interacting systems to a system of divisions', *European Journal of Social Theory*, 20:4 (2017), 455–72.

—— 'Intersectional individuality: Georg Simmel's concept of "the intersection of social circles" and the emancipation of women', *Sociological Inquiry*, 86:2 (2016), 216–40.

Streeck, Wolfgang, *Buying Time: The Delayed Crisis of Democratic Capitalism*, trans. Patrick Camiller and David Fernbach (London: Verso, 2nd edn, 2017).

——, *Gekaufte Zeit: Die vertagte Krise des demokratischen Kapitalismus*, Frankfurter Adorno-Vorlesungen, 2012 (Berlin: Suhrkamp, 2013).

——, 'How will capitalism end?', *New Left Review*, 87 (2014), 35–66.

——, *How will Capitalism End? Essays on a Failing System* (London: Verso, 2016).

Strydom, Piet, 'Cosmopolitanization and the Prospects of a Cosmopolitan Modernity', in Anastasia Marinopoulou (ed.), *Cosmopolitan Modernity* (Oxford: Peter Lang, 2015), pp. 73–100.

Sünker, Heinz, Dieter Timmermann, and Fritz-Ulrich Kolbe (eds), *Bildung, Gesellschaft, soziale Ungleichheit: Internationale Beiträge zur Bildungssoziologie und Bildungstheorie* (Frankfurt: Suhrkamp-Taschenbuch-Verlag, 1994).

Supiot, Alain, 'Et si l'on refondait le droit du travail…', *Le Monde Diplomatique* (October 2017), pp. 1 and 22–3.

——, 'The Territorial Inscription of Laws', in Gralf-Peter Calliess, Andreas Fischer-Lescano, Dan Wielsch, and Peer Zumbansen (eds), *Soziologische Jurisprudenz: Festschrift für Gunther Teubner zum 65. Geburtstag am 30. April 2009* (Berlin: de Gruyter, 2009), pp. 375–93.

Sutcliffe-Braithwaite, Florence, 'Neo-liberalism and morality in the making of Thatcherite social policy', *The Historical Journal*, 55:2 (2012), 497–520.

Taylor, A. J. P., *English History, 1914–1945* (Oxford: Clarendon Press, 1965).

Taylor, Mark C., *Journeys to Selfhood: Hegel and Kierkegaard* (Berkeley: University of California Press, 1980).

Teubner, Gunther, 'Constitutional Drift: Spontaneous Co-evolution of Social Ideas and Legal Form', in Michael W. Dowdle and Michael A. Wilkinson (eds), *Constitutionalism Beyond Liberalism* (Cambridge: Cambridge University Press, 2017), pp. 79–95.

——, *Constitutional Fragments: Societal Constitutionalism and Globalization* (Oxford: Oxford University Press, 2012).

——, 'A Constitutional Moment? The Logics of Hitting Rock Bottom', in Poul F. Kjaer, Gunther Teubner, and Alberto Febbrajo (eds), *The Financial Crisis in Constitutional*

Perspective: The Dark Side of Functional Differentiation (Oxford: Hart, 2011), pp. 3–42.

——, *Critical Theory and Legal Autopoiesis: The Case for Societal Constitutionalism*, Critical Theory and Contemporary Society (Manchester: Manchester University Press, 2019).

——, 'Global Bukowina: Legal Pluralism in the World Society', in Gunther Teubner (ed.), *Global Law without a State* (Aldershot: Dartmouth, 1997), pp. 3–30.

——, 'Polykorporatismus: Der Staat als Netzwerk öffentlicher und privater Kollektivakteure', in Hauke Brunkhorst and Peter Niesen (eds), *Das Recht der Republik. Festschrift für Ingeborg Maus* (Frankfurt: Suhrkamp, 1999), pp. 346–72.

——, *Recht als autopoietisches System* (Frankfurt: Suhrkamp, 1989).

——, *Verfassungsfragmente: Gesellschaftlicher Konstitutionalismus in der Globalisierung* (Berlin: Suhrkamp, 2012).

Thompson, Michael, *The Domestication of Critical Theory* (London: Rowman & Littlefield, 2016).

Thomson, A. J. P., *Deconstruction and Democracy: Derrida's Politics of Friendship* (London: Continuum, 2005).

Thornhill, Chris, 'Contemporary constitutionalism and the dialectic of constituent power', *Global Constitutionalism*, 1:3 (2012), 369–404.

——, 'The Future of the State', in Poul F. Kjaer, Gunther Teubner, and Alberto Febbrajo (eds), *The Financial Crisis in Constitutional Perspective: The Dark Side of Functional Differentiation* (Oxford: Hart, 2011), pp. 357–93.

——, *A Sociology of Constitutions: Constitutions and State Legitimacy in Historical-Sociological Perspective* (Cambridge: Cambridge University Press, 2011).

——, *A Sociology of Transnational Constitutions: Social Foundations of the Post-National Legal Structure* (Cambridge: Cambridge University Press, 2016).

——, 'A Tale of Two Constitutions: Whose Legitimacy, Whose Crisis?', in William Outhwaite (ed.), *Brexit: Sociological Responses* (London: Anthem Press, 2017), pp. 77–89.

Tocqueville, Alexis de, *L'Ancien Régime et la Révolution*, ed. J. P. Mayer (Paris: Gallimard, revised and corrected edn, 1967).

Todd, Emmanuel, *Après la démocratie* (Paris: Gallimard, 2008).

Touraine, Alain, *La Fin des sociétés* (Paris: Seuil, 2013).

——, *L'Après-socialisme* (Paris: B. Grasset, 1980).

Vail, Mark I., *Recasting Welfare Capitalism: Economic Adjustment in Contemporary France and Germany* (Philadelphia: Temple University Press, 2010).

Varoufakis, Yanis, *And the Weak Suffer What They Must? Europe, Austerity and the Threat to Global Stability* (London: The Bodley Head, 2016).

——, *The Global Minotaur: America, the True Origins of the Financial Crisis and the Future of the World Economy* (London: Zed, 2011).

——, 'How I became an erratic Marxist', *Guardian* (18 February 2015), pp. 29–32.

Veitch, Scott, Emilios A. Christodoulidis, and Lindsay Farmer, *Jurisprudence: Themes and Concepts* (London: Routledge, 2nd edn, 2012).

Vogel, Berthold, *Die Staatsbedürftigkeit der Gesellschaft* (Hamburg: Hamburger Ed., 2007).

Wall, Derek, *Elinor Ostrom's Rules for Radicals: Cooperative Alternatives Beyond Markets and States* (London: Pluto, 2017).

Walter, Franz, *Vom Milieu zum Parteienstaat: Lebenswelten, Leitfiguren und Politik im historischen Wandel* (Wiesbaden: VS Verlag für Sozialwissenschaften, 2010).

Weber, Max, 'Politics as a Vocation', in Hans Gerth and C. Wright Mills (eds), *From Max Weber: Essays in Sociology* (New York: Scribner & Son, 1946), pp. 77–128.

——, *Staatssoziologie: Soziologie der rationalen Staatsanstalt und der modernen politischen Parteien und Parlamente*, ed. Johannes Winckelmann (Berlin: Duncker & Humblot, 2nd edn, 1966).

Weeks, Kathi, *The Problem with Work: Feminism, Marxism, Antiwork Politics, and Postwork Imaginaries* (Durham, NC: Duke University Press, 2011).

Whittington, Valerie, 'The Challenges of Deliberative Democracy' (D.Phil, University of Sussex, forthcoming).

Willke, Helmut, *Ironie des Staates: Grundlinien einer Staatstheorie polyzentrischer Gesellschaft* (Frankfurt: Suhrkamp, 1992).

——, *Regieren: Politische Steuerung komplexer Gesellschaften* (Wiesbaden: Springer VS, 2013).

Wilson, Peter H., *The Holy Roman Empire: A Thousand Years of Europe's History* (London: Allen Lane, 2016).

Winczorek, Jan, 'Making Law Together? On Some Intersystemic Conditions of Judicial Cooperation', in Alberto Febbrajo and Gorm Harste, *Law and Intersystemic Communication: Understanding 'Structural Coupling'* (Farnham: Ashgate, 2013), pp. 229–53.

Wirtz, Thomas, 'Entscheidung: Niklas Luhmann und Carl Schmitt', in Albrecht Koschorke and Cornelia Vismann (eds), *Widerstände der Systemtheorie: Kulturtheoretische Analysen zum Werk von Niklas Luhmann* (Berlin: Akademie Verlag, 1999), pp. 175–97.

Witte, John, *Law and Protestantism: The Legal Teachings of the Lutheran Reformation* (Cambridge: Cambridge University Press, 2002).

Woodward, Susan L., *The Ideology of Failed States: Why Intervention Fails* (Cambridge: Cambridge University Press, 2017).

Yusuf, Hakeem O., *Colonial and Post-Colonial Constitutionalism in the Commonwealth: Peace, Order and Good Government* (London: Routledge, 2014).

Zagorin, Perez, *Rebels and Rulers, 1500–1660 Vol.1, Society, States and Early Modern Revolution: Agrarian and Urban Rebellions* (Cambridge: Cambridge University Press, 1982).

——, *Rebels and Rulers, 1500–1660 Vol.2, Provincial Rebellion: Revolutionary Civil Wars, 1560–1660* (Cambridge: Cambridge University Press, 1982).

Žižek, Slavoj, *The Sublime Object of Ideology* (London: Verso, 2nd edn, 2008).

Zweifel, Thomas D., *International Organizations and Democracy: Accountability, Politics, and Power* (London: Lynne Rienner, 2006).

Index

EU authorised representative for GPSR:
Easy Access System Europe, Mustamäe tee 50,
10621 Tallinn, Estonia
gpsr.requests@easproject.com

www.ingramcontent.com/pod-product-compliance
Lightning Source LLC
Chambersburg PA
CBHW051959270326
41929CB00015B/2719